THE GROWTH OF THE INTERNATIONAL
ECONOMY, 1820–1960

THE GROWTH OF THE INTERNATIONAL ECONOMY 1820-1960

AN INTRODUCTORY TEXT

BY
A. G. KENWOOD AND A. L. LOUGHEED
University of Queensland

'The Causes which determine the economic progress of nations belong to the study of international trade . . .'
A. Marshall, *Principles of Economics*, 8th edn
reprinted (London, 1959), p. 255

London
GEORGE ALLEN & UNWIN
Boston   Sydney

First published in 1971
Fifth impression 1977

© George Allen & Unwin (Publishers) Ltd, 1971

ISBN 0 04 330174 6 hardback
ISBN 0 04 330175 4 paper

Printed in Great Britain
in 10 point Times Roman
by Lowe & Brydone Printers Limited, Thetford, Norfolk

Contents

Tables

Diagrams

Introduction

The exchange of goods and services is the means through which independent economic units enter into economic relations with one another and become part of a local or national economic community. As exchange passes beyond a country's boundaries, national economic systems become parts of a broader regional, continental or world economy. Flows of commodity trade are not the only economic links forged between nations, however. People are also highly mobile, and the long evolution of trade from primitive barter to our modern worldwide network of commodity exchange has made necessary an intricate system of international credits, loans and investments. It is these flows of trade, labour and capital that constitute the vital processes of the international economy. Obviously, therefore, any study of the growth of the international economy must be concerned with the measurement and comparison of the rate at which these processes go on over time. It must also be concerned with examining the ways in which the international economic system is organized to carry out these vital processes, and how the structure, organization and functioning of these processes change as the international economy expands. In the final analysis, however, the international economy is studied not as an end in itself, but rather as a means to an end, for in studying its expansion in recent times, we are analysing one of the most potent causes of modern economic growth.

The international economy encourages national economic growth in two ways: by providing opportunities for international specialization; and by acting as a mechanism for diffusing between nations the apparatus and/or benefits of modern industrial technology. Since specialization implies trade and cannot occur without it, and since specialization and division of labour are a major cause of increased productivity and rising *per capita* real incomes, some comment is called for on the nature of the basis of trade between countries before we say something briefly about the international economy as a means of spreading industrialization.

International trade arises simply because countries differ in their demand for goods and services and in their ability to supply them. So far as supply is concerned, the basis for trade is to be found in the uneven distribution of economic resources among the nations of the world, coupled with the fact that commodities and services require different proportions of these economic resources in their production. This uneven distribution of resources is partly a matter of climate and geography, and partly a result of each nation's historical development, which has left it with a certain stock of capital and a population trained and educated in numerous techniques and skills. Whatever their origin, however, each country's endowment of land, minerals, skills, and machinery equips it to produce certain goods and services more efficiently (cheaply) than others. For differences in the relative supplies of different productive resources within a country will mean differences in their relative prices and therefore differences in the costs of producing various goods and services.[1] Considering these elements alone, each country would tend to specialize upon those products best suited to its factor endowment, which means those using little of its scarce factors but drawing heavily upon the cheap and abundant ones. Thus differences in relative factor prices based on the relative abundance or scarcity of economic resources within countries will mean differences in international costs of production and therefore differences in commodity prices. It is these differences in commodity prices that are a basic cause of trade between nations.

However, the international structure of commodity prices and the pattern of foreign trade based on it are not fixed for all time. Over time, changes occur in the distribution of economic resources between countries which alter the comparative cost structure and modify the pattern of world trade. Any one country's factor endowment can change radically from internal causes, as technological progress occurs, as population changes, as domestic capital is accumulated, and as the economic extent of the land is modified. It can also change from external causes, by virtue of international movements of labour and capital and the spread of technical knowledge. The effect of such changes on a nation's relative factor endowment should be obvious. The principal basis for its specialization and the character of its trade are altered. In analysing the growth of the international economy, therefore, we must consider how changes in factor supplies, technical progress, increasing productivity, and changes in demand can transform the structure of comparative costs. For changes in comparative costs affect the pattern of international trade, while developments in international trade in turn influence the economic growth processes in the world economy that bring about changes in the international distribution of economic resources.

Whatever the structure of comparative costs at any particular point in time, the size of the trade flows between nations will also

[1] What is important is the relative, not absolute, supply of the factors of production. Thus China is a country large in area, but, relative to its population's demand for food, land is scarce and capital is relatively even more scarce. On the other hand, Belgium may have a small population in absolute size, but its labour supply relative to the country's land and capital may be the most abundant factor.

depend upon the existing level of transport costs. Since trade is based mainly on international price differences, it may be severely limited in situations where transport costs largely offset the price advantage of low-cost producers. In other words, the basis for trade, whether international or interregional, lies in comparative cost differences which are not neutralized by transport costs. It follows therefore that any reduction of transport costs due to technical improvements in the carriage of goods enhances the opportunities for trade by allowing international cost and price differences to become more apparent in world markets.

One apparent failure of the factor proportions theorem just outlined is that it does not provide an adequate explanation for the comparative advantage which industrialized nations appear to possess in different industries. This is brought out clearly by the fact that, in this century, trade has tended to expand fastest between the advanced industrial nations, many of which have roughly similar factor endowments. The need to explain the trade advantage of industrial countries has led consequently to emphasis being placed on factors other than simple resource scarcity. One approach to the problem stresses the importance of economies of scale. The technical superiority of certain large indivisible units of capital or the use of specialized labour, both of which depend on the existence of large markets, suggests that a large country, especially one with a big population and high *per capita* incomes, will be more fruitful for the development of large-scale industry than a smaller country with a similar level of income. Hence the scale economy explanation essentially asserts that the country with the largest domestic market tends to specialize in those commodities which exhibit the *greatest* scale economies.

The growth of trade between industrial nations has also been explained in terms of the technological gap between nations created by the discovery of new products and new processes of production. According to this theory, trade consists of the impermanent commerce which originates solely in the temporary technological superiority gained by the nation making the industrial breakthrough. In other words, the innovating country's export trade in the new product will last until such time as other countries adopt the new techniques or produce the new product on a scale sufficient to supply their domestic markets and make them independent of imported supplies. The period it will take for the manufacture of a new product to spread from one country to another will obviously depend upon a variety of factors, including the threat which new products pose to existing goods and the lure of the high profits to be earned in the new line of production. At the same time, technological gap trade may be prolonged by the fact that the innovating country enjoys a peculiar advantage in harvesting scale economies. This advantage arises because the markets for new products expand rapidly at first. The innovator can thus more confidently erect large plant and secure an entrenched position in domestic and export markets than can successor firms abroad. In this respect the technological gap theory is an improvement on the scale-economy theory, since according to the former a small country which innovates may yet build a large plant, whereas the latter theory simply asserts that the country with the largest home market builds the biggest plant, regardless of when it begins production. Finally, it should be noted that while the technological gap theory implies that trade between industrial nations is only a temporary thing, the fact that innovation and technical progress are continuous processes means that trade between advanced industrial nations may well persist and even grow over time.

Another explanation of the rapidly expanding trade between industrial nations stresses the importance of domestic demand as a determinant of the products which a country will export. Only after the new product is firmly established in the domestic market, it is argued, will the entrepreneur be ready to respond to profit opportunities in foreign markets. Moreover, since income, more than any other variable, appears to determine the consumption and purchasing habits of broad sectors of the population, countries having similar income levels are likely to trade with each other more intensively than countries having different income levels. This explanation of the basis of trade between nations is, of course, dramatically opposed to the factor-endowment theory which implicitly argues that trade between capital-rich (high-income)and capital-poor (low-income) countries tends to be the more promising for the trading partners than exchange of goods between countries whose average income levels are similar, where labour and capital may be expected to be distributed in similar proportions. But having made this point, it should also be noted that none of the alternative theories just discussed completely dispenses with the factor proportions approach. Indeed, over time, a country's comparative advantage in certain industrial activities may be largely a matter of historical accident, in the sense that past international specialization based on relative factor endowment may lead to a strengthening and developing of natural skills, innovative capacity, and investment activity along lines which are different from those of other countries. Consequently opportunities for technological gap trade may emerge and economies of scale assert themselves in the production of commodities and services which will have a ready market in other countries with similar income levels.

Whatever forms the basis of trade between nations, however, there is no doubting the gains from specialization, which come about because trade between countries provides the opportunity for an international division of labour that leads to a better allocation of economic resources and greater productive efficiency in every country. Indeed, it was these gains from trade, in the form of the extra output made possible by international specialization, and their distribution among trading nations, that formed the basis for the advocacy of a policy of free trade between countries during the nineteenth century. But past experience indicates that the emergence of a truly international economy did much more than just provide a large market suitable for increased specialization, for it also provided, through international flows of capital and labour as well as of goods, a mechanism for the diffusion of modern industrial technology and a means of transmitting economic growth from industrializing countries to the less developed areas of the world. In short, the expansion of the international economy after 1820 was a major cause of modern economic growth. But in emphasizing its functioning as an 'engine of growth', we should not forget the fact that an expanding international economy is both a cause and an effect of national economic growth. For while the technological diffusion and increased specialization facilitated by an expanding international economy may provide considerable stimulus to the economic growth of a country, that country's growth, in turn, may, through its increased demand for foreign goods, capital and labour, promote closer economic relations at the international level.

Given the main purpose of this book, which is to describe the growth and assess the economic significance of the international economy in the period between 1820 and 1960, its contents fall easily into three parts. The first part contains a discussion of the forces responsible for the expanding international flows of trade, labour and capital in the years up to 1913, and an examination of the functioning of the international economy as an 'engine of growth' during these years. The impact of World War I on the workings of the international economy is analysed in the second part, and in the light of this analysis an attempt is made to account for the partial collapse of the international economy during the 1930s. Finally, in the last part, we describe the efforts made in the 1940s and 1950s to place international economic relations on a firmer footing, partly by rectifying some of the deficiencies in the system that had become apparent in the difficult years of the thirties.

Part I

THE INTERNATIONAL ECONOMY
1820–1913

Chapter 1

THE CAUSES OF THE GROWTH OF THE INTERNATIONAL ECONOMY IN THE NINETEENTH CENTURY

To understand why a truly international economy first evolved during the nineteenth century it is necessary to examine the economic, technical and other changes which were responsible for the massive expansion of capital movements, migration and foreign trade that occurred during these years. For it was through these flows of money, men and goods that countries hitherto economically independent were fused into the international economy.

TECHNOLOGICAL PROGRESS: INDUSTRY AND AGRICULTURE

The industrial revolution, which began in Britain in the late eighteenth century and which spread first to Europe and then to the United States during the nineteenth century, enormously increased the opportunities for trade between countries, for the new technology presupposed a wide variety of resources and an expanding market. But except for a few favoured countries, such as the United States, most industrializing nations during the nineteenth century had to look outside their own borders for markets in which to sell the surplus output yielded by modern industry, and for the additional supplies of raw materials that were needed when domestic production of these inputs failed to keep pace with rising industrial demand. A similar situation arose in the new centres of primary production overseas, where the use of modern farming techniques produced agricultural surpluses for which markets had to be found abroad. At the same time, the apparatus of improved farming often had to be imported, along with the transport equipment necessary to the opening up of new areas of primary production.

Success in the search for foreign markets for manufactured goods depended very much on whether the new techniques resulted in a new product or in the cheapening of an existing one. Obviously trade in a new product will grow fastest when many countries are unable to produce it for themselves but want to consume it. For this reason, the rather limited spread of industrialization before 1913 must have given a powerful impetus to the growth of trade in industrial goods during the nineteenth century. On the other hand, where innovation involves the cheapening of old goods the effects on trade are often less clear. Thus foreign trade in cheap machine-made articles often increased at the expense of trade in hand-made substitutes. This happened with British cotton textiles and Indian calicoes during the late eighteenth and early nineteenth century, though on balance the revolution in textile manufacturing that occurred in Britain at this time led to a net increase in the volume of cotton goods traded internationally. In other instances, however, where, for example, synthetic substitutes for natural products were discovered, a decline in trade could result from the introduction of the technical improvement.[1]

Taken generally, however, technical progress in the nineteenth century tended to be pro-trade biased. Innovation was widespread, and the opportunities for trade multiplied accordingly. Before 1870 the important innovating industries were textiles (especially cotton) and iron, with steam the new source of power. After 1870 the focus of technical change began to shift, as increasing emphasis came to be placed on the production of steel, machine tools, electrical engineering products, and chemicals. Electricity emerged as a new form of energy and the internal combustion engine as the basis of a new means of transport. The outcome of all these developments was a flood of new goods, including railway equipment, steam-ships, steel and electrical products, plant and machinery of all kinds, and a growing variety of other manufactured products. In addition, many of the articles already traded internationally became cheaper, especially cotton cloth. The result was a rapid expansion in foreign trade in manufactures.

Part of this trade in manufactures was necessarily of a temporary nature, since it was linked with the spread of industrialization. For, while technical progress in the form of new or cheaper goods undoubtedly favours trade, the diffusion of technology, by encouraging imitation in production and the substitution of domestically produced goods for goods previously imported, tends to be biased

---

[1] Even so, certain other influences could offset the trade-reducing impact of the innovation. Thus the Germans were responsible for a long series of major discoveries which led to synthetic dyes replacing those made from vegetable products. But the fact that by 1900 German producers controlled some 90 per cent of the world market in dyestuffs indicated a substantial increase of trade in the synthetic product, since consumers of dyestuffs in other countries were mainly dependent on German sources of supply.

strongly against trade. Within a limited area the diffusion of the industrial revolution that began in Britain was fairly rapid. By 1850 it had penetrated into France and Belgium. Half a century later it had reached Germany, the United States, Sweden, Russia and Japan. In certain lines of foreign trade, for example, textiles and clothing, the trade reducing effect of technical diffusion soon became apparent. On the other hand, the spread of industrialization may have increased the world innovatory capacity, and there is some evidence of shifts in innovatory capacity occurring after 1870 from Britain to the U.S. and Germany. If increased innovation meant fresh opportunities for trade, shifts in the centre of innovatory activity were obviously important in influencing the geographical pattern of world trade. In short, despite the spread of industrialization, nineteenth century technical progress tended, on balance, to favour the expansion of world trade while at the same time bringing about changes in the direction and composition of trade between countries.

Besides providing expanding opportunities for the international exchange of manufactured goods, modern industrial technology also created increased opportunities for trade in raw materials. In the early stages of the industrial revolution, when textile production expanded rapidly, and machinery continued to be constructed largely of wood, agricultural raw materials dominated these exchanges, especially raw cotton and timber. Later on, however, as industrial technology continued to evolve, manufacturing industry came to rely more on minerals and relatively less on agricultural raw materials. This growing industrial dependence on mineral resources was reflected both in a widening of the range of minerals for which an industrial use was found and in the development of mass consumption of a few of them. While the output of coal and iron ore increased substantially throughout the nineteenth century, after 1850 the output of other metals, such as copper and zinc, grew even faster, and other previously little used minerals such as petroleum and aluminium, had achieved a considerable economic importance by the beginning of the twentieth century.

As industrial growth accelerated in the last quarter of the nineteenth century, the consumption of raw materials increased phenomenally. Between 1880 and 1913, petroleum production doubled every 8·6 years, copper every 13 years, pig iron, phosphates, coal and zinc, every 15–17 years, and lead and tin every 20 years. In the circumstances, the tendency to exhaustion of the more readily available supplies of less common metals and fuels was to be expected, and their costs of production rose accordingly. In the search for new and cheaper supplies of minerals that followed, the

United States emerged as a major producer, capable of supplying not only most of its own needs but also of providing a surplus for export to other industrial nations. Russia, too, possessed great, though widely dispersed, mineral resources, and Canada, South Africa, Australia, Chile, Malaya, and a number of other countries emerged as other important mineral producers. Indeed, a feature of the growth of world mineral production during these years was the constant shifting of the centre of world supply of these materials from one region to another. Such shifts were recorded for various minerals, including copper and iron ore, and for precious metals, such as gold. Quite obviously, these production shifts had important repercussions on the pattern of world trade, and they also exerted a significant influence on the international flows of labour and capital before 1914.

A similar situation to that found in mineral production developed in agriculture, when the spread of industrialization and the rapid growth of population brought about a phenomenal increase in the demand for foodstuffs and agricultural raw materials, a series of shifts in the geographical sources of supply and, consequently, great changes in the volume and commodity structure of foreign trade. Simultaneously, technological progress and the opening up of new regions cheapened many agricultural products and provided conditions under which mass markets could be supplied with many items formerly classified as luxuries. More and better farm implements and machinery, the use of chemical fertilizers, improved stock-breeding and new methods of checking plant and animal diseases—all made significant contributions to the growth of agricultural output. Many of these innovations originated in Europe and eventually diffused to countries overseas. Others were developed in the new farming regions themselves, where labour shortage, drought, short growing seasons and other problems called forth fresh invention and innovation to deal with them.

The growing demand for tropical products, which accompanied industrialization and the rise of real incomes in Europe and North America, led to a rapid expansion of plantation agriculture in the period after 1850. In the old established areas of European enterprise the growth of output was achieved primarily by the more efficient use of an abundant labour force. Elsewhere it was obtained either through improvements in peasant farming or through the spread of the plantation system, which brought with it better farming methods, higher-yielding plant strains, and the greater use of machinery, particularly in the preliminary processing operations. The plantation system also encouraged the introduction of new crops. Rubber trees, for example, were introduced into Malaya from Brazil in 1877.

Rubber cultivation spread rapidly from there to the Netherlands East Indies and French Indo-China, and by the end of the century south-east Asia had become the chief source of the world supply of natural rubber. In contrast to rubber, the centre of world coffee production shifted in the opposite direction, from Asia to Latin America, following the emergence of Brazil as the world's greatest coffee producing country. Rice, sugar, tea, tobacco and cotton production were similarly affected by these production shifts as their output grew in response to the expanding demand for primary products in industrial Europe and North America.

TECHNICAL PROGRESS: TRANSPORT AND COMMUNICATIONS

Through cheapening and speeding up the movement of goods and people, improved transport and communications played a vital role in the growth of the world economy in the nineteenth century. By promoting the exchange of a growing volume of goods; by expanding markets, as well as opening up new sources of supply of many products; by permitting the concentration of certain types of production in fewer centres, thereby encouraging specialization and assisting the realization of economies of scale; and by allowing a greater interregional flow of men and capital, the new forms of transport and communications made possible that growing economic interdependence of the whole world which is so remarkable a feature of nineteenth-century economic development. Moreover, by making possible a significant relocation of economic activity throughout the world, transport improvements contributed substantially to the rising productivity that lay behind the growth of real incomes in the world economy during these years.

Of these improvements, the application of steam to land and sea transport was of critical importance. On land, steam was rapidly adapted to the railway, which quickly supplanted the existing means of transport. The earliest railways were built in Britain and the eastern United States, but they quickly spread, first to Europe and then to the other continents of the world. The extent of this dispersion in the nineteenth century is shown in Table 1.

In Europe the spread of the railway led to the formation of new states, such as Germany and Italy, and the creation of the large markets necessary for industrialization. In North America and Russia similar developments occurred, but on a grander scale. Here the railway permitted the political domination of whole continents by a single government while at the same time opening up the untapped wealth of virtually empty territories. Outside North America and Europe, railways were essentially instruments of the

TABLE 1. *Railway Route Mileage, 1840–1910*

| | '000 miles | | |
	1840	1870	1910
Europe	2·6	65·4	212·1
North America	2·8	55·4	265·8
Latin America	0·1	2·4	60·7
Asia	—	5·1	59·5
Africa	—	1·1	23·0
Oceania	—	1·1	19·3
World	5·5	130·5	640·4

Source: W. S. and E. S. Woytinsky, *World Commerce and Governments* (New York, 1955), p. 341; W. Woodruff, *Impact of Western Man* (New York, 1966), p. 253.

expansion of the world economy. Financed largely by European capital, the railways of Latin America, Asia, Africa and Australasia were built primarily to assist in the export of the continents' agricultural and mineral products and, since the abilities of the different countries in these continents to supply the required primary products varied, it is not surprising to find that railway developments were not uniform either within the continents or between them. In Latin America, only Mexico, Brazil, and Argentina had networks of any importance, whereas in Africa half the continent's railways at the end of the century were to be found in the Union of South Africa. In Asia, two-thirds of the railway mileage in operation at the end of our period were in India, where railways had been built chiefly to ensure political control of the sub-continent. Elsewhere in Asia, railway development had barely begun outside Japan, where over 7,000 miles of railway track had been built by 1914.

Compared to the railway, the steam-ship was slow to establish its supremacy at sea, where the relatively high standard of perfection achieved by the sailing-ship during the nineteenth century made it a formidable competitor. By 1869, however, the iron steam-ship had made serious inroads on the traffic of the sailing-ship. The coastal trade had early been taken over, while the ocean passenger service and the carriage of mail overseas also passed quickly to steam. With freight, progress was much slower. The steam-ship cut sharply into the North Atlantic carrying trade, but the Far Eastern trade remained exclusively the preserve of the sailing-ship. Here the opening of the Suez Canal in 1869, by providing a shorter route to the East, well served by conveniently located and efficient coaling stations, hastened the replacement of sail by steam. Later, the introduction of the compound engine, which significantly reduced coal consumption, and the conversion from iron to steel in ship-building that took place in the 1880s, made possible a continuous increase in the carrying capacity of the steam-ship and so increased its competitive power further. From 27m. tons in 1873, the amount of total world freight carried in steam-ships rose to 63m. tons in 1898, while the steam-ship proportion of the total world shipping tonnage grew from just over 12 per cent in 1870 to almost two-thirds of the total in 1900.

Despite the rapidly increasing demand for shipping in the nine-teenth century, capacity grew sufficiently quickly to bring about a secular decline in ocean freight rates. This decline took place in two phases: between 1815 and 1851, and between 1870–3 and 1908–9. In the first period of decline, freight rates were particularly affected on outward cargoes (from Europe and the United Kingdom), on the Baltic and Mediterranean routes, and on the North Atlantic run. The causes of the decline in freight rates at this time included technological improvements in sailing-ship design and construction, the increased utilization of ships that resulted from improvements in cargo handling and dock facilities, the reduction of time in ballast, and increased knowledge, particularly of winds and currents. In the second period, the greatest decline occurred in the freight rates on long hauls. In bringing about this fall in rates, the steam-ship exercised a decisive influence, although the performance of sailing-ships continued to improve well into the last quarter of the nineteenth century. This lowering of transport costs was of vital significance for the growth of world trade, especially after 1870. Since only those goods that can bear transport costs and still be cheaper than some part of domestic production in the importing country will be traded, a reduction in transport costs will obviously widen the range of internationally traded goods by allowing foreign goods to become even lower in price relative to domestic production. By widening the range of international commodity exchange, and by permitting heavy or bulky products to enter into foreign trade, transport improvements provided a great stimulus to the growth of world trade in the nineteenth century.

In the task of cheapening and speeding up the movement of men and goods the railway and steam-ship were supported by a series of developments in related activities. The growth of merchant fleets was accompanied by harbour improvements, the building of docks and warehouses, and the introduction of new machines and methods for the rapid handling of cargoes. Sea transport was also speeded up by the cutting of ship canals. Here the two outstanding feats were the opening of the Suez Canal in 1869, and of the Panama Canal in

1915. Other important developments during these years included the completion in 1872 of a new waterway connecting Rotterdam to the North Sea, the opening of the Manchester Ship Canal in 1894 and the Kiel Canal in 1895. The telegraph system was another development of immense significance for the growth of world trade. In particular, world commodity markets could become a reality only with the introduction of the telegraph and the spread of its use across the continents. By the turn of the century new developments in the field of transport and communications of considerable significance for the future were already apparent. The internal combustion engine offered an alternative form of land transport, although its ability to compete for traffic with the railways still seemed doubtful. The same could be said of aviation and the passenger traffic on the high seas. Meanwhile, oil began to be used to drive ships, although only some 2 per cent of world shipping was oil-fired in 1914. The telephone had emerged as an improvement on the telegraph, and the invention of the wireless set in 1896 was another step in the direction of bringing the peoples of the world closer together.

THE ACCUMULATION OF CAPITAL

The importance of capital accumulation for increasing production has long been recognized by economists. Capital accumulation facilitates the introduction of new techniques and provides tools and equipment for a growing population. It also brings about, through increases in the supply of tools and machinery per worker, the use of more efficient 'roundabout' methods of production. In particular, the process of industrialization, with its emphasis on more mechanized methods of production, a rapidly growing consumption of raw materials, and the need to supply wider markets, results in substantial additions being made to a country's stock of capital equipment. At the same time, technical progress and continued population growth make necessary a continuous increase in this capital stock if living standards are to be maintained or raised.

Any long-term analysis of the process of capital accumulation is made extremely difficult by the formidable conceptual problems involved in appropriately defining and measuring capital. Moreover, the task of amassing enough empirical evidence to justify definite conclusions concerning the changing level and structure of capital formation over time has barely begun. Yet while the available empirical data are limited to only a few countries, it is possible to use this material to make a few generalizations concerning the process of capital accumulation during the nineteenth century.[1] In

[1] For details of the available estimates of capital formation, see S. Kuznets,

Britain, for example, the transition from a pre-industrial to an industrial society was neither sudden nor did it involve any dramatic rise in the rate of capital accumulation. Most of the upward shift in the level of national investment associated with the industrial revolution in Britain seems to have occurred in the four decades between the mid-1830s and the mid-1870s, when capital formation rose from some 7–8 per cent of national product in the early thirties to perhaps 14 per cent in the 1870s. This upsurge in the rate of capital accumulation was the result of heavy investment in domestic railways, the coal, iron and textile industries, shipping and its ancillaries, such as docks and harbours, plus substantial investment overseas. After 1875 capital accumulation continued at a high level, with the decline in the relative importance of railway investment being offset by much higher levels of investment in residential building activity and in industry, commerce and finance. Meanwhile, land as a percentage of total national capital declined continuously throughout the nineteenth century from being over one-half of the total capital stock in 1798 to just on 7 per cent of the total in 1912.

In other industrializing countries the process of capital formation and the consequent changes in the structure of the capital stock were similar to those experienced by Britain, although for various reasons the late industrializers probably achieved a high level of capital accumulation much more quickly than did Britain. But the demand for capital goods was not restricted to the industrial or industrializing countries. The spread of the railway to all corners of the globe set up a growing demand for railway equipment of all kinds, and efforts to exploit the natural resources of the newly settled continents created a heavy demand for agricultural machinery, mining equipment, and related types of capital goods. The consequent growth in the world stock of capital provided many fresh opportunities for international trade. The need of developing countries to import machinery and equipment during the early stages of industrialization created a growing demand for the manufacturing output of those countries already industrialized, as did the demand for capital goods by the primary-producing regions of the world. Moreover, differences in the rates of saving relative to investment possibilities in different countries provided profitable opportunities for lending capital on a large scale, which provided a means of financing the purchase of capital equipment needed by the various borrowing

Modern Economic Growth (New Haven, 1966), pp. 75–81. The countries covered include Britain, Belgium, Norway, West Germany, the United States, Australia and Japan.

countries. In other words, the volume of world trade in the nineteenth century was kept at a high level by two closely connected facts: first, the fact that the new countries, whether industrializing or primary producing, keenly desired a type of good that the older industrialized countries were well fitted to supply, and, secondly, the fact that the old countries did not demand immediate payment for these goods, but were willing in effect to supply them on credit, so that the volume of trade was continuously larger than it would have been had it depended solely on the opportunities for simultaneous barter.

THE GROWTH OF WORLD POPULATION

Economic growth in the nineteenth century was also accompanied by a rapid increase of population. World population grew from just over 900m. in 1800 to approximately 1,600m. in 1900. At the same time, the distribution of world population changed in a number of significant ways as the following table shows.

TABLE 2. *Growth and Percentage Distribution of World Population, 1800–1900*

	Numbers (millions)		Percentage distribution	
	1800	1900	1800	1900
Africa	90	120	9·9	7·5
North America*	6	81	0·7	5·0
Latin America	19	63	2·1	3·9
Asia†	597	915	65·9	56·9
Europe (including Russia)	192	423	21·2	26·3
Oceania	2	6	0·2	0·4
Total	906	1,608	100·0	100·0

Source: A. M. Carr-Saunders, *World Population* (Oxford, 1936), pp. 30–45.
Notes: * North America = north of the Rio Grande.
　　　　† Excluding Asiatic Russia.

Population grew fastest in the regions dominated by Europeans. In 1900 Asia still remained, as she does today, the most densely populated continent in the world. But in the nineteenth century her relative position had declined, as had that of Africa, because the populations in the other continents, especially North America and Europe (including Russia) were growing faster. The cause of the rapid increase of population in Europe was a familiar one, death rates were falling while birth rates continued at a high level. In North America, Latin America and Oceania, apart from high rates of natural increase, heavy inflows of migrant population, particularly from Europe, contributed to bring about even faster rates of population growth in these regions than were to be found in Europe.

The rapidly growing world population had a number of important consequences for world trade. In itself a growing population would have meant some increased demand for those commodities already traded internationally. Taken in conjunction with changes in the other factors of production, however, it greatly enhanced the possibilities of trade. For example, in Europe, with the possible exception of Russia, the land : labour ratio became less favourable as population grew, despite improved farming techniques and the reclamation of waste lands. Land became scarce and rose in price, so that agricultural products became more expensive relative to those obtained from other countries overseas. As agricultural price differences widened, therefore, the opportunities for trade increased correspondingly, while in those countries where the growth of domestic production of foodstuffs failed to keep pace with population increase foreign imports had to be relied on increasingly to fill the gap. Moreover, the unfavourable land : labour ratio in Europe had another consequence for the intenational economy. It forced people from the land into the towns and, when domestic urban employment was unavailable, overseas to the new regions of primary production. In these areas, where labour was short, the rapid growth of indigenous population, aided by immigration, served only to create more favourable conditions for the exploitation of economic resources, particularly natural resources, which had hitherto remained unworked partly because of the lack of labour.

THE SUPPLY OF NATURAL RESOURCES

Even if precise measurement of natural resources in economic terms is difficult, if not impossible, the available evidence suggests that a substantial increase in the world supply of natural resources occurred during the nineteenth century.[1] Within Europe the supply was added

[1] Difficulties of measurement arise for many reasons. For example, acreage will not do for land, since different areas of land vary significantly in their climatic features, location and natural fertility. Moreover, once land is worked it becomes impossible to separate it from other factors, and especially from capital. Measurement over time is complicated by the fact that technical change may alter the economic value, if not the physical characteristics, of a given resource. Thus petroleum deposits became much more valuable following the invention of the motor-car. Finally, the fact that resource discovery and depletion may take place

to by the cultivation of previously unworked land and the discovery and exploitation of new sources of mineral supply. But by far the largest addition to the world supply of natural resources came from the opening up of the vast, fertile and mineral-rich continents of the Americas and Oceania. Virtually uninhabited, these regions also afforded an enormous increase in living-space for the growing flood of migrants from Europe. By 1800 the European-occupied areas in these continents were already more extensive than the whole of western Europe, whose settled area at this date has been put at between 650,000 and 790,000 square miles. In the course of the next hundred years a further 8–9m. square miles was added to these European territories overseas, approximately an eight to nine-fold increase in the occupied area, while the degree of land use became, in every way, a great deal more intense.

Apart from people's willingness and ability to move to these new lands, the key factors in opening them up included an increased knowledge of their natural resources—land, minerals, climate, and so on—and their economic accessibility, which largely depended on the availability of cheap and adequate transport. Also important was a sufficiency of capital to clear and work the land and exploit its mineral wealth. In all these respects the Americas and Oceania were particularly fortunate, for they possessed a variety of natural resources, which, for the most part, were easily accessible and capable of development by known techniques requiring moderate amounts of capital.

In Asia and tropical Africa, on the other hand, the opening up of new lands and the development of new sources of raw materials was a much slower process than elsewhere. Climatic and topographical difficulties, inadequate knowledge, and institutional resistance to change provided the main obstacles to development in these regions. Where development in these continents did occur, however, the availability of natural resources appears to have been the chief factor influencing the location of what have been described as 'export economies'. Situated for the most part in the tropics, the location of these largely plantation and mining activities was determined not by the relative supply of the various factors of production which existed within a country's borders, but by the location of the least mobile factors of production, such as climate, soil conditions, or mineral deposits, and by accessibility to markets, which if overseas, meant access to ocean-going transport. Labour, capital and entrepreneurship were internationally mobile and could be applied almost any-

---

simultaneously makes it hard to decide whether the supply of natural resources available to a particular country has increased over time or not.

where in the world, so that choice of these industry locations was based on other cost considerations. The most fertile lands and the most promising mineral deposits could be chosen and those requiring the lowest transport costs worked first.[1]

THE GROWTH OF REAL INCOMES

Compared with previous periods, there was a marked rise in real incomes in the nineteenth century as a result of the increase in productivity brought about by new production methods, better organization and improved transport. Despite the obvious difficulties in measuring this improvement in statistical terms and the consequent approximate nature of the available national income estimates, they suggest a three-fold classification of countries based on the annual rates of growth of real incomes which they experienced in the course of the nineteenth century. Heading the list are those primary producing countries which experienced rates of growth in real income per head in the region of 1½ per cent per annum. These included the United States, and after 1850, Canada and Brazil. *Per capita* real income in Argentina may also have risen this fast in the period after 1880. In Australia, on the other hand, the rate of growth of *per capita* real income was somewhat slower than 1½ per cent per annum, and that of New Zealand substantially so. In New Zealand, real income grew at 4·6 per cent per annum, but with population also growing rapidly (4·1 per cent per annum), there was only a 0·5 per cent rise in real income per head. The explanation of this slow growth of *per capita* income in New Zealand seems to be the high income level already attained by the mid-1860s, when average living standards appear to have been significantly higher than those in Australia, which in turn were significantly higher than those in either the United States or Britain. A further substantial rise in real income from such a high base with immigration running at a record level was clearly difficult. Australia's performance was similarly affected by a high initial *per capita* real income, but in addition she experienced a severe and prolonged depression in the 1890s which depressed average real income to such an extent that they did not regain their 1891 peak until 1909.

In Europe, only Sweden and Denmark appear to have experienced rates of growth of real income per head comparable with those of North America. Most other European countries recorded growth rates of between 1 and 1¼ per cent per annum. In Britain and France *per capita* real incomes grew at 1¼ per cent per annum during the nineteenth century, and in Germany in the years after 1870. In

[1] J. V. Levin, *The Export Economies* (Cambridge, Mass., 1960), Chap. IV.

B

Tsarist Russia, real income per head may have risen by 1 per cent or more annually over the period 1800–1914, and in Holland by rather less than 0·9 per cent over the same period. In Italy, where the backward south acted as a drag on economic growth, product per man-year grew by only 0·7 per cent in the period between 1863 and 1913.

The third group consisted of those countries making up the greater part of Asia, Africa, and Latin America, where the annual rate of growth of *per capita* real income was 0·5 per cent or less. Few statistics are available for these countries. In India, where conditions were more favourable to growth than anywhere else in Asia outside Japan, average *per capita* income rose at about 0·4 per cent over the period 1857–63 to 1896–1904. Elsewhere the world output appears to have grown sufficiently fast enough to maintain a slowly growing population. Even if *per capita* real incomes grew in these countries during the nineteenth century, a rate of 0·5 per cent per annum would seem to be the upper limit to what was attainable given their prevailing economic circumstances. The one exception to this generalization was Japan whose total product grew at 4·4 per cent per annum over the period 1880 to 1913. After allowing for population growth, Japanese real income *per capita* grew at the astonishingly high rate of 3 per cent per annum.

Changes in income levels have much to do with changes in demand and consequently with changes in the structure of output and the composition of foreign trade. As incomes rise, there is an increased demand for capital goods, manufactured consumer goods, and services, and a relatively slow expansion in demand for food, textiles and clothing. Moreover, rising living standards, involving as they do changes in tastes, incomes and, consequently, in consumption patterns, not only influence the structure of domestic output but also affect the volume and composition of foreign trade. Thus the shift in the diet of the United States and other Western nations from cereals towards meat and dairy products as the standard of living rose was important both for the domestic producers of these commodities and for the trade flows that existed between these countries. Another example associated with the rise in real incomes is the increased demand for colonial products. Items of trade, such as sugar, tobacco, tea, coffee and cocoa, largely luxuries to previous generations, came to be regarded as necessities during the nineteenth century, while the consumption of tropical fruits also became important for the first time towards the end of this period.

The particular importance of the influence of *per capita* income levels on trade in manufactured goods has been stressed by S. B. Linder, who argues that exports can be developed only in those products for which there is a significant home market. In other words, countries typically export goods that fit into the standard of living attained by broad numbers of their own population. This certainly appears to have been the case with the manufactured consumer and producer goods exported by Britain during the nineteenth century, and it also fits the experience of most other countries too. Moreover, as C. P. Kindleberger has pointed out, Linder's theory may also apply to declining export markets. Thus Britain lost the market for low-grade cotton textiles primarily because of foreign competition but partly because her living standards had risen to the point where these goods were unimportant items of consumption and domestic demand had shifted to higher qualities. On the other hand, the Japanese invasion of this export market was achieved by a textile industry which was supported by a growing domestic demand for low-grade cotton cloth. Linder's hypothesis that trade flows are related to the world structure of *per capita* incomes also leads us to expect large volumes of trade among nations with high *per capita* incomes and small trade flows between rich and poor countries, which is exactly what has tended to happen over the past two hundred years or so. The general validity of Linder's theory has yet to be established empirically, but as the above necessarily limited observations show, it does have an attractive plausibility, particularly as an explanation of the rapid growth of trade in manufactures between high income countries.[1]

THE SPREAD OF ECONOMIC FREEDOM

The period between 1820 and 1913 was characterized by the gradual liberalization of controls over the flows of capital, labour and trade that were to link the countries of the world more closely together as the nineteenth century progressed. The gradual removal of restrictions on the movement of people, both within and between countries, while encouraging international migration, also gave to these movements of population their distinctive feature, namely, their quality as a free movement of individuals, almost entirely without control from either the receiving or sending countries and undertaken almost entirely by single individual or family units. Controls over financial

[1] S. Burenstam Linder, *An Essay on Trade and Transformation* (New York, 1961), especially Chap. 3. See also Kindleberger, *Foreign Trade and the National Economy*, (New Haven, 1962), pp. 58–9. In a number of ways Linder's theory succeeds where the factor proportions theory fails. This is particularly so with respect to prediction of trade flows, where emphasis on differences in factor proportions lead to the false predictions of a large flow of trade between rich and poor countries, and declining trade among industrial countries.

transactions were also minimal. Short and long-term capital could move unsupervised in any direction and these movements could take any form. Direct foreign investment was undertaken, and was often encouraged by the governments of the receiving countries. Foreign securities were freely traded on most stock exchanges. Repatriation of profits was unhampered, and the fear of confiscation of foreign investment almost completely absent. In the form of gold coins, foreign currencies mixed freely with the domestic currencies of many countries. Moreover, like migration, individuals (and enterprises) dominated international financial and commercial transactions before 1914, and only rarely were dealings conducted among countries acting as whole. Finally, whereas international trade had to overcome tariffs during the latter part of the nineteenth century, these were exceedingly low by comparison with those introduced during the interwar years. Furthermore, quotas, import prohibitions and other quantitative restrictions on trade hardly existed before 1913, nor did ideas of economic self-sufficiency, towards the furtherance of which these restrictions on trade were often introduced.

This increase in the degree and extent of economic freedom obviously contributed greatly to bringing about the formation of an international economy during the nineteenth century, although the true extent of that contribution is difficult to measure, because the spread of economic freedom was only one factor operating simultaneously with many others, and because in many instances its influence was dependent on the existence of these other factors for its full realization. For example, increased freedom to move was not in itself sufficient to generate mass migration, for, amongst other things, migration also depended on the existence of cheap and speedy transport facilities. This general conclusion is equally true of all the other influences at work taken individually. What is also apparent, however, is that, taken together, these influences brought about the powerful expansion of foreign trade, capital flows and population movements by means of which the integration of the international economy was achieved during the nineteenth century. It is to a consideration of the forging of these international links of capital, men and trade that we now turn.

SELECTED REFERENCES

Ashworth, W., *A Short History of the International Economy since 1850* (London, 1962), Chaps. I–VI.
Habbakuk, H. J., *and* Postan, M. (eds.), *The Cambridge Economic History*

of Europe, Vol. VI, 'The Industrial Revolutions and After, Part I' (Cambridge, 1965), Chaps. I–IV.

Kindleberger, C. P., *Foreign Trade and the National Economy* (New Haven, 1962).

North, D. C., 'Ocean Freight Rates and Economic Development 1750–1913', *The Journal of Economic History*, Vol.XVIII, No. 4 (Dec., 1958), pp. 537-55.

Woodruff, W., *Impact of Western Man* (New York, 1966), Chaps. V and VI.

Chapter 2

INTERNATIONAL LONG-TERM CAPITAL MOVEMENTS, 1820–1913

Specialization in production along the lines of comparative advantage was a major feature of the nineteenth-century international economy, and it was brought about partly by the mobility of capital (and labour) from country to country. In particular, the outflows of men and money from Europe to the vast, fertile and mineral-rich continents overseas helped provide the increased supplies of foodstuffs and raw materials needed to feed Europe's growing population and industry. Consequently the growth of trade and real income in the world economy that occurred at this time was determined in part by an international redistribution of capital and labour on a scale unique in history. Thus during the century ending in 1913 some £9–10,000m. were invested abroad and some 45–46m. people moved overseas. This movement of capital and population from regions where they were relatively abundant to regions where they were relatively scarce was a necessary condition for the expansion of the international economy.

International movements of capital occur when the residents of one country acquire assets in another (or reduce their liabilities there). Transactions of this sort can occur in a number of ways. For example, a resident in Britain may purchase securities in an American business or the bonds of an American government; or he may export goods to the United States and leave the proceeds on deposit in that country; or, if he owns a business in the United States, he may 'plough back' the profits of the enterprise instead of withdrawing them as dividends. What all these transactions have in common is the fact that some person (an individual or a firm) resident in Britain acquires either the paper assets of, or property ownership rights in, the United States.

One basic distinction between different types of international capital movements is that between long and short-term transactions. This distinction gives rise to problems of definition, but these can be safely ignored here by assuming that the foreign long-term capital investment discussed in this chapter consists of capital invested in the expectation that the investment will not be liquidated in the near future and that it will earn income over an appreciable period.[1] While it is our intention here to concentrate on an examination of foreign long-term capital movements in the nineteenth century, the methods adopted in compiling the estimates of foreign investment used in this chapter are such that the figures may occasionally include short as well as long-term capital flows. This fact, however, does not weaken in any way the analysis that follows.

THE GROWTH OF FOREIGN INVESTMENT

At the beginning of the nineteenth century the total value of foreign investment was small, and its economic impact on both the borrowing and lending countries insignificant. It was a business activity undertaken almost exclusively by a few privileged European trading and financial organizations with foreign interests. From the end of the Napoleonic Wars, however, foreign investment assumed a new character and an increasing significance. This change came about for a number of reasons. The establishment and growth of specialized financial institutions in both borrowing and lending countries, such as commercial banks (operating in foreign exchange) and investment houses, made foreign investment easier and less risky, while the accumulation of savings by a middle class willing to invest them abroad supplied the funds needed for an expansion of foreign lending. The flow of funds from savers in one country to borrowers in another was also facilitated by the appearance of more sophisticated financial instruments, such as credit money and bills of exchange. In addition, capital markets, such as 'the City' in London, became much more diversified in their business dealings, thereby aiding the expansion of international trade and the growth of foreign investment.

[1] Conventionally, capital lent for less than one year is said to be short-term; that lent for longer than this is described as long-term. The chief difficulty found in implementing this seemingly simple and clear-cut distinction is that the form of the commercial instrument used is not an entirely reliable guide for allocative purposes. Thus, nominally long-term investments, such as government bonds, may in fact be held for short periods if they are readily marketable. This has led some writers to think of the distinction in terms of the investor's motives. The definition used above is conceived largely in these terms.

Long-term investment may also be classified into 'direct' and 'portfolio'. Direct investment occurs when a company in one country sets up a subsidiary, or acquires a controlling interest in a domestic business, in another country. Portfolio investment consists of capital flows from one country to another over the use of which the investors do not have any control, for instance investment in foreign government loans, in the purchase of a small proportion of share capital in a foreign company, or deposits in foreign financial institutions.

From the end of the Napoleonic Wars until the mid-fifties about £420m. ($2,050m.) was invested abroad. By 1870 the total value of these investments had more than trebled. But the great era of international lending occurred after 1870, with the capital outflow becoming a flood during the decade before World War I. By 1900 foreign investments totalled £4,750m. ($23,000m.), and they rose rapidly during the next few years to reach £9,500m. ($43,000m.) in 1914.[1]

DIRECTION OF FOREIGN INVESTMENT

Capital Exporting Countries

Britain was the major source of supply of foreign capital during the nineteenth century, and France another foreign lender of substance during these years. After 1870, however, when the outflow of loanable funds from the capital-rich countries accelerated tremendously, Germany and the United States became major investing countries and by 1914 together accounted for one-fifth of the total value of the assets owned abroad by all the capital exporting nations. Belgium, the Netherlands, and Switzerland formed another important group of countries willing to place large surplus savings at the disposal of investors in other countries. But as Diagram 1(a) demonstrates, Britain remained by far the most important single source of foreign funds after 1870, with a record as a foreign lender unsurpassed in the whole history of international investment. Thus between 1870 and 1914 the annual outflow of capital from Britain for investment overseas averaged approximately 4 per cent of national income. Even more striking is the fact that the annual outflow of capital from Britain averaged close to 7 per cent of her national income over the years 1905 to 1913, and reached a phenomenal 9 per cent in the latter year.

Capital Importing Countries

Diagram 1(b) shows the distribution of foreign investments in 1914 by recipient region. From it we see that Europe received the largest slice of this investment. Most European countries received some capital from abroad at one time or another during the nineteenth century, but by 1914 Russia and the Balkans (including Turkey) were the major borrowers, mainly from France and Germany. Next in order of size of capital inflow was North America. Two-thirds of its share went to the United States, and the remainder went to

---

[1] The total value of foreign investments is the gross amount owed by other countries to lending countries. Some lenders, for instance, the United States, were net borrowers during the period, since they borrowed much larger amounts of foreign capital than they lent abroad themselves.

Diagram 1: Distribution of Foreign Investments, 1914

(a) By Investing Regions

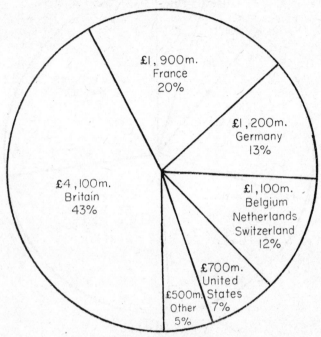

£1,900m.
France
20%

£1,200m.
Germany
13%

£4,100m.
Britain
43%

£1,100m.
Belgium
Netherlands
Switzerland
12%

£700m.
United
States
7%

£500m.
Other
5%

Total: £9,500m.

Canada. Argentina, Brazil and Mexico were the most attractive countries in Latin America for foreign investors, and together they accounted for over 80 per cent of the foreign capital directed to that region. In Asia the bulk of funds went to India, Ceylon, China and Japan, each of which received £200m. or more. By 1914, the Union of South Africa had absorbed approximately 60 per cent of the total funds entering Africa. Egypt accounted for another quarter to a third, and the colonies of Britain, France, Germany and Belgium for most of the remainder. Australia was the major recipient of funds exported to Oceania. If the countries comprising the 'regions of recent settlement'—the United States, Canada, Argentina, Uruguay, South Africa, Australia and New Zealand—are taken together, they absorbed about 40 per cent of the capital invested abroad by 1914.

Changing Direction of Investment

Table 3 and Diagram 2 show the changing geographical pattern of

Diagram 1 (b) By Recipient Regions

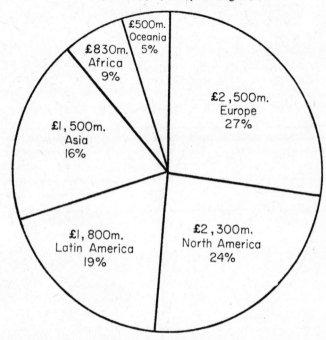

Total : £9,430m.

Source: W. Woodruff, *Impact of Western Man* (London, 1966), pp. 154–5

British foreign investment over the period 1830 to 1914. The bulk of Britain's foreign investment in 1830 was to be found in Europe and Latin America, where British lending during the 1820s had been used primarily to stabilize currencies and to maintain the political *status quo*. In addition the boom of the mid-twenties in Britain had stimulated substantial direct investment in Latin American mining activity. In the late 1820s, however, financial reverses in Europe and Latin America left much of the newly incurred debt in default, and consequently the British investor turned his attention to the United States, where canal and railway building financed by the issue of state and municipal securities created a demand for foreign funds. Unfortunately North America proved little more reliable than South America as a borrower, and in the difficult years that followed the financial panic of 1837, the state governments were forced to stop interest payments and two states repudiated their debts outright. As a result of these further financial set-backs, and because domestic economic activity was running at a high level after

1845, interest in foreign investment waned in Britain during the 1840s, although the domestic railway boom of the mid-decade did give rise to railway construction by British contractors in Europe and the colonies. By the mid-fifties, therefore, the distribution of Britain's overseas investment had changed significantly. The share of the total to be found in Europe and in Latin America had declined, while that of the United States had increased substantially. The flow of funds to the rest of the world continued to be insignificant.

Between the mid-fifties and 1870 another major change in the regional distribution of British capital occurred. Empire countries increasingly attracted British funds away from Europe and Latin America, whereas the United States was barely able to maintain its relative share of the total capital outflow from Britain. These changing preferences of British investors were neither fortuitous nor largely the outcome of conscious political planning on the part of the investing country. Rather they were the result of the changing circumstances confronting British railway builders and investors on the Continent who found their profits being squeezed by increasing competition from French, Belgian, and German entrepreneurs. In addition, the unsettled conditions in the United States prior to, and during, the Civil War combined to turn the British investor away from that country. By 1870 Empire countries

TABLE 3. *British Foreign Investment, 1830–1914 (Regional Distribution)*

	1830	1854	1870	1914
	%	%	%	%
Europe	66	55	25	5
United States	9	25	27	21
Latin America	23	15	11	18
British Empire: India			22	9
Dominions	2	5	12	37
Other regions			3	9
Total	100	100	100	100
Total investment (£m.)	110	260	770	4,107
($m.)	536	1,266	3,750	20,000

Sources: L. H. Jenks, *The Migration of British Capital to 1875*, 3rd edn. (London, 1963), pp. 64 and 413; A. H. Imlah, 'British Balance of Payments and Export of Capital 1816–1913', *Economic History Review*, (August 1952), pp. 208–39; C. H. Feinstein, *Home and Foreign Investment, 1870–1913* (Cambridge, 1960); W. Woodruff, op. cit., pp. 154–5.

accounted for a third of all British foreign investments. Investment had been heaviest in India, where some £95m. was invested in railways alone between 1845 and 1875, but the volume of investment in Canada, Australia and New Zealand was also growing during these years.

The trend towards investment in Empire countries intensified to such an extent after 1870 that close to one-half of the total British capital abroad in 1914 was located in these countries, with the bulk of it invested in the Dominion countries. Australasia during the 1880s and Canada after 1904 were the most attractive Empire regions for British investors during this period, while India's relative share declined considerably. The United States continued to receive a high proportion of British capital outflow, chiefly in the form of portfolio investment in railroad companies, and Latin American countries, especially Argentina and, to a lesser extent, Brazil, once again gained favour in the London capital market. On the other hand, Britain's European investments had become relatively unimportant

Diagram 2: British Foreign Investment, 1830–1914
(Regional Distribution)

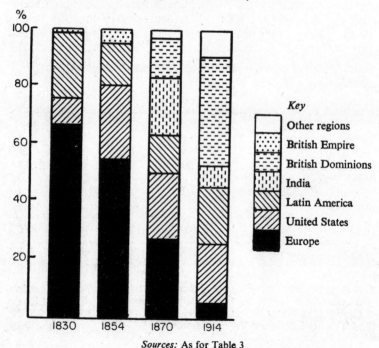

Sources: As for Table 3

by 1914, chiefly because the Continent had become better able to supply its own capital needs, and while the percentage share going to the rest of the world had trebled between 1870 and 1914, in absolute terms its amount remained small.

French foreign investment during the period 1816 to 1851 amounted to 2,500m. francs (£98m.), the bulk of which was to be found in Spain, the Italian States and Belgium. There was some French investment in the United States in the late 1830s, but French capital played only a minor role in development there before 1880. Europe continued to absorb the largest share of the French capital outflow in the thirty years after 1851, while the Ottoman Empire and Egypt also emerged as major borrowers at this time. About a third of the new capital was invested in railway building, particularly in the Iberian and Italian peninsulas, in Central Europe, and in Russia. A large part of the foreign government loans was lost in the defaults of the seventies, with losses particularly severe in the Near East, but by the early 1880s a revival of French foreign investment was well under way.

In the subsequent period up to 1914, the direction of the outflow of investible funds from France changed radically, as Table 4 and Diagram 3 illustrate. The Mediterranean, Near Eastern, and Central European countries lost their previous attractions for French

TABLE 4. *French Foreign Investment, 1851–1914 (Regional Distribution)*

Region	1851 F.000m.	%	1881 F.000m.	%	1914 F.000m.	%
Mediterranean[1]	1·5	60	6·9	39	7·3	14
Central Europe[2]	0·3	12	3·1	18	4·1	8
Eastern Europe[3]	—	—	1·3	7	14·7	28
North-West Europe[4]	0·6	24	1·2	7	4·1	8
Near East[5]	—	—	3·5	20	5·9	11
Colonies	—	—	0·7	4	4·5	9
Western Hemisphere	0·1	4	0·9	5	8·3	16
Other regions	—	—	—	—	3·8	6
Totals (F.000m.)	2·5	100	17·6	100	52·7	100
(£m.)	98		688		2,073	

Notes: 1. Italy, Spain, Portugal. 2 Austro-Hungary, Germany, Switzerland. 3. Russia, Rumania, Greece, Serbia. 4. Belgium, Luxemburg, Netherlands, United Kingdom, Scandinavia. 5. Ottoman Empire and Egypt.
Source: R. E. Cameron, *France and the Economic Development of Europe 1800–1914* (Princeton, 1961), pp. 79, 85 and 486.

Diagram 3: French Foreign Investment, 1851–1914
(Regional Distribution)

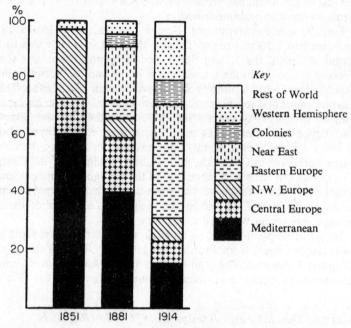

Key

Rest of World

Western Hemisphere

Colonies

Near East

Eastern Europe

N.W. Europe

Central Europe

Mediterranean

Source: As for Table 4

investors who transferred their attentions towards Russia and the Balkans. In addition, from the late nineties, non-European countries, chiefly in Latin America, increased their relative share of the available funds. In contrast with the attitudes of British investors, the French colonies were not considered favourably by French capital owners, and only Algeria, and to a lesser extent Indo-China, received the benefits of capital inflow. By 1914, therefore, approximately three-fifths of the total French capital outflow was located in Europe, 16 per cent in the Americas, and slightly more in Asia, chiefly in Turkey.

German foreign investment only assumed significance in the 1880s, when government securities issued by the Balkan countries, Turkey, Spain, Portugal and Italy were subscribed to in Germany at a time when Paris hesitated to lend in these directions. In addition, loans were extended to Argentina, Venezuela and Mexico, and United States railroad bonds were also popular. Following the defaults associated with the financial crises of the 1890s, German foreign lending declined until the early years of this century when the German investor turned away from Europe and towards the United States and the German colonies. By 1914 about half the German foreign investments had been absorbed by European countries, with Austro-Hungary accounting for a substantial part of this capital, and the rest being fairly evenly spread over Russia, Turkey, the Balkans, Spain, Portugal, France, and Britain. Of the 11,000m. marks (£540m.) invested outside Europe, about 70 per cent went to the Americas and Africa, and Asia (especially the German colonies there) obtained most of the remainder.

Before 1870 United States foreign investment was little more than $75m. (£15m.), and was mostly confined to direct investment in mining and manufacturing ventures in Canada, Mexico, and South America. By 1899, however, investment in Europe had considerable attractions for American businesses and 80 per cent of the $685m. (£140m.) held abroad, mainly in the form of direct investment, was located in Canada, Mexico, and Europe. This proportion of total foreign placements of funds declined progressively after 1899 to 66 per cent in 1914, when the total United States foreign investment reached $3,514m. (£717m.). During this period of greatly accelerating foreign investment, South America and Asia became important recipients of United States direct investment. Manufacturing, the mining of industrial metals, and agricultural enterprises consumed the bulk of the capital outflow.

DETERMINANTS OF CAPITAL OUTFLOW

Before a country could undertake a massive foreign investment programme a number of conditions had to be fulfilled. First, a considerable degree of economic growth had to be achieved in the country to ensure that domestic savings were accumulated fast enough to provide the surplus of funds. Second, there had to exist abroad a number of government or business enterprises willing and anxious to borrow, or alternatively, numerous opportunities for profitable business ventures for direct investment. Third, some form of machinery was required to ensure that the transfer of funds from savers in one country to borrowers in another proceeded with a minimum of friction—in other words, a fairly diversified capital market was needed and one capable of undertaking foreign investment. Finally, an incentive to invest abroad had to present itself.

Undoubtedly the prospect of earning a higher rate of return on one's investment by placing it abroad rather than at home is a major determinant of the volume of foreign lending. For this reason we would expect to find that investment abroad tends to increase at times when domestic economic activity in the capital exporting country is depressed and investment at home is thus relatively unprofitable. On the other hand, investment in foreign extractive and other industries could be expected to rise at a time when business activity in the industrial capital exporting country was high and incomes rising, since foreign resources required tapping to feed domestic industries with raw materials and income earners required greater quantities of imported consumer goods, especially foodstuffs. However, attempts to establish statistically the nature of the relationship between expected rates of return and their effects on the volume of investment at home and abroad have not been very successful.[1] This is probably because of the very simple models used in these tests, which fail to consider the many other influences, including political factors, acting upon capital flows. Even so, changes in relative interest rates and rates of return on investments in the capital exporting and capital importing countries—after allowance for changing risk premiums—must have been important determinants of both the willingness to invest abroad and the desire and ability to borrow abroad during the nineteenth century.[2]

Another important determinant of the volume and direction of foreign investment during these years was the growth and altering structure of the international economy. The industrialization of Europe and the growth of its population created a steadily growing demand for raw materials and foodstuffs, much of which had to be imported. At the same time, important advances in technical knowledge, especially in transportation and communications, and the existence of underpopulated and land-rich countries in other continents provided the means whereby these demands could be met. The greater part of the foreign investment undertaken during the nineteenth century was concerned with promoting this international specialization between an industrial centre located in Europe (and, later, in the United States) and a periphery of primary producing countries. Apart from being suppliers of foodstuffs and raw materials, these peripheral countries were also important markets for manufactured goods. Their significance as markets provided another incentive for investment in them, especially after 1880, when, because of the industrialization of Germany and the

---

[1] See, for example, A. I. Bloomfield, *Patterns of Fluctuation in International Investment before 1914*, Princeton Studies in International Finance, No. 21 (Princeton, 1968), especially pp. 35–40.

[2] The relationship between capital movements and the terms of trade, which forms one aspect of this problem of relative rates of return in capital exporting and capital importing countries, is discussed in Chapter 10, pp. 165–66.

United States and the spread of protection, Britain lost many of her traditional export markets in Europe and North America. Increasingly during these years British foreign investment was directed to the Empire, which also now became one of its most important export markets.

The amount of technical and capital assistance that can be used effectively by a country is often spoken of as its capacity to absorb capital. Obviously, while it is not possible to measure exactly what the 'absorptive capacity' of an individual country is at a particular time, it is possible to list certain conditions that are necessary for the productive utilization of capital, whether of domestic or foreign origin. Absorption capacity will be low, for example, when there are inadequate transport facilities, administrative and organizational bottlenecks, deficient qualities of entrepreneurship, a lack of complementary natural resources, scarcities of trained manpower, narrow localized markets, and so on. In respect of these conditions during the nineteenth century some countries, notably the United States, Canada, Australia, Argentina, Brazil, and a number of European countries, were better placed than others, for example, China, India, Egypt, and most of Africa. It is not surprising therefore to find that by 1913 almost two-thirds of the total foreign investment undertaken during the nineteenth century was to be found in the first-mentioned group of countries, whose capacity to absorb this capital was helped by the international flows of labour that accompanied these movements of foreign capital.

Institutional developments and the spread of protectionism were other important influences at work determining the volume and direction of foreign investment, especially after 1870. The growth and development of financial institutions in both lending and borrowing countries, the movement towards free trade by the 1870s (although reversed in later decades), and the establishment of the gold standard, all contributed in varying degrees to the marshalling of domestic savings in lending countries, the rapid transfer of these funds to borrowing countries, and the relatively efficient distribution of the acquired loans to the investors in the latter countries. Especially after the 1870s, foreign direct investment expanded for yet another reason, namely, to avoid high tariffs on imports by setting up factories in the tariff-raising countries. This was largely the reason for German direct investments in the United States, Russia, and a number of other European countries, for British direct investments in Europe and the United States, and for American investments in Canada and Europe.

Finally, political factors influenced foreign investment in a number of ways. Before 1850, British loans to Greece, Belgium and several

Latin American republics were made partly because of the sympathy existing in Britain for the rebel states. However, this attitude did not prevent the British investor from advancing loans to other European governments for counter-revolutionary purposes or for other uses aimed at preserving the *status quo* in European politics. The pattern of French investment before 1850 was also largely determined by political considerations, as well as geographical proximity and cultural and religious affinities to the borrowing countries. In these years 95 per cent of French holdings of foreign government securities were those of Spain, Portugal, the Italian States, Belgium and Austria. After 1850, political considerations continued to exert some influence on the direction of foreign investment, but they became an important determinant only after 1890, when the need to build up military alliances in anticipation of a future power struggle led to numerous foreign loans being negotiated. The French invested heavily in Russian government securities, and by 1914 10,000m. francs (£390m.) was owed to French investors. For similar reasons, Russia also received substantial British loans in the years leading up to 1914. Much German investment at this time went to Austro-Hungary and certain of the Balkan countries. Moreover, the political rivalry which arose in Europe late in the nineteenth century manifested itself in a burst of imperialism and rapid colonization in much of Africa and Asia. This development was accompanied by a flow of funds into these regions either to exploit their natural resources or to establish European control over them.

THE USE OF FOREIGN FUNDS IN BORROWING COUNTRIES

During the nineteenth century, foreign investment went into three major fields: government loans, transport and communications, and manufacturing and extractive industries. Compared with most other capital-importing regions, European borrowing tended to be dominated by government loans. Frequently, in the first half of the century, these loans were used to support the extravagance or inefficiency of courts and governments, or for war, defence, insurrection, or counter-revolutionary purposes. Towards the end of the century, as the European power struggle gathered force, loans from the west European capital exporters to the governments of Russia, central Europe, and the Balkans tended once again to be utilized mainly for military purposes. Of greater economic significance, however, was the heavy investment in railway construction. From the 1840s the desire of railway builders, at first in Britain, and later in France and Germany, to cover the European continent with a railway network provided most European countries with the usual economic (and military) benefits to be derived from improved transportation.

Foreign investment in railways was also important for the opening up of other continents. By 1914, $4,000m. (57 per cent) of the total United States foreign debt of $7,000m. was in the form of railway securities held abroad, more than half of them in Britain. The British also invested heavily in Indian, Canadian and Australian railways; while in Latin America, Asia and Africa railway building absorbed a large share of the investment funds flowing from Britain and Europe to these regions in the period after 1870. In addition to providing many countries with more unified domestic markets, this railway investment accelerated their integration into the international economy by allowing cheap and rapid transport of commodities produced in the interior of each country to the seaboard for shipment abroad. In this way international capital movements provided the basis for an expanding foreign trade.

If other forms of investment in public works were of minor significance when compared with the railways, they were nevertheless important to many countries. The provision of port facilities was a valuable supplement to the railway construction in the Great Plains regions. Canals were built in the United States in the 1820s and 1830s largely with the aid of British capital, and the provision of water and sewerage, roads, bridges, public buildings, telegraph and telephone facilities, gas and electricity financed with foreign funds formed important services for the inhabitants of countries which were experiencing the general benefits of expanding international investment.

For the most part the flow of funds into the manufacturing and extractive industries took the form of direct investment, the extent of which was small in the years before 1870. British capital and enterprise were involved in textile and iron manufacturing on the Continent at this time, and there was also some British capital invested in mining activities in Sweden, Italy and, later, Spain. French industrial investments were concentrated largely in Belgium and Germany, where they were to be found in mining, the metallurgical industries and glass manufacture. After 1870, however, the level of foreign investment in manufacturing and mining increased substantially. In Europe, Germany and France invested heavily in a wide range of manufacturing and mining enterprises in Austria, Italy, Spain and Sweden, but the most striking benefits to be derived from direct investment in Europe accrued to Russia, where a number of industries, including chemicals, metal fabricating, textiles and metal refining were financed by foreign capital after 1880. Foreign investment in oil production, and copper, gold and lead mining also contributed significantly to Russian development. As a result, Russia recorded one of the highest annual average rates of growth of gross national product in Europe between 1870 and 1914.

In the United States there was some private portfolio investment in manufacturing after 1870, where foreign investors, mainly British, contributed funds to such firms as U.S. Steel, Eastman Kodak, United Fruit Company, and General Electric. Direct investment by British, Belgian and Dutch firms also went into American oil production, especially after 1901. In Canada, American direct investment expanded production in several spheres of manufacturing, chiefly steel, sugar refining, paper and pulp, and mineral refining.

Direct investment in mining and manufacturing also occurred in Latin America and, to a lesser extent, in Australasia and parts of Asia. But these investments remained of minor significance when compared with the much heavier foreign industrial investment in Europe and North America. Even in the latter continents, however, the importance of this type of investment should not be exaggerated. As we have already seen, the bulk of foreign lending went into railways and other forms of social overhead capital. Consequently, if foreign lending was of any great significance to the industrial development of the borrowing countries, it made its main contribution indirectly, in the sense that better transport facilities widened domestic markets and thereby encouraged the growth of manufacturing industry, and because the availability of foreign capital for investment in overhead capital meant that domestic capital resources were released for use in other forms of domestic economic activity, including manufacturing and mining.

In concluding this section a brief comment on foreign investment in primary production is relevant. British foreign investment in agricultural and pastoral industries tended to occur in an indirect manner, especially in Australasia and South America, where financial institutions, both British and domestic, accumulated savings through deposits in Britain and lent them to primary producers in the countries concerned. In addition, American direct investment was responsible for the establishment or expansion of agricultural industries in Canada, Mexico, Cuba, and South America. Direct investment, of the colonial type, was instrumental in expanding plantation crops such as sugar, rubber, coffee, tea and cocoa, and in developing various mining ventures in Latin America, Africa, Asia, and Oceania. British, French and German investors were particularly active in these areas.

ECONOMIC CONSEQUENCES OF FOREIGN INVESTMENT

For capital-exporting countries there were risks involved in all types of investment, particularly those involving the postponement of interest payments and repudiation of debts. During several periods of the nineteenth century foreign investors either lost their capital through default or were compelled to wait many years before even interest payments were resumed. This happened to British investments in Europe and Latin America in the 1820s, in the United States in the thirties, and in several areas of the world in the 1890s. French investors also burnt their fingers in the United States in the late thirties and in Europe in the seventies, and German investors were estimated to have lost through repudiation or default in the early 1890s as much as 10 per cent of their total capital abroad at the time.

The profitability of investing abroad to a large extent depended on the uses to which the funds were put in the recipient countries. If invested in economically useful and desirable fields, such as in overhead capital or in industrial enterprises located in the growth sectors of the borrowing economy, the likelihood of default was diminished (but not eliminated), for such investments favourably affected growth rates, and at the same time tended to expand exports (or more occasionally reduce imports), so that the means for paying income to foreign investors was provided by the use of the funds. Countries which 'wasted' their loans from abroad in uneconomic pursuits, such as wars, speculation, or to support the extravagance or inefficiency and corruption of courts and governments, tended on the whole not to provide such a mechanism for servicing the foreign debt. Thus default or repudiation was often a virtual certainty. But while much foreign investment was lost in this way, the bulk of it was used productively, and the investment income from abroad, especially after 1870, was of such a size that it tended almost to equal or to exceed the total annual outflow of foreign capital. In other words, for most capital exporting countries during these years, and especially for Britain, the income receipts on past foreign investment provided the funds out of which new loans for foreign borrowers were provided.

The lending countries also received substantial indirect benefits from their foreign investments. For numerous non-European countries, foreign capital inflow led to an acceleration of international specialization of production, chiefly in the development of the Great Plains regions. By lending surplus savings to these regions to set up railway systems and thereby directly effecting a rapid extension of the land frontier, European countries provided for themselves additional sources of supply of cheap foodstuffs and raw materials which ensured that the industrialization of their economies would take place with a minimum of friction and bottle-necks. Such benefits substantially outweighed the occasional losses through default and repudiation, for which irrational actions of the lenders themselves were partly to blame. Indeed, the speedy return of investors to foreign lending after each international financial crisis had passed is indicative of the benefits to be derived from such activity.

The economic impact of foreign lending on the capital-importing country depended on the uses to which the funds were put. In a number of countries capital inflows (accompanied by immigration) acted as a major force producing rapid and sustained economic growth so that by 1914 these countries were among the most economically highly developed in the world. When countries used their foreign loans efficiently the problem of servicing the debt incurred by borrowing, that is, of meeting the interest payments and the eventual repayment of the loan, was unlikely to produce any significant balance of payments difficulties. Thus over time, the only determinant of the borrowing country's capacity to repay was the loan's contribution to the productivity of the economy as a whole and the capacity of the system to skim away part of the increased productivity in taxes or pricing for transfer abroad. In so far as the loans to borrowing countries (largely primary producers) were used to increase the output of primary products and lower their costs of production, an expansion of exports could be expected which, as long as it grew faster than the long-run rate of growth of imports, would produce a balance of payments surplus out of which interest payments and debt redemptions could be met. Where foreign loans were wasted in uneconomic uses, balance of payments difficulties for the borrowing country were inevitable, followed by non-payment of interest on the debt and possibly even default.

Generally speaking, foreign investment bestowed other benefits upon many borrowing countries. It facilitated the diffusion of technological knowledge from the lending to borrowing countries, thus increasing the likelihood of an increase in productivity. At the same time, the capital flows produced real flows of resources from lenders to borrowers by ensuring that the latter's imports of goods and services could continuously exceed exports for a considerable period of years. To the extent that capital goods increased relative to consumer goods in imports, the growth of productivity in the borrowing country was further enhanced. Thus, for many countries, the diversion of funds received into economically desirable avenues of investment assumed a major role in the development of their economies, even if, at times, the inflow exceeded the absorptive capacity of the industries concerned, and if, occasionally, sudden cessation of capital inflow led to short-run balance of payments crises. But as the loans made their impact felt on the economy and as each country's total production rose so too did savings out of incomes rise. As time passed the rate of savings in many capital importing countries accelerated. Although for most countries the growth of domestic savings did not lead to a reduction of capital inflow, foreign capital tended on the whole to be used in certain different ways, especially in the provision of public works, so that the extra savings could be used to increase production in other sectors of the economy, for example, manufacturing and commerce. Nevertheless, there was often much overlapping of the two types of investment in certain industries. It remains true, however, that the ability of domestic income earners to accumulate savings stemmed in part from the use of foreign funds in the economy.

Finally, direct investment made some contribution to the growth of production in a number of countries. This was a particulary attractive form of foreign investment activity for industrializing countries in the nineteenth century because it provided a combination of capital with technological know-how and entrepreneurial ability. In the early stages of industrialization in both Europe and North America this type of investment played an important and valuable part. In primary producing countries, however, particularly those in Asia, Latin America and Africa, the concentration of direct investment in export industries, such as plantation crops and mining, in general did little to improve local living standards, and most of the benefits derived from such ventures tended to accrue to the foreign investors in the capital-exporting countries.

With the exception of government loans used for military purposes and those frittered away on the upkeep of courts and other royal extravagances, the international capital flows in the nineteenth century aided the economic growth of both borrowing and lending countries. The recipient countries used the capital to construct social overhead capital and to increase their output of export products. The lending countries were at the same time able to intensify their movement towards industrialization by ensuring rapidly growing supplies of cheap raw materials to feed their factories, and of cheap foodstuffs for their increasing urban populations. The receipts of interest and dividend payments by the capital exporting countries rapidly grew to such levels as to provide a revolving fund out of which further capital was quickly made available for re-investment abroad. Although the mechanism of international investment occasionally broke down, when the whole period before 1914 is considered, the international flows of capital, and the benefits this investment produced in the form of high rates of economic growth in many countries and a rapidly rising volume of international trade, constituted one of the most significant forces at work in welding together the international economy during these years.

SELECTED REFERENCES

Cairncross, A. K., *Home and Foreign Investment 1870–1913* (Cambridge, 1953).

Cameron, R. E., *France and the Economic Development of Europe 1800–1914* (Princeton, 1961).

Feis, H., *Europe the World's Banker 1870–1914* (New Haven, 1930).

Hall, A. R. (ed.), *The Export of Capital from Britain 1870–1914* (London, 1968).

Hobson, C. K., *The Export of Capital* (New York, 1914).

Imlah, A. H., *Economic Elements in the Pax Britannica* (Cambridge, Mass., 1958).

Lewis, C. (assisted by Karl T. Schlotterbeck), *America's Stake in International Investments* (Washington, 1938).

Royal Institute of International Affairs, *The Problem of International Investment* (Oxford, 1937).

Saul, S. B., *Studies in British Overseas Trade 1870-1914* (Liverpool, 1960).

Woodruff, W., *Impact of Western Man* (New York, 1966), Chap. IV.

Chapter 3

INTERNATIONAL MIGRATION, 1820-1913

If the flow of capital from Europe constitutes a remarkable chapter in the history of international economic development, so does the emigration of labour that accompanied the outflow of capital. As we have just seen, the bulk of Europe's foreign investment in the nineteenth century went to relatively sparsely populated areas where labour was scarce. To these regions also went millions of emigrants from Europe. As entrepreneurs and workers, they complemented and helped to make productive the capital that was flowing to these new countries overseas.

EUROPEAN MIGRATION 1821–1913

When it comes to an examination of the volume, composition and direction of these intercontinental flows of population, difficulties inherent in definition, coverage and techniques of data collection and reporting make it hazardous to chart the course of the streams of migration that constitute this extensive redistribution of population. Inevitably these difficulties become more acute the further back into the nineteenth century we go. But thanks to the diligent and cumulative efforts of some of the world's leading demographers, the nature and direction of these intercontinental population flows can now be indicated with a considerable degree of confidence.

Taking the emigration statistics first, these suggest a total population outflow overseas of some 46 millions during the period 1821–1915. The mass of the migrants, some 44 millions originated in Europe (see Diagram 4), the remainder coming chiefly from Asia. The bulk of the European movement took place after 1880, although with every decade the tide of population movement increased in volume, rising from an average of over 110,000 a year in the period 1821–50 to 270,000 in 1851–80, and to over 900,000 in 1881–1915 (see Table 5). In total some 11–12 million Europeans emigrated before 1880 compared with 32 millions after that date. This acceleration in the rate of emigration from Europe after 1880 was

Diagram 4: Emigration from Europe, 1821–1915

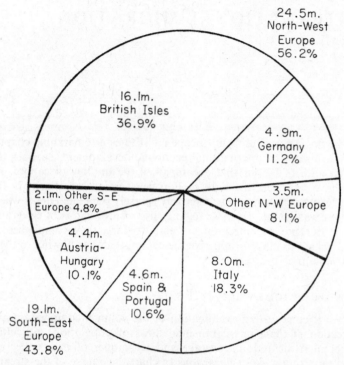

Total Outflow: 43·6m.
Source: As for Table 5

coupled with a significant shift of the source of the population outflow. Before 1880 most of the emigrants came from northern and western Europe; after that date the majority were from southern and eastern Europe.

Over the whole period the British Isles was the principal source of supply of people, accounting for approximately 37 per cent of the total outflow from Europe.

The other major sources, in order of their importance, were Italy, Germany, Austro-Hungary, Spain, Russia (including Poland), and Portugal. Emigration from Britain was heavy throughout the nineteenth century, whereas the outflow from Italy became substantial only after 1880. Then it grew rapidly, and in the first decade of this century it was heavier even than the outflow from Britain (3·6m. compared with 2·8m.). German emigration, which along

Diagram 5: International Immigration, 1821–1915

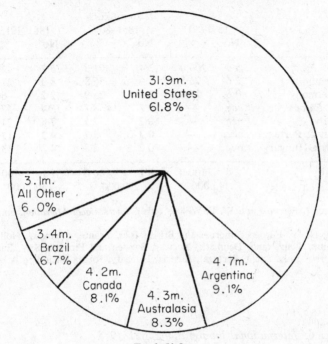

Total: 51·5 m.
Sources: As for Table 6

with the British accounted for the bulk of the European outflow before 1880, became relatively less important after that date, owing chiefly to the alternative domestic employment opportunities afforded by rapid industrialization.

The immigration statistics, which probably give a fuller and truer picture of intercontinental population movements during these years, show a gross inflow of just over 51 million (Diagram 5 and Table 6). Not all of these immigrants settled permanently in the countries to which they travelled, but owing to lack of adequate information on the numbers returning home, the extent of the net movement is difficult to gauge. Of the total gross immigration recorded between 1821 and 1915, about 62 per cent entered the United States, 9 per cent Argentina, 8 per cent Canada, and approximately 7 per cent Brazil. Taken together, the Americas received more than 85 per cent of the recorded immigration before 1915. The greater part of the remainder consisted of migrant flows

TABLE 5. *Emigration from Europe, 1821–1915*

	1821–50		1851–80		1881–1915	
	No	%	No	%	No	%
N.W. Europe	*3·4*	*100·0*	*7·4*	*91·3*	*13·7*	*42·7*
Britain	2·6	76·5	4·6	56·8	8·9	27·7
Germany	0·6	17·6	2·1	25·9	2·2	6·9
S.E. Europe	neg.	—	*0·7*	*8·7*	*18·4*	*57·3*
Italy	neg.	—	0·2	2·5	7·8	24·3
Spain & Portugal	neg.	—	0·3	3·7	4·3	13·4
Austria-Hungary	neg.	—	0·2	2·5	4·2	13·1
Total	3·4	100·0	8·1	100·0	32·1	100·0
Annual averages	113,000		270,000		917,000	

Source: I. Ferenczi and W. F. Willcox (eds.), *International Migration*, op. cit., Vol. 1.
Note: N. W. Europe comprises the British Isles, France, Germany, Holland, Belgium, Switzerland, Denmark, Norway, Sweden and Finland; S.W. Europe comprises Italy, Spain, Portugal, Austria, Hungary, Russia (including Poland).

TABLE 6. *International Immigration, 1821–1915*

Country of Immigration	1821–50		1851–80		1881–1915	
	No	%	No	%	No	%
United States	2·38	67·0	7·73	68·1	21·76	59·4
Canada	0·74	20·8	0·82	7·2	2·59	7·1
British W. Indies	0·08	2·3	0·27	2·4	0·53	1·4
Brazil	0·02	0·6	0·45	4·0	2·97	8·1
Argentina	—	—	0·44	3·9	4·26	11·6
Australia ⎱	0·19	5·4	0·79	7·0	2·77	7·6
New Zealand ⎰			0·25	2·2	0·26	0·7
All others	0·14	3·9	0·60	5·3	1·50	4·1
Total	3·55	100·0	11·35	100·0	36·64	100·0
Annual averages	118,000		378,000		1,046,857	

Source: I. Ferenczi and W. F. Willcox (eds.), *International Migration*, op. cit., Table 6, pp. 236–88; United States Bureau of Census, *Statistical Abstract of the United States;* G. W. Roberts and J. Byrne, 'Summary Statistics on Indenture and Associated Migration affecting the West Indies 1834–1918', *Population Studies* (July, 1966) pp. 125–34.

to Australiasia and the temperate part of Africa. By and large, the British migrants went to the Dominions and to the United States, the Italians to the United States and Latin America, the Spaniards and Portuguese to Latin America, and the Germans to the United States and, in smaller numbers, to Argentina and Brazil. Despite the weakness and deficiencies of the migration statistics, the predominant flow of population—from Europe to the Americas, and to the United States in particular—is so great that no reasonable estimates of error can alter the picture presented above.

MIGRATION AND ITS CAUSES

In discussions of population movements a distinction is often made between 'push' and 'pull' migration. During the first sixty years of the nineteenth century there is no doubt that the forces operating to generate intercontinental movements of labour were mainly of the 'push' type, in the sense that the migrant was driven from his homeland by adverse economic conditions or other circumstances rather than attracted to his country of destination by the more or less vague expectations of a future improvement in his lot. At the same time the motives for moving were as various as the types of individuals involved. But where a few sought freedom for political or religious principles, judging by the figures alone, most migrants left for reasons which, although social in their implications, were basically economic in origin.[1]

The root causes of the rise of mass emigration from Europe in the years between 1815 and 1870 were the demographic and technical revolutions that were currently transforming the economic and social life of western Europe. Basically it was an outflow of rural population brought about by the classical Malthusian situation of a rapidly growing population pressing on limited means of subsistence. Under the pressure of population increase, the land was subdivided until holdings became too small even in good years to support those who cultivated them. Even when improvements in agricultural methods increased productivity, this tended simply to strengthen the trend towards what List graphically described as a 'dwarf economy' (*Zweigwirtschaft*) of tiny marginal holdings.[2] In Ireland and in other countries on the Continent, notably Germany and Scandinavia, the introduction of the potato in particular facilitated the uneconomic subdivision of the land. Where suste-

---

[1] The chief example of migration because of religious persecution is the flight of 1½m. Jews from Russia to the United States in the fifteen years preceding World War I.

[2] F. List, *The Land System, Dwarf Economy, and Emigration* (Stuttgart, 1842).

nance could be obtained from the potato crop supplemented by the milk of cows or goats, and when no obstacle existed to the minute subdivision of holdings, there was virtually no check to population growth except famine.

Famine finally overwhelmed Ireland in the years 1845–7, and in the space of a few years the country lost about a fifth of its population by emigration, starvation or disease. Even prior to 1847 emigration had drawn off considerable numbers of the Irish population, but now the losses were much higher, reaching an average of 200,000 a year from 1847 to 1854. If, in subsequent years, the outflow was never again as great as it had been during the forties and fifties, it was heavy nevertheless, being 540,000 in the 1870s and 700,000 in the 1880s, and, in the period up to 1890, the Irish continued to contribute to the British emigration to the extent of one-third to one-half of the total annual outflow.

Alternative employment opportunities for displaced rural labour were to be found in urban manufacturing industry or in the construction of railways, but until the last quarter of the nineteenth century the pace of industrialization in most of Europe was decidedly slow. Even when it accelerated, the tendency was for emigration to increase in volume, at least in the short-run, as countries experienced the disrupting effects of industrialization and the introduction of capitalistic forms of agricultural production. Adding to these difficulties in the 1870s and early 1880s was the inflow of cheap American grain which depressed prices and made much of European agriculture unprofitable. Where, as in Britain, the farmer remained unprotected against this competition the result was a partial collapse of agriculture and a massive outflow of rural population overseas.

There was also growing emigration from the countries of southern and eastern Europe after 1880, as they began for the first time to experience on a widespread scale the socially-disruptive effects of population growth and economic and technical change. Italy emerged as second only to Britain in importance as a source of emigrants at this time, and after 1900 sent more people overseas than any other European country. There was also heavy emigration from Spain, Portugal, Austro-Hungary, and Russia, and whereas for the latter two countries political oppression provided further stimulus to emigration, the bulk of the population movement that occurred during these years took place because of the pressures of rural overcrowding. In short, whatever the diversity of their places of origin, most European migrants during the nineteenth century were rural workers. Either they were peasants displaced from the soil by the great transformation of European agriculture of these years, or they were artisans similarly displaced by the conversion of handicraft work to factory production.

AIDS TO MASS EMIGRATION

Financial Assistance

The willingness to emigrate under pressure of adverse economic circumstances was not in itself sufficient to bring about a mass outflow of population from Europe. Willingness to move had to be backed by ability to do so. This latter problem, which involved basically the cost of movement, became apparent quite early in the nineteenth century, when the poor and destitute came to constitute a growing proportion of the total emigration from Europe. The high peak in this outflow of pauper labour came with the Irish famine of the late 1840s, which had the effect of removing from the land the poorest inhabitants or those who had been living on the margin of subsistence.

During these early years the growing outflow of peoples from Europe was made possible partly because the climate of public and official opinion became more favourable to the emigration of the poor. This was shown not only by the removal of restrictions on emigration in countries such as Britain, Germany and Sweden, but also by the fact that the state and other interested bodies, such as philanthropic organizations, emigration and colonization societies, trade unions, and even individuals, appropriated money to pay the costs of emigration of poor people. In Britain, particular importance attaches to the Colonial Land and Emigration Department, which was established in 1840 for the purpose of organizing the sale of land in Australia and New Zealand as a means of raising money to assist emigration to these colonies. As a result of its efforts some 339,339 emigrants went to Australasia between 1847 and 1869 at a cost of £4·9m., of which £532,000 was raised by the emigrants or their friends and the rest came from colonial funds. More limited financial aid was provided by the parishes, which were empowered by the British Parliament in the 1830s to raise money on the security of the local rates to assist the emigration of the locally unemployed. Additional help came from philanthropic individuals and societies, as well as from landlords seeking to escape the excessive burden of the poor rate caused by unemployment, while in the towns the trade unions were also active in supporting the emigration of out-of-work members. On the continent, a somewhat similar system of private and state assistance for emigrants developed in Germany, especially after the uprisings of 1848, when state governments came to look on emigration as a means of getting rid of a potentially dangerous proletariat. Only in Baden, however, was there a serious programme of state subsidization of emigration during these years.

As publicly subsidized emigration declined in importance after the 1850s, financial aid to migrants came increasingly from governments and private persons or groups in the receiving countries. In particular, assisted immigration remained important throughout the rest of the nineteenth century for Britain's Australasian colonies and for some Latin American countries, all of which suffered under the twin handicaps of distance and North American competition in their quest for migrants. Thus between 1861 and 1900 the total number of assisted immigrants entering Australia was more than 388,000, compared with a net gain through immigration of some 767,000. In the next decade only 17,700 assisted immigrants reached Australia, but in the following four years (1911–14) they amounted to almost 145,000 out of a total net gain from the United Kingdom of 198,500.

In Brazil, free passage, free land, and sometimes free machinery, seed and livestock, as well as monthly cash allowances to tide immigrants over the initial period of settlement were powerful incentives which eventually attracted a steady stream of migrants to the country. In Sao Paulo, for example, where the treasury began defraying transportation costs from southern Europe to the Brazilian coffee plantations in 1887, the number of immigrants reached large proportions. Out of almost 1½m. entering the state between 1890 and 1913, 65 per cent were subsidized. Liberal financial assistance to cover the costs of travel and settlement was also provided by the Argentinian government, which further encouraged immigration into that country by offers of exemption from military service and immunity from discriminatory taxes.[1]

Another form of financial help to migrants which originated abroad was the remittances sent home by prosperous and successful settlers which could be used towards paying the fares of relatives and friends who wished to emigrate. The full extent of these remittances is not known, but a few examples of these financial flows between countries are sufficient in themselves to make us aware of the contribution they must have made towards bringing about the large-scale movement of people that took place after 1860. For the United Kingdom, the annual inflow of remittance money from the United States varied considerably, but between 1848 and 1879 the total amounted to over £21m., enough to emigrate comfortably no less than two million people. Towards the end of the nineteenth

---

[1] Free land or land obtained against a nominal fee was also made available in the United States, following the passage of the Homestead Act of 1862, and in Canada after the Dominions Act of 1872.

century it was estimated that 79 per cent of the British migrants going to the United States had their fares paid by friends and relations already settled there. Equally striking is the estimated two billion dollars remitted to Italy between 1901 and 1923, 80 per cent of which derived from America. Much of this money represented savings repatriated by Italians returning to their homeland, but some of it was undoubtedly used to finance part of the heavy emigration from Italy that took place during the early years of this century.

Thus while government assistance to migrants was important for some countries, for example, Australia and Brazil, its overall impact on the volume and direction of international migration before 1913 should not be exaggerated. The great bulk of the migrants had to depend on their own resources or those of their families and friends, including people already settled overseas, to finance their movement abroad. At the same time, the fact that so many people were able to emigrate was in no small way due to the availability of cheaper and more accessible transport.

Cheap Transport

In the development of cheaper, faster and more accessible transport the operative factors were the unprecedented expansion of commerce that took place in the nineteenth century and, after 1850, the spread of steamship travel. In the early years of the century it was the growth of the Canadian timber trade and the expansion of the trade of the United States with Europe, particularly in cotton, which gave rise to a considerable increase of unused space on return journeys, so that shipowners increasingly looked to emigrants to provide part of the return freight. As this passenger trade grew in size, intensive competition between the shipping companies brought fares tumbling down. At Liverpool the cost of steerage passage to New York fell from £12 in 1816 to just over £3 thirty years later, and comparable reductions occurred at the other ports of north-western Europe with connections in the New World. But cheaper fares were small compensation for the terrors associated with travel in overcrowded, badly-provisioned, and often unseaworthy boats, and it was not until the 1840s that interested governments were able to secure better treatment and more comfortable travelling for the migrants. However, the final solution to this problem came only with the growth of the steam-ship trade, which reduced travelling time substantially and placed the passenger trade in the hands of the more reputable steam-ship companies.

The spread of steam-ship travel was rapid after 1850, and although sailing-ships still handled about one-half of the emigrant trade in the 1860s, by 1873 the proportion had been reduced to less

C

than 4 per cent. Apart from encouraging emigration by speeding up travel, the steam-ship companies played a direct part in inducing migration, for in their bid to ensure full passenger lists their ticket agents combed Europe for migrants, conducting extensive propaganda campaigns in favour of settlement overseas.[1] At the same time, government regulations and competition between steam-ship companies resulted in continuous improvements in passenger facilities. Despite the better facilities and the long-run decline in the purchasing power of money, the cost of steerage passage varied very little after 1850. Thus in 1913 steerage rates were £5 10s and £6 15s., compared with an average cost of emigrating Irishmen in 1855 of £5 10s per head.

ECONOMIC CONSEQUENCES OF MIGRATION

Immigrant Countries

The essential economic function of international migration in the nineteenth century was to redistribute some of Europe's agricultural population to new primary producing regions overseas, where physical and social conditions enabled it to produce more per man than it would have done had it remained at home. Sometimes this result was achieved directly, but not always. Many immigrants, although drawn from largely agricultural economies, contributed to the development of new countries by taking non-agricultural jobs in them, thus releasing more of the native population to expand agriculture. A minority of migrants possessed industrial skills and were responsible for the introduction of new manufacturing techniques. But the chief contribution of immigrants to industrial development in these countries was to be found in the numerical addition to a country's population they made, first as newcomers, and later, through the high birth-rates they sustained, as parents. These growing numbers provided both the labour force and the large and expanding market so essential to industrialization and large-scale production.

Whatever the occupational destinations of the migrants, there was a direct connection between immigration and economic growth in the receiving countries. Each inflow of population acted as a powerful force in pushing up the rate of growth of investment, income and employment. Whether these upsurges in economic growth caused the inflow of foreign population or whether immigration stimulated

---

[1] Steam-ship companies and railway construction companies in the United States attracted thousands of emigrants by paying much of the prospective emigrant's fares. At one time a single transatlantic steam-ship company had no fewer than 3,400 agents arranging passages and advancing money from America to emigrants from the British Isles.

economic expansion—and there is evidence that both causal sequences operated during the nineteenth century—the contribution of the immigrants to economic growth was obvious. As entrepreneurs, they brought to the recipient countries the capital and knowledge that formed the basis of a wide variety of new manufacturing industries, including, amongst others, textiles, furniture, chemicals, glass-making, and brewing, and as artisans, they supplied the technical skills necessary to make these new industries an initial success. A more characteristic contribution, however, was of another order. Often lacking even the minimum of skills, the bulk of the immigrants fed the construction industries with the man power needed to build railways and other transport facilities, and to erect cities and equip them with public utilities, sanitation, and other urban requirements. In addition, where, as in the United States, mechanized production was introduced on a large scale, immigrants provided the factory workforce necessary for rapid and sustained industrial growth.

European agricultural skills could not always be put to use overseas. Only rarely, therefore, did immigrants become frontiersmen or pioneer farmers. In more settled areas, however, many European agricultural techniques proved immensely valuable. The introduction of sugar beet and 'everlasting' clover, the growth of wine production, and the diffusion of novel methods of wheat growing are only a few instances of the contributions made by immigrants to the growth of overseas agriculture during the nineteenth century. Moreover, in the neighbourhood of the growing cities, the immigrants often became involved in various types of market-gardening and small-scale intensive agriculture to which native farmers were not accustomed, thus developing a pattern of agriculture that was of genuine importance in the economy, and one that was responsible for bringing about subsequent changes in local consumption habits.

However, immigration involves costs as well as benefits to the receiving country, and the heavy pressures exerted on a country's existing supplies of housing, educational, and transport facilities during periods of heavy immigration are characteristic of these. Furthermore, since the majority of immigrants are wage earners, the likely impact of immigration on the wage system of the receiving country must assume considerable importance in any discussion of the economic consequences of migration. Indeed, the threat, real or otherwise, to the living standards of the indigenous population posed by immigrant labour was the occasion for violent anti-immigration demonstrations in many countries during the nineteenth century. Examination of the available evidence suggests that there was no marked tendency for wages *in general* to fall in the pre-1913 period. But since it is practically impossible to eliminate the effect on the wage level of all the other interacting and continually changing forces, such as technological progress and rising productivity, the spread of industry, and the growth of new employment opportunities, it remains a matter of conjecture whether in particular countries immigration did in the long run have an unfavourable effect on the general wage level in receiving countries. On the other hand, if we concentrate on the wages earned in specific occupations, there is some evidence to suggest that heavy immigration did adversely affect wage levels in certain occupations. Thus in America, the real wages of unskilled workers remained relatively constant in the periods of heavy immigration after 1880, whereas other incomes increased steadily in real terms. Indeed, the 'pick and shovel' man received only slightly more in the United States than in Europe, compared with the wide differentials between American and European earnings in other occupations and skills, a fact which was put down by contemporary American observers to the enormous influx of immigrants. We also find evidence in Argentina and Brazil of heavy immigration retarding the growth of real incomes in certain occupations. But this tendency was not due solely to the increased supply of labour in the market because of immigration. Difficulties are also apparent on the demand side, where the *latifundia* system, which placed the ownership of the land in a few hands, and the slow growth of industry limited the expansion of employment opportunities in both agriculture and manufacturing.

Emigrant Countries

Economic benefits and losses were also experienced by the countries losing population. They suffered a money loss in the capital or property which emigrants took with them as well as the loss of human capital represented by the money expended in rearing, educating and training the emigrant. But the extent of the losses should not be exaggerated. Many of the emigrants were desperately poor, and the majority of them had little or no marketable skills. Even when they possessed skills they were often unsuitable to their new environment. On the other hand, the losing country also benefited from its emigrants in a number of ways. There was the money gain in remittances and in the savings brought back to the country by repatriates, and they sometimes returned with new knowledge and new ideas which could be put to profitable use in the home country. Furthermore, where, as in Ireland, the loss of population was heavy and sustained, there is evidence that emigration did contribute in part to raising real wages and, perhaps more importantly, to increasing the degree of regularity in employment. For the most part, however, emigration operated largely as a safety valve for people stranded in declining occupations and places. It did little to raise the real incomes of growing populations or to expand employment opportunities in losing countries, for these improvements depended more on the spread of industrialization, technical progress, and the growth of productivity than on a simple loss of population. In other words, emigration remained throughout the nineteenth century a palliative rather than a solution for the problems of social and economic change.

INTRACONTINENTAL MIGRATION

The large-scale movement of population was not confined to exchanges between continents. Within the new continents opened up by the migration of largely European peoples, substantial shifts of population brought about the occupation of extensive areas of new land. Whereas at the beginning of the nineteenth century the European outposts overseas consisted largely of islands and tide-water settlements, in the following century whole continents were conquered in the Americas and Australasia, as the local populations, supported by a growing influx of migrants, turned inland and developed the natural wealth of these largely unoccupied lands. The existence of unoccupied land in parts of Eastern Europe also brought substantial internal migration within Europe during these years. Much of this movement of population was directed towards Russia, where 4·2m. foreigners settled between 1828 and 1915. Two-thirds of these came from Europe, mainly from Germany and Austria. The remainder came from Asian countries bordering on Russia, especially China, Japan, Persia and Turkey. There was also a significant eastward movement of Russians into Asia. Of the 7m. involved in this long-distance internal migration roughly three-quarters were peasant settlers, the rest, numbering 1·3m., were prisoners and exiles. These migrants settled mainly in Siberia, others went southwards into the steppe country, others to eastern Asia and Turkistan. The bulk of the movement took place after 1890. This movement of population into Asiatic Russia forms part of the general redistribution of Asian population that took place during these years, the nature and direction of which is the subject of the following section.

ASIATIC MIGRATION AND TROPICAL DEVELOPMENT

The Demand for Asian Labour

As the free movement of European peoples across the Atlantic grew in volume, the centuries old forcible transfer of Africans to the tropical regions of the New World finally came to an end. Despite its legal abolition in a number of countries, the African slave trade was growing rapidly in the early decades of the nineteenth century, and by 1840 it was estimated to have been almost double what it had been in 1807.[1] During the next decade, however, Britain's efforts to suppress the trade achieved considerable success, and by 1850 the traffic to Brazil was virtually finished and nearly half of the West African coastline was closed to the slave trade. There was some revival of slaving in the fifties, due mainly to the expansion of cotton production in the United States during these years, but the outbreak of the American Civil War quickly put an end to the illegal trade there, as well as in numerous other countries, such as Cuba, where it had been carried on under the protection of the American flag.

The abolition of slavery in the period before 1870 resulted in a serious shortage of labour in the tropical plantation economies, and this was partly responsible for the growing volume of Asiatic migration during the nineteenth century. But while some of these migrants (which included mainly people from India and China, and, after 1870, Japan) went to other continents, the bulk of the population movement was confined to Asia and its adjacent islands. Indian migrants, largely indentured labourers, went to the West Indies, Mauritius, South Africa, and South America, and still larger numbers were imported into the plantation and mining economies of Ceylon, Malaya and the East Indies. Chinese intercontinental migration, which was on a considerable scale between 1848 and 1873, was broadly similar in direction and character to that of Indian emigration during these years, but with a somewhat larger number of 'free' Chinese emigrating to countries such as the United States and Australia. Nearer home, the Chinese went chiefly to south-east Asia, including Burma, Siam, Indo-China, and Malaya, and to the East Indies, the Philippine Islands and Formosa. The bulk of the Japanese indentured labour went to Hawaii. Large numbers of Japanese also emigrated to Asiatic Russia, America, and Korea.

Under the system of indenture, the labourer undertook to work for a fixed period of anything up to five years in return for the cost of his passage, a fixed wage, and certain other amenities such as free housing and medical care. On expiration of his contract the labourer could renew it or settle permanently in the receiving country by taking up alternative employment. After 1857, Indian indentured labourers, who were employed largely in other colonies of the British Empire, could also return home at the expense of the colony which had imported them. From the start the system of indentured labour was subject to grave abuse, and in extreme cases work on the plantations was little better than slavery. The governments of the

[1] The increase was from 100,000 to 200,000 a year, of whom 150,000 were carried across the Atlantic and 50,000 went to the Arab world.

countries involved in this exchange of labour endeavoured to control the worst of the abuses, and from time to time the emigration of indentured labour was suspended. Even so, the problem of ensuring fair treatment for indentured labour continued to exercise the minds of government officials well into the twentieth century.

The Volume and Direction of Asian Migration

Adequate statistical records exist for only some of the intercontinental flows of Asian migrants. One well-documented movement was that directed to the West Indies, where the freeing of the slaves in 1833 left the sugar plantations with a severe labour shortage. Of the 536,000 mainly indentured labourers introduced into the colony in the period 1834 to 1918, some four-fifths (430,000) came from India. Other British colonies outside Asia to which Indians migrated in any numbers during these years were South Africa and Mauritius. Although the full extent of the population inflow into the colonies is not known, a total of 161,000 Indians was recorded in the South African census of 1921. Within Asia, Indian migrants went chiefly to Ceylon and Malaya. In Ceylon, the immigrant labour worked mainly in the coffee and tea plantations, and, although for the majority of them their stay was only temporary, the net inflow of Indians into Ceylon between 1839 and 1913 amounted to over 1·8m. persons.

Like the Indian emigration, the bulk of the Chinese migrants went to other parts of Asia. The Straits Settlements received 5·7m. Chinese between 1881 and 1915, and large numbers of Chinese also went to Siam after 1885 so that by 1922 their numbers in that country totalled 1½m. A further quarter of a million Chinese emigrated to the Philippine Islands before the American take-over of the islands from Spain in 1898 resulted in the application to the Philippines of the Chinese exclusion Act already in force in the United States. Next to Asia, the Americas attracted the most Chinese. Thus some 18,000 Chinese entered the West Indies under contract between 1852 and 1884, and by 1862 there were over 60,000 Chinese in Cuba. In Peru, where as a result of an immigration law passed in 1849 large numbers of Chinese were brought into the country to work on plantations and on the guano beds, the numbers of Chinese entering the country between 1849 and 1874 have been variously estimated at between 80,000 and 100,000. Gold discoveries in California were responsible for the early flows of Chinese into the United States, and by the end of the century over 300,000 had entered the country, mainly in the years before 1882, when a reaction against the use of Chinese labour in railway construction and other forms of employment led to the passage of an Act of exclusion. Gold also brought an influx of Chinese into Australia in the 1850s, and by 1861 they numbered 38,298. But with the decline in alluvial gold mining, and following the restrictions placed on Chinese immigration by the various Australian colonies, which culminated in the Commonwealth Immigration Restriction Act of 1901, the number had declined to 22,000 by 1911.

Japanese emigration was not legalized until 1885, when an agreement was signed by the Japanese government and certain Hawaiian sugar plantation owners under which Japanese contract labourers were permitted to emigrate to Hawaii. An Imperial edict legalizing emigration of Japanese labourers in general soon followed. Consequently, between 1885 and 1907 approximately 540,000 Japanese emigrated, of whom one-third went to Hawaii and a further 14 per cent each to the United States and Korea. Other countries receiving more than 10 per cent of the outflow included Asiatic Russia and China. In the following period 1908 to 1924 a further 643,000 emigrants left Japan. Of these, 38 per cent went to Asiatic Russia and about a fifth to the U.S. Smaller numbers went to Hawaii, China, Brazil and Peru. After 1907 Japanese immigration into the United States slowed down, following the conclusion of the so-called 'Gentlemen's Agreement', under which the Japanese government undertook to limit the issue of passports valid for continental America to certain selected groups of Japanese migrants. Complete exclusion followed in 1924.

SELECTED REFERENCES

Berthoff, R. T., *British Immigrants in Industrial America, 1790–1950* (Cambridge, Mass., 1953).

Davie, M. R., *World Immigration* (New York, 1936).

Ferenczi I., *and* Willcox, W. F., *International Migration* (2 vols., New York 1929–31).

Handlin, O., *The Positive Contribution by Immigrants* (Paris, 1955).

Isaac, J., *Economics of Migration* (London, 1947).

Johnson, C., *A History of Emigration from the U.K. to North America, 1763–1912* (London, 1913).

Scott, F. D. (ed.), *World Migration in Modern Times* (Englewood Cliffs, 1968).

Walker, M., *Germany and the Emigration, 1816–85* (Cambridge, Mass., 1964).

Woodruff, W., *Impact of Western Man*, (New York, 1966) Chap. III.

Chapter 4

COMMERCIAL POLICY IN THE NINETEENTH CENTURY

A country's commercial policy determines the nature of its trading relations with the rest of the world. For this reason it is necessary to examine commercial policy in the nineteenth century in some detail before turning to look at the trade flows which, along with the movements of labour and capital, link countries together internationally. Although protectionism was widespread before 1850, and was revived again after 1880, during the intervening period there was a general reduction of restrictions on trade. This movement towards freer trade took place at two levels. At the national level it involved the economic unification of a number of nation states which later came to play a prominent part in international economic affairs. At the international level it involved the widespread adoption of free-trade policies, which reached a peak in the third quarter of the nineteenth century, and which marked the end of the system of privileged trading blocs and restricted commerce characteristic of the growth of the colonial empires of Britain, France, Holland and Spain in the period before 1800. At both levels the advantages of free trade provided the rationale for the movement towards closer economic relations between the areas concerned.

In Britain, France, and the United States economic unification had been completed by the beginning of the nineteenth century. Elsewhere, however, economic fragmentation was the rule. This was particularly so in Europe, where, as a result of the Congress of Vienna (1815), Germany was organized as a loose federation of thirty-nine states each economically independent of the others, and Italy was similarly fragmented into a number of politically and economically independent states. Since national economic unification was an indispensable prerequisite for the economic development of these countries, as well as for the growth of a world economy, the economic integration of Germany through the German *Zollverein* (1834) and the emergence of a unified Italian state in 1861 were important landmarks in the growth of the international economy. They were not the only examples of national economic integration in the nineteenth century, however, for they were preceded and followed by similar movements in many other European and overseas countries.

Equally striking was the movement towards free trade that reached its peak in the 1870s. Adopted initially by Britain, the policy of free trade between nations gained wide acceptance on the Continent in the years after 1860. Even so, universal free trade was not attained at this time despite the favourable circumstances, and only Britain and Holland adopted policies of complete free trade. Nevertheless for a comparatively brief period in the 1860s and the 1870s the world came close to attaining the ideal trading conditions postulated by classical economic theory.

BRITAIN ADOPTS FREE TRADE

In Britain, the intellectual foundations of the case for free trade were laid down by Adam Smith in his work *The Wealth of Nations* published in 1776. Smith's analysis was not without its weaknesses, however, and it was left to other economists, notably David Ricardo (*Principles of Political Economy and Taxation*, 1817) and John Stuart Mill (*Principles of Political Economy*, 1848) to complete the theoretical system justifying free trade begun by Smith. The theory of international trade developed by the classical economists consisted of an explanation of the bases of the gains from trade and of the way in which these gains would be distributed among the trading nations. According to the theory, nations, like individuals, should specialize in the production of those goods which they can make with relatively greatest efficiency. This would make it possible for them to produce a larger output of goods through a more efficient allocation of resources, with the possibility of exploiting unused economies of scale as an added advantage. In short, the gains from trade consist of the *extra* output generated by international specialization. Moreover, it is the existence of this extra output which makes it possible for each trading country to benefit from the international exchange of commodities. The conclusion of classical trade theory, that every trading nation stood to benefit from international specialization and exchange, explains why the doctrine of free trade exerted such a powerful hold over economic thought in the nineteenth century and why it is still widely advocated today.

The apostles of free trade in Britain had an early success when the Eden Treaty of 1786 relaxed some of the tariff on trade between Britain and France. But this trend towards trade liberalization was reversed during the wars with France, when the need for war finance led to a substantial rise in the British tariff. After the war these trade barriers were only slowly dismantled, despite demands for greater trade liberalization by the supporters of free trade. Two problems made the adoption of complete free trade impracticable at this stage in Britain's political and economic development, however. First, the government lacked an alternative source of revenue to protective duties. More importantly, the full realization of free trade depended upon the repeal of the Corn Laws, which by placing a duty on imports of wheat, protected British farmers from foreign competition.Such legislation, however, was hardly expected from a government which drew its support largely from the agricultural interest. Even so, a start was made in the years of expanding trade after 1823, when budget surpluses temporarily overcame the revenue difficulty, thus enabling Huskisson as President of the Board of Trade to make a cautious beginning at fiscal reform.

However, the crucial moves towards free trade were made in the 1840s. In his budget of 1842, Sir Robert Peel abolished the outstanding export duties on British manufactured goods and reduced the import duties on no fewer than 750 articles in the customs list. To makes up the expected loss of revenue the income tax, which had been levied during the Napoleonic Wars and then abandoned, was reintroduced for three years. The next step was taken in 1845 when with the renewal of the income tax for another three years, Peel swept away 520 customs duties and abolished the remaining export duties on raw materials.

With the income tax likely to replace customs duties as a source of government revenue, free trade for Britain now depended on the abolition of the Corn Laws. But the agricultural interest in Britain remained staunchly protectionist, and despite various attempts at reform the Corn Laws remained largely unimpaired at the beginning of the 1840s. Britain's economic circumstances were changing, however. Since the end of the eighteenth century Britain's growing population had made her increasingly dependent on imported wheat, and by the 1840s she was feeding between 10 and 15 per cent of her population on foreign wheat. Britain was also changing politically, for the growth of manufacturing industry was shifting the balance of political power from a rural to an urban electorate, where industrialization was creating a new economic interest which demanded 'cheap bread' and an end to agricultural protection. In support of these demands the Anti-Corn Law League, first set up in 1838, maintained an unrelenting attack on agricultural protection. Despite the brilliance of its campaign, however, it was not the League but the catastrophic Irish famines of the years 1845–6 which made the repeal of the Corn Laws inevitable. In the face of mass starvation restrictions on the free import of food could not be tolerated and the Corn

Laws were finally abolished in 1846, though a brief respite from foreign competition was afforded to British farmers by not making the Act fully effective until 1849, when, except for a registration fee of one shilling, corn came into Britain free. In that year another pillar of protectionism was removed with the repeal of the Navigation Laws which threw the carrying trade as well as the import of corn open to all nations.

In the course of the next twenty-five years Gladstone completed the movement towards free trade in Britain. He carried through further tariff reductions in 1853, and equalized the duties on sugar in 1854. For the next few years the necessity of financing the Crimean War (1854–6) delayed further progress. Finally, in 1860, Gladstone introduced the first of the great series of budgets which completely freed Britain's foreign trade. In that year the number of dutiable items was reduced to 48, and most of the remaining food duties were abolished. Only those on sugar and confectionery remained an important source of revenue. All preferential duties admitting imports from British possessions at a favourable rate were also abolished at this time. Subsequent budgets put timber on the free list in 1866, removed the registration fee on corn in 1869, and freed sugar of duties in 1875, but for all practical purposes it was the budget of 1860 that marks Britain's emergence as a free trade nation within the international economy.

THE SPREAD OF FREE TRADE

Inspired by Britain's example, the classical economists believed that the rest of the world would subsequently move towards complete free trade to the mutual benefit of all concerned. For a brief period after 1860 this dream of universal free trade appeared to be approaching reality, as the policy of trade liberalization spread to other countries through the negotiation of commercial treaties and tariff agreements. The manner in which this trend towards free trade was brought about and the extent to which foreign trade was liberalized during these years will be examined shortly. First of all, however, a brief comment on the economic unification of Germany is called for as an example of the operation of the free-trade principle at the national level.

The Zollverein

Prussia played the major role in the economic and political unification of Germany. Beginning in 1819, a series of treaties was signed with other German states which culminated in 1831 in the formation of the Prussian Customs Union, the first common market of any significance. Meantime, a similar union between Bavaria and Würtemburg in 1827 led eventually to the establishment of the Bavarian Customs Union. Finally, in 1833, the Prussian and Bavarian Customs Unions decided to unite to form the *Zollverein*.

The *Zollverein*, which came into existence on January 1, 1834, included eighteen states with a total population of 23·5 million people. The fundamental principles of the union, as with all the previous customs unions, was a common tariff (based in the main on the rates in force in Prussia) against all states outside the Union, and the abolition of all duties on goods passing between the various member states. Complete economic integration was not attempted, and each state kept its own commercial code, patent laws and government monopolies. As for the proceeds of the customs duties, these were divided amongst the states in proportion to population. After its formation new states were admitted to membership of the *Zollverein* so that by 1852 it included all the states that were eventually to constitute the German Reich.

The Cobden–Chevalier Treaty (1860) and its consequences

The Cobden–Chevalier Act of 1860, which represented the culmination of the trends towards trade liberalization evident in both France and Britain during the 1850s, was the first of a series of commercial treaties which in effect converted the greater part of Europe into low tariff blocs in the 1860s. In Britain, the only duties on manufactures with any perceptible protective quality in the 1850s were on luxuries like lace, cambric handkerchiefs, carpets and shawls, and the long untouched series of silk duties. These protective duties interfered almost exclusively with trade between Britain and France. Hence the importance of the Cobden–Chevalier Treaty. By it Great Britain agreed to abolish all duties on manufactured goods, to lower the duty on brandy to the colonial level, and to reduce the import duties on wines. These concessions were offered to all countries alike, but would in fact be most beneficial to France. On the other hand, France made concessions only to Great Britain. These included reductions of the duties on British coal and coke, bar and pig iron, steel, tools and machinery, yarns, and manufactured goods of hemp and flax.

A number of important results followed from the Anglo-French treaty of 1860. First, it inaugurated a chain of other tariff treaties negotiated in a free-trade spirit, for France now began to conclude similar commercial treaties with other countries for the reciprocal relaxation of tariffs. These included agreements with Belgium and the *Zollverein* in 1862; with Italy in 1863; with Switzerland in 1864;

with Sweden, Norway, the Hanse towns, Spain and Holland in 1865; with Austria in 1866; and with Portugal in 1867. Even Britain, despite her inability to offer tariff concessions once she had completed her free-trade programme, secured treaties with Belgium (1862), Italy (1863), and the *Zollverein* and Austria (1865).

Second, the countries whose economies were linked by low-tariff treaties in the 1860s soon began to co-operate in other matters necessary for the further expansion of international trade. Many conventions were signed during these years to facilitate international communications—railways, canals, telegraphs, postal arrangements and so on. In 1868 the Rhine—a vitally important commercial link in western Europe—was at last declared a freeway for ships of all nations. Other agreements liberalized navigation on the rivers Scheldt, Elbe, Po and Danube. In 1857 Denmark and the principal maritime powers agreed to the abolition of the Sound dues. By establishing the Latin Monetary Union in 1865, France, Italy, Switzerland and Belgium agreed to standardize the value of their coinage, which besides temporarily stabilizing the international bimetallic standard, naturally facilitated commerce between these countries.

Finally, the Anglo-French treaty of 1860 included a most-favoured nation clause, which also became a feature of most of the following series of commercial treaties. Under this clause the reductions granted by Britain in its tariff against particular classes of goods imported from France were extended to goods of those classes imported into Britain from all other countries. The importance of the most-favoured nation clause lies in the encouragement it gave to trade to expand on a multilateral basis. It prevented discrimination because the reduction of duties to one country meant that they were automatically reduced to all other countries enjoying most-favoured nation treatment with the country reducing them. By including the clause the treaty of 1860 left a permanent mark on commercial policy, and the existence of the treaty clause became a potent means of restraining tariff increases during the latter part of the nineteenth century. Its use demonstrated conclusively that bilateral trade negotiations are the most effective of all methods of tariff reduction, provided they aim at multilateral trade.

Perhaps the most questionable use to which the most-favoured nation clause was put was in opening up trade with the East. Here trade concessions granted initially to Britain and the United States by China and Japan respectively were later extended to all other western countries through the use of the principle of most-favoured nation treatment. As a consequence of these trade treaties with the western powers, which amongst other things stipulated the rates of duties to be levied on their imports and exports, both countries were temporarily deprived of their right to determine tariff policy, a loss of sovereignty that for China continued until 1930.

British Colonial Commercial Policy

The adoption of free trade also brought about a change in British colonial commercial policy. Under Huskisson, the British colonial system had been transformed from a monopolist into a preferential system, with British goods receiving preferential treatment in the colonies and colonial produce gaining tariff preference in the British market. In the next thirty years or so, however, the preferential system was gradually dismantled, and the colonies were free to follow their own independent commercial policies. The reactions of the colonial governments to this new situation were varied. The removal of preferential duties on wheat in 1849, and the complete abolition of those on timber in 1860 placed Canada in a difficult position. Unable to withstand European competition in the British market, she now looked to trade with the United States as an answer to her problems. In 1855 a reciprocal trade treaty was signed with the United States and, despite its abrogation in 1866, trade between the two countries grew rapidly. In Australia the British preferences were swept away in 1851 and the colonies were free to pursue their own commercial policies, with New South Wales favouring free trade, Victoria protectionism, and the others emphasizing the levying of duties for purely revenue purposes. New Zealand's early tariffs were also designed to raise revenue and had little protectionist bias. In South Africa, the abandoment of preferential wine duties in 1860 left the country virtually free to fix its own tariff. In 1866-7 a protective tariff was introduced without any opposition from Britain. The commercial policies adopted by the colonies were of little immediate economic significance for Britain, however. As the dominant industrial power in a world moving towards free trade, her colonial monopoly was no longer valuable when a world market lay within her grasp. Only after 1880 when the competition of the newly-industrializing nations became acute, was there a revival in the importance of the imperial market.

THE ECONOMIC CONSEQUENCES OF FREE TRADE

Stimulated by its release from restrictions, international trade grew apace. The available, admittedly rough, estimates suggest that the value of international trade doubled between 1830 and 1850, and at least trebled and may have nearly quadrupled in the next thirty years. In *per capita* terms world trade grew at a decennial rate of 33 per cent between 1800 and 1913, and reached a peak rate of growth of 53 per cent per decade in the period 1840–70. The rapid expansion of foreign trade that occurred in the third quarter of the nineteenth century was of course not solely due to the advent of free trade, and it is difficult to disentangle its effects on trade from those of the other important influences at work during these years. Even so, free trade played its part, and in two respects at least the commercial policies adopted during these years continued to influence economic events in the protectionist period that followed.

The first of these long-run effects of free trade relates to the use of the most-favoured nation clause in the commercial treaties and agreements entered into during these years. The unconditional form of the clause, by which each country received without any question of reciprocal concessions whatever tariff reductions were granted by every country with which it had a treaty, was a potent means of restraining tariff increases during the latter part of the nineteenth century. In addition, many important treaties which ran for long periods contained provisions binding rated items against increase. These provisions had the effect of preventing any increase of duties on a large list of imports. Moreover, since every country had many treaties containing such provisions and expiring at different dates, it became difficult for any of them to embark upon wholesale tariff increases. In short, the most-favoured nation clause placed certain limits on the spread of protectionist policies in the period after 1880. The second long-run effect was more general in its influence, and concerns the part played by free-trade policies in generating the atmosphere of freedom in which economic affairs were conducted in the nineteenth century. Despite the restrictions increasingly placed on trade in the period after 1880, this 'atmosphere' of freedom persisted up to 1913. In particular, the setting out of the legal rights of aliens in many of the commercial treaties negotiated during these years enabled trade to expand in a world where the rights of the private traders and of private property were guaranteed by an extensive network of treaties. In short, these treaties created a stable world, in which traders were free to come and go, to organize and invest abroad, almost as freely and safely as in their own countries.

THE RETURN TO PROTECTION

For the classical economist, as for many economists today, universal free trade took on the form of an eternal truth, independent of time or place. Yet in a very real sense the doctrine was a product of its time, for it became the creed of a nation confident in its own power to defeat all rivals in the drive for markets and forced by natural circumstances to depend on the rest of the world for a large part of its supply of food and raw materials. But if free trade had an obvious appeal for the industrially successful nation, it was the failure of the doctrine to deal with the problem of economic development and the complicated relations between advanced and backward economies that formed the basis of the criticisms levied against it by nineteenth-century protectionists such as List, Hamilton and Carey. The controversy is by no means settled even today.

The Case for Protection

The basis of the protectionist argument is to be found in Alexander Hamilton's famous *Report on Manufactures* (1791), which remains one of the most elaborate general arguments for protection ever written. In his report to the American Congress, Hamilton stressed both the desirability of national self-sufficiency in manufacturing, and the importance of a sizeable non-agricultural consuming class for a stable and prosperous agriculture. Manufacturing industry, he argued, should be encouraged to grow by the use of a system of bounties and subsidies, and behind a protective tariff, which would free domestic manufacturers from foreign competition, and thus enable them to expand the scale of their operations, thereby achieving economies comparable to those enjoyed by foreign competitors. In this way the 'infant industries' would quickly attain maturity, and would then be able to produce at least as cheaply as foreign manufacturers.

Strongly influenced by Hamilton, the German Friedrich List (*The National System of Political Economy*, 1841) was highly critical of the classical theory of free trade. In particular, he reproached the classical economists with having purposely ignored the differences in economic strength between the nations which they had invited to trade freely with one another on an equal footing. A country's commercial policy, List argued, was related to its level of economic development and it was therefore wrong to advocate one policy as being universally applicable. He concluded that while free trade is beneficial during the early and later (commercial-industrial) stages of development, the transition from an agricultural to an industrial society could be achieved only through a policy of protection. List therefore demanded an 'educational' tariff on the products of infant industries designed to protect them for a limited period of time from the competition of foreign industries not naturally more efficient but simply more advanced in development.

While Hamilton and List advocated protection only as a temporary 'educational' measure, another American, Henry Charles Carey, went beyond both in demanding protection as a permanent feature of economic policy. Like Hamilton, Carey stressed the fundamental community of interest between agriculture and manufacturing by maintaining that all industrial growth is determined and limited by the available surpluses of agricultural products. In the event, it was this combination of agricultural and manufacturing interests that provided the broad support for the protectionist policies adopted by the United States.

Protection in the United States

While the debate on protection was going on in the United States in the 1790s, the wars between France and England, by blocking the accustomed channels of trade and production, provided a practical illustration of the 'benefits of protection'. The wartime shortages gave an enormous stimulus to those branches of American industry, such as cotton, wool and iron manufactures, whose products had previously been imported. But with the end of the war in Europe came the threat of renewed British competition and a demand for protection from the newly expanded industries. The Tariff Act of 1816 provided the required protection, and for the next twenty years the United States followed a continuous policy of protection, moderate at first, but becoming strongly protective after 1824. Protectionist pressures moderated in the 1830s, after the passing of the Compromise Tariff Act of 1833, which provided for a gradual and steady reduction of duties in the years up to 1842, and although tariffs were raised for a while after 1842, liberalization was resumed in the Tariff Act of 1846, and reinforced by that of 1857. Consequently, for a few years, the United States came as near to free trade as it had been since 1816.

Although the trend towards freer trade was reversed in 1861, when the Morrill Act restored the moderately protective tariff level of 1846, it was the substantial rise in duties needed to pay for the Civil War which laid the foundation of the future American system of protection. During these years the average rate on dutiable commodities rose to 37 per cent in 1862, and to 47 per cent in 1864. After the war there was a call for tariff reform, but the war tariff remained the basis of the American protective system until the passage of the Act of 1883, when the general tariff level was lowered some 5 per cent. Thereafter the tariff level was pushed up twice in rapid succession. In 1890 the McKinley Act raised the average level of tariffs to 50 per cent. High duties were placed on textiles, iron, steel, glass, and tin plate, and to appease the farmers, who were facing increased competition from Canadian imports, tariffs were imposed on a number of agricultural products. The Democrats brought about a downward revision of the tariff in 1894, lowering the average level to 40 per cent, but the Republicans speedily reversed the trend with the

Dingley Tariff (1897), which not only restored the McKinley rates, but also raised the average level even higher, to 57 per cent. No further change of any significance took place in the American tariff until 1913, when a Democratic administration passed the Underwood–Simmons Tariff Act, which eliminated specific duties, added over 100 items, including sugar and wool, to the free list, reduced tariffs on nearly 1,000 classifications and increased them on a few others, mostly chemicals. The result of these changes was to reduce the rates of duties on dutiable imports to the extremely low average of 16 per cent. Unfortunately, this trend towards free trade in the United States had little opportunity to be tested, for within a year, war had broken out in Europe. The experiment was not to be repeated again until after World War II.

Protection in Europe

In Europe a number of economic and political developments combined to bring about a return to protection after 1880. Economically, it was the desire for industrial development and the competition engendered by successful industrialization that was responsible for the growing demand for protection. Backing up the economic case for protection was the revival of nationalism in the late nineteenth century associated with the emergence of new nation states, such as Germany and Italy. In addition to embarrassing foreign industrial competition, increasing tariffs provided the larger revenues needed to meet the rising expenditures on armaments caused by the growing military rivalry between the states of Europe, as well as expenditures on education, public health and social services, which were in part social manifestations of the nationalist feeling. While nationalism and protectionism are not inevitably associated with one another, in nationalism we do have a force providing at least a predisposition toward protection. Taken together, nationalism and the lag in industrialization made protection inevitable.[1]

What actually started the swing to protectionism in Europe, however, was neither of these broad economic and political factors, but two specific economic developments of the 1870s. One was the large inflow of cheap grain into Europe from the United States and Russia; the other was the depression of 1873–9, the longest and deepest period of stagnant trade the world had yet experienced. Farmers and industrialists alike clamoured for relief, and the demands of this coalition of young industry and injured agriculture gave the initial stimulus to protection. Once started, this swing to protectionism was supported and maintained by the deeper forces

[1] See also P. T. Ellsworth, *The International Economy* 1st edn. (New York, 1950), pp. 360–3.

of nationalism. Over time, pressure groups and vested interests grew in political power, and were often able to influence parliaments into granting greater protection to further their own self-interests. Protection also tended to spread across the board, as concessions to one group of industries made it difficult for governments to refuse similar privileges to others. Furthermore, from the 1890s, rate setting tended to become competitive. This tendency arose out of the two-tiered framework yielded by the commercial treaty system developed during these years. Under this treaty system, high general duties were levied on imports from non-treaty countries, and lower rates were applied to dutiable commodities from countries with which treaties had been concluded. As these treaties were renegotiated periodically, immediately before renegotiation, an extensive upward revision of the general (or maximum) tariff of each treaty country was legislated so as to ensure that negotiations would not result in a "treaty" (or minimum) tariff detrimental to the country's industries. Such a procedure tended to produce higher all-round protection and, in some cases, tariff warfare, detrimental to all concerned. Taken together these developments produced a swing to protection within Europe that became more pronounced as we approach 1913. Over the whole period 1880–1913, only Britain, Holland and Denmark steadfastly adhered to free trade.

Stimulated by the depressed conditions in industry, the increased competition from imported grain, and the financial needs of the imperial government, protectionist sentiments gained ground in Germany in the late 1870s. Finally, in 1879, moderate tariff protection was extended to both agriculture and manufactures. Raw material imports, however, remained duty-free. Two major upward revisions of duties on grain followed in 1885 and 1888, but the next general revision of the tariff did not come until 1902. By then, the rate increases in the United States, France, and Russia, together with the lapse of various treaties in which German duties were fixed by agreement, furnished an additional motive and a suitable opportunity for more protection. The new general tariff introduced much higher rates, particularly on finished manufactures, and was more detailed and specialized than the 1879 tariff. The duties on semi-manufactures were kept low, and raw materials continued to be admitted duty-free. A higher level of protection for agriculture was also provided, with increased duties on grain and livestock. The new system remained in being until it was swept away by the outbreak of war.

Many other countries followed Germany's example. Italy commenced the 1870s with a moderate tariff, but new legislation in 1878 substantially increased protection for manufacturing industry. A year later protection was extended to agriculture. In 1887 rates were raised to a high level and these remained in effect until after the war. The Swiss did not adopt a general tariff until 1884, when duties were imposed which remained only moderately high despite an upward revision in 1891. In 1906, however, new legislation provided high duties on foodstuffs and considerable increases in rates on manufactures. On the other hand, Russia reverted to protection as early as 1868, when manufactured imports were subjected to heavy duties in an effort to promote domestic industrialization. This Act was not superseded until 1891, but in the interim several all-round increases in duties occurred. The 1891 tariff legislation introduced a maximum–minimum rate structure for purposes of tariff bargaining, and placed duties on raw materials and semi-manufactures. The duties on coal, steel, machinery, and chemicals were raised so high that import of these goods practically ceased. Further increases of duties in 1893 and in the early 1900s maintained Russia's position as the most highly protected country in the world.

The demands made by French industrialists for protection were hampered by the persistence of a strong free-trade sentiment and by the existence of long-term commercial treaties which effectively pegged the French tariff at a low level. But in the 1880s, growing dissatisfaction in agriculture brought the farmers into line with the industrial advocates of higher tariffs, and in 1890 the combined protectionist forces gained political power. The Méline Tariff of 1892 meant higher duties all round, including an average increase of 25 per cent on duties on agricultural products, and some substantial increases of rates on manufactures. A two-tier system of maximum and minimum rates was introduced for treaty purposes, with the minimum rates themselves amply protective. A general revision of the new tariff structure did not occur until 1910, and then it was aimed primarily at covering the many new products, such as chemicals and electrical and rubber goods, that had been developed in the intervening years. The Tariff Act of 1910 predominantly favoured manufacturing industry, and only a few increases were granted on agricultural products. There were few reductions, and raw materials generally were exempted from duties.[1]

THE ECONOMIC CONSEQUENCES OF PROTECTION

Given the multitude of influences at work in the international econ-

[1] Inter-country comparisons of tariff severity are difficult to make, but one estimate for the early years of this century puts the average tariff in Russia at 28 per cent, in the United States at 18·5 per cent, in France and Germany at 9·8 per cent, and in Austria at 7·5 per cent. See C. F. Bastable *The Commerce of Nations* (London, 1923), p. 106.

omy during these years, the effect of the return to protection on the character and the volume of foreign trade after 1880 is not easily determined. However, taking into account the many strong 'trade-creating' forces at work in these years, the moderate level of the protective tariff in some countries, and the existence of commercial treaties that lowered them in many others, and remembering that, if tariffs discouraged some forms of international exchange, they also tended to stimulate rivalry in open markets, the conclusion that tariffs probably did not seriously hinder the growth of international trade in the period before 1914 seems a reasonable one. Indeed, world trade grew steadily between 1870 and 1914, averaging some 3·4 per cent annually over the entire period, and was growing faster than total world production which averaged 2·1 per cent per annum.

If world trade did not suffer unduly from the return to protection, the trade of individual countries may well have done so. Britain's export trade, in particular, could be expected to suffer from the protective tariffs imposed by the newly-industrializing nations. Here woollen exports were the biggest losers, since their best markets were situated in the United States and Europe, where competition and protection were most severe, and since alternative markets were mostly lacking. In contrast the cotton textile industry overcame its difficulties by exporting finer quality cottons to protected markets and by expanding the sales of cheaper cottons to the newly-developing countries where the protected cotton industries of Europe and America were rarely able to compete. Apart from the possibility of switching exports to unprotected markets, there are other reasons for not exaggerating the impact protection had on the overall level of British exports. Tariffs remained for the most part moderate, and Britain could always depend on the most-favoured nation clause embodied in the commercial treaties of the day to shield her from the worst excesses of her competitors. Moreover, where a long-run decline in British exports did occur it was more often because of a loss of competitiveness than because of protection. Thus tariffs may have initially lost Britain markets for iron and steel manufactures in the United States and Germany, but later, when American and German producers surpassed the British in efficiency and competitiveness, they became unnecessary to keep British exporters out of these markets. Yet the changes in the composition of British exports due to the tariff were not without their problems for the future, for the shift was towards products which were less profitable and prospectively less capable of expansion. Exports of semi-manufactures grew in importance relative to exports of finished goods, and coal exports expanded rapidly after 1880. The forced specialization on quality products, and semi-manufactured goods, like yarn and pig iron, meant production to satisfy a more volatile demand, thus introducing a greater degree of instability in the British export sector than may formerly have existed. Moreover, the profits of further fabrication, which had previously accrued to Britain, were now passing to those countries which used British semi-manufactures to turn them into finished products. For the time being, however, the shift into new export lines was made without any great difficulty, and British exports continued to grow.

Although agricultural products became more highly protected as time passed, for much of the period between 1880 and 1914 raw materials and foodstuffs, with the exception of grain into Continental Europe, were comparatively free from restrictions, and consequently the 'regions of recent settlement' were not impeded in their growth by prohibitive tariffs. In any case, there was always the British market, the largest in Europe, into which primary producing countries enjoyed freedom of entry for their exports, for Britain's response to the decline in the world price of wheat after 1880 was to complete the liquidation of agriculture as an economic sector of any importance. France, Germany and Italy, as we have seen, responded to the new situation by imposing tariffs in an attempt to maintain the relative price of wheat and to protect grain producers. Denmark, however, did not impose a tariff on wheat. Instead it converted from the growing of grain to animal husbandry and specialization in dairy production. In carrying out this economic transformation, proximity to expanding industrial markets for dairy products in Britain and Germany was particularly helpful. The possibility that other countries, such as France and Germany, could have successfully adopted a similar policy of allowing free imports of grain and transferring domestic agricultural resources out of grain into livestock remains, however, a debatable point. But the failure of the British farmer to adjust quickly to the changed market situation contrasts sharply with the Danish success.

As for manufacturing industry, there is no doubt that the raising of tariff barriers in the United States, Germany and elsewhere initially contributed to its growth in these countries. But by the 1890s the 'infant industry' argument in favour of manufacturing protection was becoming somewhat threadbare, and the case for protection was being based on a variety of other arguments, such as self-sufficiency, maintaining employment levels, industrial diversification, protection of living standards and wage levels, and so on, some of which were of dubious economic merit. Indeed, the need for protection at all, even for infant industries, was questioned. Thus one survey of American protection before 1913 produced the conclusion that the protected industries in the United States had either always had comparative advantage over foreign competitors or they were never able to achieve comparative advantages even with tariff protection. Australian experiences of protection during these years suggests a somewhat similar conclusion, since manufacturing developments in protectionist Victoria do not appear to have been markedly different in rates of growth from those in free-trade New South Wales. Manufacturing industry in both colonies progressed whether tariffs were present or not.

Protection does appear to have had some influence on the structure of industry, however. In both the United States and Germany the big industrial concern came to dominate manufacturing, and the resulting concentration of economic power contrasted sharply with the diffusion of economic power characteristic of the early stages of the British industrial revolution. As the amount of capital tied up in a particular venture increased, management became less willing to allow the success of the business to be decided by the uncontrolled operation of market forces. Through trusts, holding companies, and business combinations of various kinds, new large business enterprises endeavoured to control the competitive process in an attempt to fix prices and maintain or increase the return on their investment. Protected by tariffs, producers in the United States and Germany were able to eliminate domestic competition and create monopoly markets free from competition. In free-trade Britain, on the other hand, the threat of foreign competition was ever present and attempts at the monopolistic concentration of production were therefore less likely to succeed.

Monopolistic activities also spilled over into the international field in the form of international cartels. At the beginning of the present century it was estimated that at least forty of these cartels were in existence, and in 1912 the figure was put at 100. They covered industries such as shipping, armaments, steel rails, electric bulbs, aluminium, calcium carbide, plate glass, tobacco, enamelware, and bottles. While international monopolies are not incompatible with free trade, the fact that they appeared in industries dominated by a few large firms suggests that protection, since it played some part in creating national monopolies, also contributed indirectly to creating conditions favourable to the international restriction of competition. Moreover, irrespective of the causes of the growth of these international cartels, their fundamental objectives—the control over prices, markets, supply, and technological change—are deterrents to specialization and trade, not only in products directly under their control, but also in other products manufactured in part from cartelized material. To what extent these cartels did restrict world trade in the period before 1913 is difficult to estimate, and therefore their significance should not be exaggerated. Mere numbers tell us little about their economic significance, which can be gauged only by estimating the proportion of total world trade formed by the commodities under their control, a calculation which has not yet been made. Moreover, the fact that Britain was not a member of most international cartels greatly limited their economic power, because the exercise of their monopoly powers was always subject to the threat of competition from Britain.

One final economic by-product of protection may be touched on briefly. This is the tendency for the existence of tariff barriers to stimulate direct foreign investment in protectionist countries. Since the aim of protection is to exclude foreign products from the domestic market of the country imposing the tariff, foreign firms can overcome these trade barriers by setting up branch factories in the markets concerned. Although not widespread before 1913, there were occasions when this kind of direct investment was undertaken. For example, the American tariff of 1883 hit certain cheaper cotton exports from Britain severely. As a result several Lancashire cotton firms set up branches in the United States. Part of the American direct investment in Canada during the pre-1913 period was also due to the existence of the Canadian tariff. While these examples could be multiplied, this type of investment remained comparatively rare before 1913, and direct investment, motivated partly by protection, was not undertaken on a large scale until after World War I.

SELECTED REFERENCES

Ashley, P., *Modern Tariff History* (London, 1910).
Condliffe, J. B., *The Commerce of Nations* (London, 1951), especially Chaps. VI–IX.
Ellsworth, P. T., *The International Economy* 3rd edn. (New York, 1964), Chap. 12.
Isaacs, A., *International Trade: Tariff and Commercial Policies* (Chicago, 1948).
Saul, S. B., *Studies in British Overseas Trade 1870–1914* (Liverpool, 1960), especially Chap. VI.
Taussig, F. W., *Tariff History of the United States* 8th edn. (New York, 1931).
Tracy, M., *Agriculture in Western Europe* (New York, 1964).

Chapter 5

FOREIGN TRADE IN THE NINETEENTH CENTURY

The task of charting the growth and changing nature of world trade during the period 1820 to 1913 has been helped enormously by Professor Kuznets' pioneering work in assembling and analysing the available statistical material, and the following discussion of foreign trade developments in the nineteenth century owes much to his latest work in the field.[1] The discussion itself will be limited to a consideration of commodity trade, since long-term data on the international flows of services (freight earnings, insurance and banking, tourism, etc.) are scarce. An analysis of the available services data suggests, however, that earnings on services tend to rise proportionately to commodity trade. Moreover, the average proportion of services to commodity trade is, for all but the smallest of countries, limited to between a tenth and one-sixth. Even so, it should be kept in mind that for some countries, for example Britain, services income played an important part in covering deficits on commodity trade, and that for others an export surplus on commodity trade could quickly disappear once payments for services are taken into account.

THE GROWTH OF WORLD TRADE BEFORE 1913

Two broad conclusions are suggested by the trends in the foreign trade statistics available for the period 1800 to 1913: first, that the period was characterized by high rates of growth in foreign trade, and second, that world trade grew at much higher rates than world output during these years. For long sub-periods, of thirty years or more, total foreign trade grew at rates ranging from 29 to 64 per cent per decade, and, on a *per capita* basis, from 23 to 53 per cent per decade. The highest decadal growth rates, whether measured in total or *per capita* terms, were registered in the sub-period 1840–70,

[1] S. Kuznets, 'Quantitative Aspects of the Economic Growth of Nations: X-Levels and Structure of Foreign Trade: Long-term Trends', *Economic Development and Cultural Change*, Part II (January, 1967).

with growth rates tending to rise throughout earlier decades and to decline thereafter. At the same time, world output per head appears to have grown at an average rate of 7·3 per cent per decade between 1800 to 1913, whereas *per capita* world trade averaged 33 per cent per decade over the same period.

The net result of these changes was a marked rise in the proportion of world trade to world product. By 1913, the volume of foreign trade *per capita* had grown to over 25 times what it had been in 1800, whereas world output per head had grown only 2·2 times over the same period. This means that during the period 1800–1913 the foreign trade proportion, that is, the ratio of world trade to world product, rose to over 11 times its initial level.[1] Moreover, if, as seems likely, the world proportion of foreign trade to product was about 33 per cent in 1913, it must have been barely 3 per cent in 1800. What brought about this marked rise in the world foreign trade proportion? Partly responsible for this development was the introduction of new nations into the network of world trade during the nineteenth century. More important were the growing propensity to trade displayed by countries during these years, particularly the older and more developed nations of the world, and the emergence of major technological and institutional forces, discussed earlier, which tended to foster a faster rate of growth of trade between countries than growth of output within them.

This marked rise in foreign trade proportions was characteristic of groups of countries and of countries taken individually. They rose markedly in both the developed and underdeveloped parts of the world, with the relative rise in the foreign trade proportion greater for the latter than for the former group of countries, which is not surprising seeing that many of these countries were integrated into the world trading network for the first time during the nineteenth century.[2] Looking at individual countries, the foreign trade proportions of the industrial European countries and Japan rose substantially between 1800 and 1913, while they declined slightly for the younger overseas countries, such as the United States and Australia, which already had high foreign trade proportions at the beginning of our period. In the circumstances, these 'new' regions could hardly be expected to become even more dependent on foreign trade once their domestic economies became more broadly based. This was particularly so with the United States with its abundant

[1] The foreign trade proportion is given by the ratio 25 : 2·2.

[2] Kuznets, op. cit., p. 15. Kuznets includes in the developed countries Canada, the U.S., Europe, Australia, New Zealand, and, after 1880, Japan and the Union of South Africa. The underdeveloped countries cover Africa (excluding South Africa after 1880), Asia (excluding Japan after 1880), and Latin America.

natural resources, while in both Australia and America, transport developments seem to have encouraged higher rates of growth of domestic output than of foreign trade. In Europe, on the other hand, limited raw material supplies and rapidly growing population appear to have increased the continent's dependence on foreign trade throughout the century, so that the foreign trade proportions of European countries grew rather than declined or remained stable.

THE DIRECTION OF WORLD TRADE BEFORE 1913

The distribution of world trade by geographic region over the period 1876 to 1913 is shown in Table 7, while Diagram 6 illustrates the position in 1913. As can be seen from the table and diagram, Europe dominated world trade in the nineteenth century, when it consisted largely of intra-European trade and Europe's trade with overseas areas, especially those settled by Europeans. This predominance was maintained throughout the period up to 1913, despite the continuous growth of the North American share of world trade, and the tendency for the European, and particularly for the United Kingdom, share to fall. In 1913 Europe (including Russia) took some 65 per cent of the world's imports and accounted for 59 per cent of its exports, whereas the North American shares were 12 and 15 per cent, respectively.

Because of the spread of industrialization and the emergence of new centres of primary production overseas, significant changes in the pattern of trade between countries and between regions occurred at this time. For European countries other than Britain, dependence on Europe for imports and for export markets was initially very marked, with the degree of dependence tending to grow as the size of the country concerned diminished. After 1870, however, as the demand for foodstuffs and raw materials drawn from overseas suppliers rose in response to industrial development and population growth, there was some decline in the degree of dependence of European countries on the continental market. At the same time, there were associated changes in the demand for primary products which had important consequences for the different trading countries. Thus from the 1820s to the mid-nineties, purchases of tropical products grew more slowly than imports of foodstuffs and raw materials coming from temperate regions. Thereafter, however, imports of tropical products from Latin America, Asia, and Africa rose significantly.

The tendency for European countries, including Britain, to draw their imports increasingly from continents other than Europe as the nineteenth century proceeded reflected the heavy dependence of overseas countries on Europe as a market for their exports. The United States was no exception to this rule. By the 1880s, over four-fifths of its exports were going to Europe, and despite a rapid expansion of American exports to Canada, Latin America, and Asia after 1895, the European share was still 60 per cent in 1913. Moreover, two-thirds of United States imports came from Europe in the 1850s, and although Europe's share declined thereafter, it remained around 50 per cent of the total after the 1870s. At the same time, significant changes in the relative importance of the different European countries supplying the American market took place. Britain's share of total imports fell from a peak of 46 per cent in the early fifties to 17 per cent in the years 1911–13. On the other hand, the share of imports coming from continental European countries, and especially Germany, continued to grow throughout the period and accounted for one-third of the total by 1913.

TABLE 7. *Regional Distribution of World Trade, 1876–1913*

| Region | Per cent 1876–80 | | | 1913 | | |
	Exports	Imports	Total trade	Exports	Imports	Total trade
Europe[1]	64·2	69·6	66·9	58·9	65·1	62·0
N. America	11·7	7·4	9·5	14·8	11·5	13·2
Latin America[2]	6·2	4·6	5·4	8·3	7·0	7·6
Asia	12·4	13·4	12·9	11·8	10·4	11·1
Africa	2·2	1·5	1·9	3·7	3·6	3·7
Oceania	3·3	3·5	3·4	2·5	2·4	2·4
World	100·0	100·0	100·0	100·0	100·0	100·0

Notes: 1. Including Russia. 2. Central and South America, including all colonial territories in the Western hemisphere.
Source: P. Lamartine Yates, *Forty Years of Foreign Trade* (London, 1959), Tables 6 and 7, pp. 32–3.

Two-thirds of Latin America's trade was with Europe, with Britain, Germany, France and Spain by far the most important of the countries concerned. If the United States is included, the share rises to 90 per cent in the years 1901–5. The trade of Africa and of Oceania was even more dependent on the European market than was that of Latin America, with Britain in particular a major source of exports to and by far the biggest importer of merchandise from these two continents. Canadian trade, on the other hand, was dominated by Britain and the United States. Whereas Britain remained the more

Diagram 6: Regional Distribution of Total World Trade, 1913

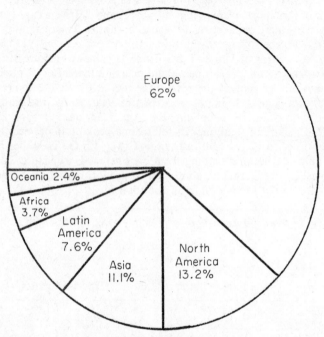

Source: As for Table 7

important market for Canadian exports throughout the century before 1913, over the years Canadian imports from the U.S. grew at the expense of those from Britain until, late in the nineteenth century, she lost first place in the Canadian market to the United States.

India, China and Britain constituted a tightly-knit trading bloc in Asia in the period before 1880. After the seventies, however, the picture begins to change. The closing down of the opium trade in the 1880s, the rise of Japan as the first Asian industrial power, and the economic penetration of China by European powers other than Britain were developments that significantly altered the pattern of international trade in the Far East. As Japan industrialized, the structure of its foreign trade was completely reversed, from one in which raw materials were exported and finished manufactures imported to one in which manufactures were exported and raw materials imported. The direction of Japan's foreign trade changed in sympathy with these developments. Asia replaced Europe and the

United States as the main source of Japanese imports, supplying almost one-half of these needs by 1913. By that date Asia had also become Japan's leading regional export market.

Despite the growing industrial importance of the United States and Japan in the late nineteenth century, the direction of world trade in the period before 1913 was dominated by Europe's ever-growing demand for foodstuffs and raw materials. Before World War I Europe absorbed more than 80 per cent of the exports of Belgium, Holland, Argentina, South Africa and New Zealand; 75–80 per cent of those of Germany, and Australia; over 60 per cent of those of France, Italy and the United States; and more than half of Canada's and India's. The foreign trade of Britain was distributed almost equally among the Empire, continental Europe and the rest of the world. Europe's share in the imports of these and other countries was somewhat less than its share in their exports. Considering both imports and exports, it appears that Britain carried on an extensive trade with all parts of the world; Canada belonged to the American economic community; China and Japan had the strongest commercial ties with Asia; and almost all other nations gravitated towards European markets.

The extent to which Europe dominated world trade before the World War I is seen even more clearly if we consider the percentage distribution of the flow of merchandise trade in 1913. Two-fifths of this trade represented intra-European exchange, slightly more than one-fifth Europe's imports from non-European countries, and 15 per cent exports from Europe to non-European countries. Thus trade among non-European countries accounted for less than one-quarter of the world trade in merchandise in 1913.[1]

THE COMPOSITION OF WORLD TRADE BEFORE 1913

The longest series of data on the composition of world commodity trade reaches back to the late 1870s, and distinguishes primary products from manufactured articles. The most intriguing feature of the series is the fact that the proportion of primary products to total trade remained remarkably constant in the period up to 1913, and beyond (see Table 8). This stability was maintained despite the spread of industrialization and the consequent decline in the relative share of primary production in total output, and despite significant changes in the composition of the export trade in primary products. Since primary products bulk large in the exports of underdeveloped countries, and since many such economies were newly integrated

[1] W. S. and E. S. Woytinsky, *World Commerce and Governments* (New York, 1955), p. 71.

into the pattern of world trade with the passing of the nineteenth
century, the stability in the share of primary products in world trade
might possibly be explained in terms of these developments counter-
acting the growth of trade in manufactures between industrializing

TABLE 8. *Share of Primary Products in World Trade, 1876–1913*

	Based on volume in current prices	Based on volume in 1913 prices
	%	%
1876–80	63·5	61·8
1886–90	62·3	62·2
1896–1900	64·3	67·7
1906–10	63·2	64·0
1913	62·5	62·5

Source: Kuznets, op. cit., Table 6, p. 33.

Diagram 7: Regional Shares of World Trade, 1876–1913
(a) Trade in Primary Products

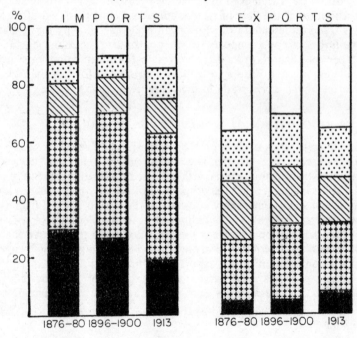

countries. But, as Kuznets has shown, the slight rise in the share in world trade of underdeveloped countries—from 27 to 28 per cent of the total—does little in itself to explain the fact of stability. Further explanation must be sought in the details of the foreign trade of the regions and countries concerned.

Table 9 and Diagram 7 show the nature of the changes in the regional distribution of trade in primary products and manufactures during the period 1876–1913. In these years the volume of the export trade in primary products more than trebled. With the exception of 'Other Europe', all regions shared in the expansion, with the growth outside Europe and North America being especially strong between 1895 and 1913. The North American share in this trade grew only slightly, whereas Europe, often overlooked as an exporter of primary products, saw its share rise to almost one-half of the world total around 1900, and then drop back to the level of the late 1870s

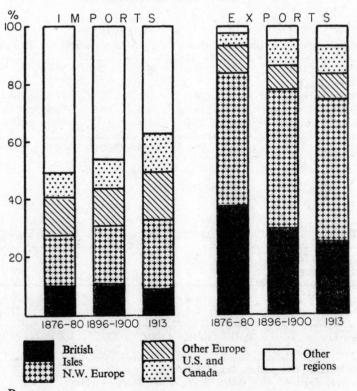

(b) Trade in Manufactures

D

by 1913. Complementing the export of primary products was the import trade in manufactures. The volume of this trade almost trebled between 1876–80 and 1913, with imports into North America more than quadrupling in volume during these years, and those of continental Europe more than doubling between 1896–1900 and 1913. With the import trade in manufactures growing so strongly in Europe and North America, the share of the underdeveloped countries in this trade actually fell in the years up to 1913.

Looking at the situation in reverse, and concentrating on those regions which predominantly exported manufactures and imported primary products, we find that the most striking features of the world export trade in manufactures was the growth of the North American share and the decline in the United Kingdom share over the whole of the period 1876–80 to 1913. Continental Europe's share remained stable, and Japan entirely accounts for the high Asian

TABLE 9A. *Trade in Primary Products: Regional Shares, 1876–1913*

| | Per cent. | | | | | |
| | 1876–80 | | 1896–1900 | | 1913 | |
Region	Imports	Exports	Imports	Exports	Imports	Exports
U.K. and Ireland	29·7	3·1	25·8	3·9	19·0	6·2
N.W. Europe[1]	39·3	22·6	45·0	27·6	43·1	25·2
Other Europe	11·2	20·2	10·4	18·1	12·3	14·7
U.S. and Canada	7·2	16·1	8·5	18·7	11·3	17·3
Rest of world	12·6	38·0	10·3	31·7	14·3	36·6
World	100·0	100·0	100·0	100·0	100·0	100·0

TABLE 9B. *Trade in Manufactures: Regional Shares, 1876–1913*

| | Per cent | | | | | |
| | 1876–80 | | 1896–1900 | | 1913 | |
Region	Imports	Exports	Imports	Exports	Imports	Exports
U.K. and Ireland	9·1	37·8	10·4	31·5	8·2	25·3
N.W. Europe[1]	18·1	47·1	20·3	45·8	24·4	47·9
Other Europe	13·3	9·2	12·2	10·3	15·4	8·3
U.S. and Canada	7·7	4·4	9·6	7·4	12·1	10·6
Rest of world	51·8	1·5	47·5	5·0	39·9	7·9
World	100·0	100·0	100·0	100·0	100·0	100·0

[1] Includes Finland, Sweden, Norway, Denmark, Germany, Belgium, the Netherlands, Switzerland, and Austria.
Source: Yates, op. cit., Tables 19, 21, 23 and 25, pp. 47–51.

proportion. The rest of the underdeveloped world was a virtual non-starter in manufacturing production and export by 1913. Turning to the import trade in primary products, the United Kingdom's share fell heavily after 1876–80, whereas because of rapid industrialization and rising real incomes, the shares of North America and continental Europe rose. The growing imports of primary products into the rest of the world after 1896 consisted primarily of food and raw materials for Japan.

Table 10 and Diagram 8, which give the respective shares of primary products and manufactures in the total trade of the developed and underdeveloped regions of the world, reveal certain other important features in the composition of world trade before 1913. First, and most obviously, the developed countries chiefly exported manufactures and imported primary products, whereas the trade pattern was reversed for the underdeveloped countries, which mainly exported primary products and imported manufactured goods. Moreover, among the developed countries we find, as we would expect that primary products are a much larger element in

TABLE 10. *Shares of Primary Products and Manufactures in Total Trade of Each Region, 1876–1913*

| | Per cent | | | | | |
| | 1876–80 | | 1896–1900 | | 1913 | |
Region	Primary products	Manufactures	Primary products	Manufactures	Primary products	Manufactures
EXPORT TRADE						
U.K. and Ireland	11·9	88·1	17·2	82·8	30·3	69·7
N.W. Europe	43·8	56·2	50·5	49·5	48·0	52·0
Other Europe	78·1	21·9	74·9	25·1	75·6	24·4
U.S. and Canada	85·7	14·3	81·0	19·0	74·1	25·9
Underdeveloped countries and rest of world	97·6	2·4	91·6	8·4	89·1	10·9
World	*61·9*	*38·1*	*62·8*	*37·2*	*61·8*	*38·2*
IMPORT TRADE						
U.K. and Ireland	85·8	14·2	82·6	17·4	81·2	18·8
N.W. Europe	60·9	39·1	62·0	38·0	59·9	40·1
U.S. and Canada	63·5	36·5	63·0	37·0	63·4	36·6
Underdeveloped countries and rest of world	30·9	69·1	29·2	70·8	40·2	59·8
World	*64·9*	*35·1*	*65·6*	*34·3*	*65·0*	*35·0*

Source: Kuznets, op. cit., Table 8A, p. 38; see also Yates, op. cit., Table 28, p. 55.

the exports of the United States and Canada, on the one hand, than of the United Kingdom and N.W. Europe, on the other. Similar differences are evident in the structure of imports, with primary products a smaller and manufactures a larger element in the import trade of the former than of the latter. Perhaps the most interesting feature of Table 10, however, is the trends in the structure of the trade in primary products which it reveals. Taking the export trade first, we notice that the shares of primary products rose for the United Kingdom and N.W. Europe, and declined for all other regions, both developed and underdeveloped. The trends in the structure of the import trade in primary products show declining shares for the United Kingdom and N.W. Europe, a stable share for the United States and Canada, and a fluctuating, if declining, share for Other Europe. It is, however, the trend in the structure of imports of the underdeveloped countries that differs significantly

Diagram 8: Shares of Primary Products and Manufactures in Total Trade of Each Region, 1913

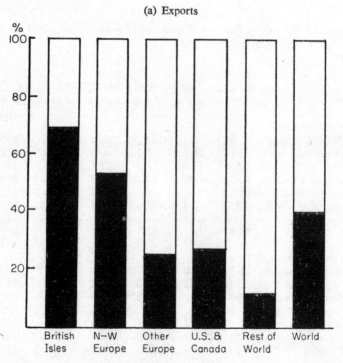

(a) Exports

Shaded Portion: Manufactures

from those of developed countries. In the underdeveloped regions imports shifted toward, not away from, primary products, the share of the latter rising from 31 per cent in 1876–80 to 40 per cent in 1913. As Kuznets points out, it is probably the slight decline in the share of primary products in the trade of developed countries combined with a rise, also slight, in the share of primary products in the trade of underdeveloped countries, plus a shift in the relative weight of different regions, for example, the rise in the weight of the United States and other developed areas overseas and the decline in the weight of the United Kingdom, which accounts for the stability in the share of primary products in world trade between 1876 and 1913.

However, this stability in shares hides significant variations in the composition of the trade in primary products and manufactures. Within the manufactures component for the developed countries, a decline in the share of textile manufactures occurred along with a

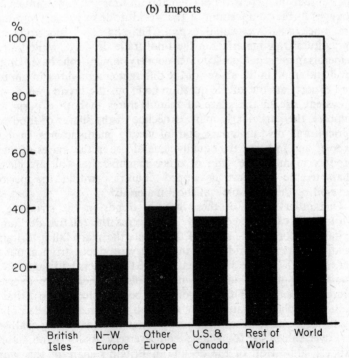

(b) Imports

Shaded Portion: Manufactures

Source: As for Table 9

rise in the share of metal manufactures, and a fairly general rise in the share of other manufactures (chemicals, paper and wood products, clay and glass products). These changes in the composition of the exports of the developed countries were partly due to industrialization and the consequent changes in the structure of domestic output that accompanied it—involving a move away from primary production towards manufacturing, and within the latter a move away from textiles to metal manufactures, chemicals, and engineering products. They were also partly caused by the extension of the international economy and the consequently greater international division of labour, which applied within manufacturing activity as well as between manufacturing and primary production. In the changed situation the developed countries found themselves at a growing comparative disadvantage in the production of foodstuffs and raw materials at the same time as their efficiency in manufacturing production was increasing.

Given the rapid expansion of metal manufacturing after 1870 and the consequent increase in the demand for ores and concentrates, the changes in the composition of the world trade in primary products are much what we would expect. The shares of foodstuffs and agricultural raw materials in the total trade declined, while that of minerals increased. Detailed inter-country comparisons based on the level and trend in the shares of the different commodities in imports and exports are out of the question here, but the broad trends—the prevalent rise in the share of manufactures in both exports and imports, the particularly marked decline in the shares of food and agricultural raw materials and of textile manufactures in both exports and imports, the equally general rise in the shares of metal product manufactures and of other manufactures—all are clearly characteristic of most developed countries within the periods covered by the available statistical material.

One other aspect of these general trends in the structure of world trade calls for comment. It concerns the relative decline of Britain in world trade after 1870. Despite the sharp fall in Britain's relative share of world trade in primary products, from about 30 per cent in 1876–80 to 19 per cent in 1913 (Table 9a and Diagram 7a), there was a marked increase in Britain's dependence on overseas sources of supply. This was only to be expected, given Britain's limited supplies of natural raw materials and her free trade policy. By 1913 seven-eighths of Britain's raw materials (excluding coal) and just over half of her food came from overseas. As for manufactured exports, almost all of the decline in Britain's share of this world market appears to have taken place after 1890. Whereas Britain seems to have held her own in textiles, chemicals and nonmetalliferrous materials, and raised her share of the world export trade in miscellaneous finished goods (furniture, leather, rubber manufactures and so forth) and drink and tobacco products, the losses arose in iron and steel, in metal manufactures, and in transport equipment. When Britain's export performance is examined in terms of the distribution of her exports between expanding, stable, and contracting commodity groups, a further weakness is uncovered. Britain was losing ground in commodity groups, such as machinery (including motor vehicles) and iron and steel, for which world demand was expanding most rapidly. On the other hand, her export expansion was occurring in those commodity groups (miscellaneous finished goods and drink and tobacco) for which world demand was declining. Her most important single export item, cotton goods, was also a commodity with a declining world market. As to the cause of Britain's disappointing export performance, some changes in Britain's overall shares of world trade in manufactures was to be expected, given the structural shifts in the commodity and area composition of trade noted earlier. Even so, the evidence suggests that Britain's export losses were overwhelmingly due to a decline in her competitiveness in foreign markets.

CONCLUSION

Between 1800 and 1913 world trade grew rapidly, far outpacing the growth of world output. This trade was dominated by Europe (including Britain), whose trade with the rest of the world consisted largely of an exchange of manufactured goods for primary products. Despite the spread of industrialization after 1850, the share of primary products in world trade remained remarkably stable, a development which is explained by a slight relative decline in demand for primary products by developed countries being offset by a moderate increase in the exchange of primary products between the underdeveloped countries. Throughout the period after the late 1870s, the share of foodstuffs and agricultural raw materials in world trade in primary products tended to decline, whereas that of non-agricultural raw materials rose. A change in the composition of world trade in manufactures is also apparent, with the textiles share declining and that of metal products and other manufactures rising.

This rapid growth of trade during the second half of the nineteenth century and the associated changes in its commodity composition and direction created a new and increasingly more complex network of economic activity and trade embracing whole continents or sub-continents. The earlier pattern of largely disconnected trading arrangements mainly centred on Britain gave way after 1860 to a new multilateral trading system based on a world-wide pattern of economic specialization. The general nature of the new pattern of world trade is clear enough. It involved an exchange of manufactured goods for raw materials and foodstuffs between the rapidly industrializing countries of Europe and North America and primary producing countries situated for the most part in the rest of the world. With the exception of Britain, the industrializing countries ran up heavy balance of payments deficits with the primary producers. Britain, on the other hand, largely because of her free trade policy, became a heavy importer of both manufactures and primary produce. She was also the most important exporter of manufactured goods to non-European primary producers, as well as the world's largest foreign lender. Consequently Britain had a trade surplus with the primary producing countries. This surplus, plus Britain's invisible earnings (payments for services, such as banking, insurance and shipping, rendered to foreigners and earnings on foreign investments), provided the foreign exchange she needed to cover her excess of imports from industrializing countries, thus providing these countries in turn with the means with which to finance their deficits with primary producers overseas. This, broadly, was the character of the multilateral system of trade settlement that had emerged by 1913. In the next chapter the growth and development of this system during the nineteenth century is examined in greater detail.

SELECTED REFERENCES

Cairncross, A. K., 'World Trade in Manufactures since 1900', *Economia Internazionale* (December, 1955). (Reprinted in Cairncross, *Factors in Economic Development* [London, 1962], Chap. 14.)

Kuznets, S., 'Quantitative Aspects of the Economic Growth of Nations: X-Levels and Structure of Foreign Trade: Long-term Trends', *Economic Development and Cultural Change*, Part II, January, 1967.

Lamartine Yates, P., *Forty Years of Foreign Trade* (London, 1959)

Saul, S. B., 'The Export Economy 1870–1914', *Yorkshire Bulletin of Economic and Social Research*, Special Number (May, 1965), pp. 5–18.

Woodruff, W., *Impact of Western Man* (New York, 1966), Chap. VII.

Woytinsky, W. S., *and* E. S., *World Commerce and Governments* (New York, 1955).

Chapter 6

THE GROWTH OF A MULTILATERAL PAYMENTS NETWORK

INTRODUCTION

An important development associated with the growth of the international economy between 1870 and 1913 was the emergence of a complex multilateral payments network, which facilitated the movements of goods, services, capital and income payments to such a degree that the braking forces of certain impediments to the growth of international commercial relations after 1870 were minimized. Before embarking upon a description of the growth and development of this network of trade and payments, however, it is necessary to define certain concepts of vital significance to the subsequent discussion.

The balance of payments of a country is a systematic record of all economic transactions between the residents of that country and residents of foreign countries during a given period of time. However, in order to simplify the following analysis, we shall assume that only commodities are traded between countries and that only gold is used to settle any outstanding trade balances. The fact that services and other 'invisible' items also enter into a country's foreign trading account, and that capital flows from country to country, does not in any way invalidate the conclusions we draw from an analysis of our highly simplified trading system, and it is always possible to extend the argument to cover all types of foreign transactions.[1]

[1] A country's balance of payments is simply a statement of its commercial and financial transactions with the rest of the world in the course of a year. This account must balance for much the same reason that the debits and credits in ordinary double-entry bookkeeping balance. It contains what are called autonomous items and financing items.

Autonomous items are classified into current account (goods and services) and capital account. The current account includes the value of commodity exports and imports, the difference between which represents the balance of trade (favourable when exports exceed imports and unfavourable when an import surplus occurs), and receipts and payments for 'invisible' items such as transportation, investment income, travellers' expenditure, and other services. The

Trade and payments patterns between countries may develop along a number of lines. A BILATERAL trade and payments system arises when the payments for commodity imports received by country A from country B are offset by payments for exports from A to B. If, under gold standard conditions, these two flows of payments do not entirely offset one another over a certain period, usually one year, then a balancing movement of gold will occur from the debtor to the creditor country.

DIAGRAM 9. *A Triangular Payments System*

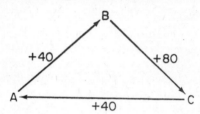

A TRIANGULAR payments system introduces a third country, C, into the international trading network. Such a system is illustrated in Diagram 9, where each country in which an arrow originates has a payments surplus with the country at which the arrow is pointed. Consequently, for each country in the system a deficit in one direction may be partly, wholly, or more than offset by its surplus in another direction. Thus A's deficit with C is just offset by its surplus with B; B's deficit with A is more than offset by its surplus with C; and C's deficit with B is partly offset by its surplus with A. It is essential to note that in the triangular payments system a large proportion of the international payments between countries will still be settled bilaterally and that it is only each country's remaining payments surpluses and deficits with other countries that will enter into the triangular system. The significance of such a triangular system is that it overcomes the need for balancing each bilateral surplus or deficit,

---

current account is favourable (in surplus) when monetary receipts for exports and invisibles exceed monetary payments for imports and invisibles. The capital account includes all autonomous capital flows into and out of the country. The balance of payments is said to be in surplus when, for autonomous items, all monetary receipts exceed all payments, and in deficit when payments are greater than receipts. The financing items offset the autonomous balance and ensure that the whole statement balances, that is, they indicate what happens to the surplus monetary receipts when the autonomous items are in surplus, and how an autonomous deficit is financed. Under the pure gold standard, the financing items normally comprised changes in the gold stocks of each country.

and thus reduces the extent of international gold flows. For example, in Diagram 9, whereas bilateral balancing would produce gold flows of 160, because of triangular settlement, a gold flow of only 40 (from C to B) would occur.

DIAGRAM 10. *A Multilateral Payments System*

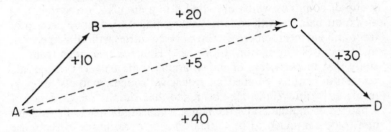

Finally, a MULTILATERAL payments system is defined as one including more than three countries or regions (A, B, C, D, etc.). In this situation, which is illustrated in a highly simplified form in Diagram 10, an extension of the 'roundaboutness' of trade settlements occurs. Once again, the fact that a country's payments surpluses in one direction can offset its deficits in another reduces the need for gold movements as a final balancing item in international transactions. Thus moving around the rim of the diagram (where the largest favourable balances are conventionally recorded) we find that the offsetting of debits and credits leads to a gold flow of only 30 compared with 100 when the outstanding balances are settled bilaterally. But multilateralism involves more than this, for each country will trade with all the other countries included in the system, that is, A will trade with C (the dotted arrow in the diagram) as well as with B and D. It is probable therefore that a multilateral payments system will include a number of triangular payments networks like ABC and ACD which will also work to reduce gold flows between countries. Thus if country A has a surplus of 5 with country C in addition to its surplus of 10 with B a gold flow of only 25 will now be needed to achieve 'world-wide' balance. It follows therefore that the larger the number of countries trading multilaterally the greater the opportunities for offsetting deficits and surpluses and, consequently, the smaller the flow of gold needed to achieve overall balance between the countries concerned. It also follows that the smaller the demands placed on the available stock of gold in the trading countries, the less is the likelihood of a country restricting its trade with other countries in order to protect its gold holdings.

In other words, the existence of a multilateral payments system is a powerful support to the growth of trade between countries.

This is the sort of payments system which Hilgerdt discovered emerging from his estimates of international trade for the period after 1870. By arranging countries according to the order and direction of their trade balances in a chosen year, he found that each country had an import balance with practically every country or group of countries which preceded it in a circular flow system and an export balance with countries succeeding it. A definite pattern of trade and payments emerged even when countries with similar economic structures were grouped together.[1] Hilgerdt concluded from his study that the servicing of unfavourable trade balances in the late nineteenth century entailed an extensive 'roundaboutness' of payments of various kinds. He also noted that, despite the existence of a pattern of multilateral settlements, a substantial part of merchandise trade continued to be settled on a bilateral basis, in the sense that the value of exports from (say) B to A was offset to some extent by B's imports from A. Hilgerdt estimated that about 70 per cent of all trade was bilateral during the late nineteenth century, and that probably a rather small proportion of the remainder was offset by foreign investment and other non-trade money flows. This meant that from 20 to 25 per cent of total world trade was multilateral in nature by World War I.

DEVELOPMENT OF THE SYSTEM

The multilateral settlement of international transactions was no new phenomenon restricted to the late nineteenth century. Multilateralism, at least of a primitive type, had been a major feature of international economic relations for centuries. Thus the triangular system comprising the United Kingdom, Western Europe and the Baltic countries had dominated Northern Europe's trade for many years, and the 'slave' triangle, linking Britain, Africa and the West Indies provided another example of this type of trading pattern. Other triangular trading systems developed during the first half of the nineteenth century. By the 1860s, for example, Britain's trade deficits with the United States were largely covered by her surpluses with Latin America, and a British deficit with China was offset by a surplus with India. But the new payments network that began to emerge after 1870 was essentially different from these earlier trading

[1] For diagrams demonstrating the nineteenth-century trade and payments systems in chosen years, see Folke Hilgerdt, 'The Case for Multilateral Trade', *American Economic Review*, Vol. XXXIII, No. 2 (March, 1943), p. 395; and S. B. Saul, *Studies in British Overseas Trade 1870–1914* (Liverpool, 1960), p. 58.

systems. Whereas the latter consisted of disconnected triangular networks centred on Britain, with each triangle arising out of an entirely different set of trading circumstances, the post-1870 variety was more complicated in nature and wider in scope. It arose partly out of the merging of some of the previously disconnected triangular systems, and partly out of the growing importance in world trade of countries and regions other than Britain. Thus by 1914, in contrast to the disconnected pattern of trading activities centred on Britain characteristic of the period before 1870, there existed a complicated system of international exchange based on a network of economic activities embracing most parts of the world. Britain still played a central role in the new system, but her trading relations with the rest of the world had undergone a profound change.

DIAGRAM 11. *The Multilateral Trade System after 1900*

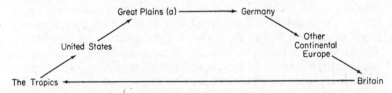

Note: (a) Canada, Australia, Argentina, etc.

Within the new system, which is described in a simplified form in Diagram 11,[1] the United States emerged as a separate link in the chain of international trade and payments in the years after the 1880s. At the beginning of that decade the bulk of American exports, which consisted predominantly of primary products, was shipped to Europe, from which region the United States also received more than half of its imports .In this way, the country experienced export surpluses with Europe (including Britain) and trade deficits with the rest of the world. As substantial domestic capital accumulation occurred, however, rapid industrialization got under way, and by the mid-nineties the United States had become a net exporter of manufactures. In consequence, by 1910–14 the early pattern of American trade had altered dramatically. Even when capital flows, interest and dividend payments and other 'invisibles' are taken into account, the

---

[1] The diagram is similar to that in Hilgerdt, op. cit., p. 395. Saul's diagram is slightly different. But it is possible to construct a number of diagrams of the network depending on the degree of generalization of regions. All would serve the same purpose, however, namely, to give a description of the multilateralism which existed at the time.

United States still had a large surplus with the United Kingdom, but compared with the 1880s its deficit with continental Europe was smaller. On the other hand, America's import surplus with the Tropics, chiefly India and Brazil, had enlarged considerably, mainly because of its increased demand for raw materials and foodstuffs. Most important of all, however, was the emergence of an American export surplus with the Great Plains countries, especially Canada, which came about largely because of their increased demand for American manufactures. It was this large and growing export surplus with the Great Plains region, rather than the credit balance with Britain or the large reductions in deficit balances with continental Europe, which financed the United States' growing deficit with the tropics.

As the United States became less dependent on the European market for its trade, the Great Plains region was drawn close to Europe by improvements in land and sea transport and by the growth of the European market for agricultural and other land-intensive commodities. As a result it quickly opened up favourable trade balances with the continent. On the other hand, despite an expansion of exports to Britain, these land-intensive countries became large debtors of Britain and tended to rely more and more on their favourable trade balances with continental Europe to finance their growing imports of British goods and the servicing of their accumulated capital debts and other 'invisibles' payments due to Britain. As the period progressed, however, it was with America that these countries came to record their largest import deficits.

After the early eighties, Germany also emerged as another link in the network of trade. Because of the rapid growth of its manufacturing industries and a relative decline in its agriculture, Germany's demand for raw materials and foodstuffs grew rapidly, and import surpluses with the Great Plains countries developed when they began to replace the United States as the German source of supply of these commodities. During the 1890s, moreover, German trade deficits with other major continental countries turned into surpluses when Germany found in these countries a ready market for its increasing exports of manufactures. These other European countries in turn increased their export surpluses with the United Kingdom, at least until 1900. Although these surpluses declined thereafter, because of heavy imports of British coal and colonial produce, they nevertheless remained fairly substantial, and produced a partial offset to the deficits which these countries had developed with Germany and the Great Plains region.

At the centre of the new multilateral trading network stood Britain, whose major contributions to its development during the period 1880 to 1914 included her growing import surplus, which declined somewhat after 1910; her free trade policy, which greatly facilitated the growth of the exports of other countries by providing a readily accessible market (partly at the expense of British agriculture); and the expansion of her international lending, which produced a favourable effect on Britain's balance of payments as income receipts from these foreign investments continuously increased.

In 1880, when foreign lending was relatively small, Britain's large deficits with continental Europe and the United States, and her smaller deficits with Australia, Canada, Egypt, and several other countries, were largely offset by favourable balances with India, South America, Turkey and Japan, with approximately one-third of British deficits with the United States and the continent being settled through India. By 1910, however, certain major changes had occurred in the British trade and payments pattern. Total negative balances with the United States had risen, Canada, the Strait Settlements, and South Africa (all recipients of large British investments) had by now become creditors of Britain, and South America was no longer a major debtor to Britain. In 1910, therefore, the settlement of British debit balances tended to flow to a large extent through the Far East and Australia. In particular, India, which offset approximately 40 per cent of Britain's total deficits, continued to provide the key to the United Kingdom's payments system by maintaining heavy export surpluses with continental Europe, the rest of the Empire, China and Hong Kong, and to a lesser extent, Japan and the United States—in other words, with many of Britain's creditors at the time. The importance of India to Britain became even more marked in the period from 1910 to 1914. The balance of payments of Australia, Brazil, Argentina and Canada all moved sharply against Britain, but fortunately for Britain the surplus with India expanded still further. While the Indian market continued to absorb large quantities of British manufactures, the entry of which into many other countries was impeded by tariff protection, Indian products exported to the continent, the United States and elsewhere attracted little tariff attention. As a result, Britain was able to absorb large quantities of foodstuffs, raw materials and manufactures from highly protected countries without having to increase her exports to these countries. Had the United Kingdom also moved towards protection during the period, international trade would undoubtedly have expanded at a slower rate, for industrial Europe and the United States would have been compelled to find other markets for their exports or to adjust their industrial structures.

When all these trends are taken into account the complexity of the multilateral payments network can be appreciated. Not only did it provide a substantial supplement to the bilateral balancing of payments, it also tended to reduce to a minimum the movement of gold for balancing purposes. It therefore facilitated the smooth working of the international monetary system, and promoted a much larger expansion of world trade than would have been possible had this trade been more dependent on the use of gold as the sole means of settling international debts. As a result numerous countries in the network were able to attain relatively high rates of growth in production and incomes through the consequent increased opportunities for trade.[1]

FOREIGN INVESTMENT AND THE MULTILATERAL SETTLEMENTS NETWORK

The growth of the multilateral payments network also facilitated the massive flows of capital and investment income which passed between countries after 1870. Although at first sight these flows appear to add strictly monetary factors to a system alleged to concentrate on 'real' flows of goods and services, it is important to note that the settlements network was to a very large extent concerned with 'real' transfers of such capital and investment income from one country to another.

When foreign capital flows from one country to another, its transfer may be effected in several ways, for example, through a shift of gold from lending to borrowing country, through an increase in the capital receiving country's imports from the lending country (or from other countries), or through a decline in the borrower's exports such that the trade balance becomes more unfavourable. Gold flows and reduced exports rarely effected the transfer during the late nineteenth century, and for the most part the transfer of capital from lending to borrowing countries took the form of increased commodity imports by capital-receiving countries. As far as British foreign investment was concerned, there were no 'tied' arrangements under which the borrowing country was committed to use the funds acquired for purchasing only British-made commodities. Nevertheless, for some borrowing countries, such as Australia before 1890, the British market was the major source of manufactured goods. But progressively after 1880, the United States and Germany made inroads into British export markets, and

---

[1] This account has not covered all triangular or multilateral settlements which arose in the various decades of this period. As Saul has shown, a more detailed breakdown of each region would reveal a much more complicated system of trade and payments than the one discussed in this chapter.

a continuously higher proportion of British foreign investment tended to be used by borrowing countries in the purchase of goods from these countries. Other lending countries probably experienced the same sort of trend as Britain, to a lesser or greater degree depending on the status of the lender among borrowing countries as a producer of manufactures.

Thus, increasingly towards the end of the period, the international transfer of foreign investments tended to be brought about in an indirect manner, and formed an integral part of the entire multilateral payments network. The importance of the network in providing a mechanism supporting the smooth flow of capital during the period is exemplified by the fact that had India not been able to absorb large amounts of British manufactures, the United Kingdom could not have invested in Canada to the extent possible after 1904, since much of the large British investments in that country was used to purchase commodities in the United States. It was only because America was experiencing a payments deficit with India, and India one with the United Kingdom, that the indirect transfer of capital to Canada operated with a minimum of friction. As for the 'real' transfer of the interest and dividends payable on British (and other) foreign investments, whenever this investment income increased and began to exceed new British capital outflows, payments, especially from the Tropics and the Great Plains countries, began to be transferred to Britain partly by way of the trade surpluses these regions had with the United States and continental Europe respectively.

CONCLUDING REMARKS

What was the significance of the multilateral settlements system for the international economy as a whole? First, it allowed countries to obtain international means of payment which could be used to acquire additional goods and services probably not available on a strictly bilateral basis; second, it permitted debt servicing to be transferred in a circuitous route from borrower to lender not possible under a bilateral system without impediments to the free flow of goods; third, it promoted the real transfer of foreign investment on a multilateral basis; and finally, it minimized gold flows for settlement purposes. One result was an enlarged volume of foreign trade. Moreover, because a country was able to finance deficits in one direction through surpluses in another, it was possible for those countries which were neither large debtors nor large creditors to aid debtor countries to pay, and creditor countries to receive, financial payments due. The world economy could thus achieve maximum benefits from trade and investment, especially when barriers to trade and capital flows were minimal, that is, under a system of free trade and convertible currencies.[1] During this period, the convertibility of currencies was generally maintained, but from the early 1880s protective tariffs became widespread in the world economy and tended to slow down the rate of growth of world trade somewhat and altered its direction considerably. In a multi-lateral trading network, the introduction of such restrictive measures on the trade between any two links in the network was likely to affect the trade of all other regions in the system, as well as the financial relations between debtor and creditor countries at opposite ends of the network. In addition, such artificial trade barriers could affect the functioning of world commodity markets and thus the prices of staple products sold in those markets. But the fact that Britain adhered to free trade, while possessing a safety valve in India when it came to a settlement of her own foreign payments, helped to minimize the restrictive effects of greater protection in the world economy after 1870. Britain's policy, even if followed unconsciously, allowed the multilateral system to grow rapidly with the minimum disruption from tariffs.

Thus while bilateral settlements between countries continued to predominate in international transactions, the growth of multi-lateralism, especially after 1870, provided the world economy with an additional mechanism for facilitating trade and payments between countries, and partly for this reason, international monetary crises were comparatively rare during these years, despite tremendous changes in the size and structure of both world produc-tion and trade. Yet the most successful years in the functioning of the multilateral trade and payments network also mark the period during which the first seeds of its future destruction were planted. For it was then that there appeared signs of a narrowing of the British payments surplus, upon the size of which the efficient func-tioning of the system so heavily depended. Although multilateralism was to survive after World War I, its destruction followed quickly in the early thirties in the face of a world-wide depression and the continued decline in Britain's international economic position.

One other feature of the functioning of multilateralism in the period before 1913 is worthy of comment. This is the extent to which foreign capital relied on the multilateral payments network for its effective transfer between countries. In the absence of such a network,

[1] Carl Major Wright in 'Convertibility and Triangular Trade as Safeguards against Economic Depression', *Economic Journal* (September, 1955), asserts that multilateral trade and currency convertibility are two aspects of the same phenomenon, each a necessary condition for the other.

capital exports would almost certainly have been lower than they were, and interest and capital repayments more difficult to effect. As we have already noted, the emergence of a multilateral payments network led to economies in the use of gold in international commercial transactions, and this fact partly explains the successful functioning of the gold standard in the period from 1880 to 1913. Nevertheless, any international payments balances outstanding after bilateral and multilateral settlements had been effected, had to be settled through the use of gold. This is a convenient point, therefore, to consider the nature and functioning of the international gold standard in the period before 1913.

SELECTED REFERENCES

Ellsworth, P. T., *The International Economy*, 3rd edn. (New York, 1958), pp. 148–55.

Hilgerdt, F., *The Network of World Trade* (Geneva, 1942).

Hilgerdt, F., 'The Case for Multilateral Trade', *American Economic Review*, (March, 1943), pp. 393–407.

Hansson, K-E, 'A General Theory of the System of Multilateral Trade', *American Economic Review* (March, 1952), pp. 59–68.

Saul, S. B., *Studies in British Overseas Trade 1870–1914* (Liverpool, 1960), especially Chaps. III and IV.

Wright, C. M., 'Convertibility and Triangular Trade as Safeguards against Economic Depression', *Economic Journal* (September, 1955), pp.422–35.

Chapter 7

THE GROWTH OF AN INTERNATIONAL MONETARY SYSTEM: THE GOLD STANDARD BEFORE 1913

Whereas trade within a country is made easy by the existence of a single currency common to all its regions, international transactions require a monetary system capable of handling trade involving the use of a variety of national currencies. Of course, this multi-currency barrier to trade can be overcome by conducting the international exchange of commodities on a barter basis, and in ancient and medieval times this type of international transaction often occurred. But bartering obviously places severe limitations on the growth of trade at any level, and so during quite early times foreign exchange markets, in which different currencies could be exchanged for one another, made their appearance thus placing foreign trade on a monetary basis. Precious metals, notably gold and silver, also came to be used to finance international trade, although their use had certain drawbacks, particularly in the high cost of transporting metals from country to country and the risks involved in such transfers. For this reason the expansion of foreign trade and commerce came to depend very much on improvements in the operation of foreign exchange markets and on the perfecting of devices to reduce the risks attached to fluctuations in the rate of exchange of one currency in terms of another.

With the growth of foreign commerce, financial innovations were quick to appear. The bill of exchange was introduced early, and by the fourteenth century a simple multilateral clearing system had been established. Much later, during the seventeenth and eighteenth centuries, the first 'forward' exchange markets were developed to overcome the uncertainty of future movements in the 'spot' rate of exchange, so reducing the risks inherent in fluctuating exchange rates. By this time Amsterdam had become the most important foreign exchange market in the world, closely followed by London, which was fast assuming a major role in world finance in the eighteenth century. At the beginning of the nineteenth century, therefore, foreign exchange markets were quite sophisticated in their operations and the financing of foreign trade and other international dealings had become quite complex. Throughout its history, the international financial system had adapted itself to meet the needs of an expanding foreign commerce and the process of adaptation continued during the nineteenth century, when a new international monetary system— the gold standard—evolved in response to the demands of a growing foreign trade and an expanding international flow of capital.

BIMETALLIC AND MONOMETALLIC STANDARDS

At the beginning of our period only Britain was on a gold standard for both domestic and international dealings. Most other major trading nations at this time were operating either a bimetallic standard, for example, France and the United States, or a silver standard, as were most other European countries.

For a country to be wholly committed to a full gold standard five basic requirements had to be met. First, the unit of account had to be tied to a certain weight of gold; second, gold coins had to circulate domestically and any bank notes in circulation had to be convertible into gold on demand; third, other coins in use had to be subordinate to gold; fourth, no legal restrictions were to be imposed on the melting down of gold coin into bullion; and finally, there had to be no impediment to the export of gold coin and bullion. Bimetallism, on the other hand, involved the employment of both silver and gold coins as standard money or legal tender under conditions similar to those just outlined for gold. Compared with the gold standard, however, a bimetallic standard had one major drawback: it worked smoothly only as long as the ratio between the values at which the two metals could be freely minted into coins approximated to their values in international bullion markets. If divergence of these values did occur, then the metal with the higher international market value would tend to be sent abroad and be replaced by the other, leaving the country with a monometallic rather than a bimetallic standard.[1] Hence the instability of the system, and

[1] Once the mint ratio and the world market ratio diverged, it paid those who could do so to engage in arbitrage at the various exchanges. Suppose, for example, that the Paris exchange is offering $15\frac{1}{2}$ ounces of silver for one ounce of gold and that an American merchant holds 1,000 ounces of gold. If the United States mint ratio is 15 to 1, he can obtain 15,000 ounces of silver for his 1,000 ounces of gold at an American mint. But if the gold is sent to Paris, he can get an extra 500 ounces of silver for it. It will pay him, therefore, to convert his gold into silver in

the periodic, but not always successful, efforts to achieve international agreement to fix the ratio of the price of gold and silver. Despite its drawbacks, however, the fear that one metal alone would fail to satisfy the world demand for money and so produce general deflation led to the widespread adoption of the bimetallic standard in the nineteenth century. In fact, for most of the time Britain alone adhered to the gold standard. It was not until the 1870s that other major trading countries began to move gradually in the same direction as that taken by Britain at the end of the Napoleonic Wars.

BRITAIN ADOPTS THE GOLD STANDARD

By the late eighteenth century Britain had moved to a *de facto* gold standard, after a long period during which silver had continuously disappeared from domestic circulation. The predominance of gold over silver had begun as early as 1717, when the gold guinea was given a value of 21s. Silver was so undervalued in terms of gold thereafter that it soon came to perform the function of a subsidiary coinage, the silver coins remaining in circulation having become so worn that it was unprofitable to withdraw them from circulation and melt them down for export. Silver's importance as a monetary unit was reduced still further in 1774, when the legal tender status of silver coins was restricted to payments up to £25. The supremacy of gold as a unit of account in Britain was assured from that year.

The movement towards the adoption of a gold standard in Britain was halted during the war years, when, as a wartime measure, cash payments were suspended in 1797 and the Bank of England freed from its obligation to convert its notes into gold. Immediately after the end of the war, however, the *de facto* gold standard of the late eighteenth century was made *de jure* by the passing of a number of Acts of Parliament. The Coinage Act of 1816 allowed for the minting of a Gold Sovereign, a 20s gold piece, the first of which was issued in the following year. The gold content of the sovereign was fixed in accordance with the mint price of gold, which had been maintained throughout the eighteenth century at £3 17s 10½d an ounce. Silver coins were legally subordinated to gold and were further restricted by being made legal tender for payments of up to only £2. In 1819 the convertibility of bank notes was restored, when an Act of Parliament committed the Bank of

---

Paris and to reconvert all his Parisian silver into gold in Washington. The final result of this process is, of course, that all gold leaves the United States and silver becomes the circulating medium. Gold was 'undervalued' and, according to the workings of Gresham's Law, that 'bad' money drives out 'good', the gold coinage does not circulate.

England to resume cash payments in gold bullion and, after 1823, in gold coin. This Act also repealed the law prohibiting the melting down of coin into bullion, and the trade in bullion was declared free. With the resumption of cash payments in 1821, Britain was legally on the full gold standard.

INTERNATIONAL MONETARY STANDARDS UP TO 1870

The task of maintaining stability within the bimetallic system, through exercising control over the world prices of gold and silver, fell to France. The performance of this function imposed few problems in the years between 1815 and 1850, when demand and supply conditions for both metals were fairly stable. There was some withdrawal of silver from circulation, as gold production steadily declined and its value appreciated relative to that of silver, but France possessed relatively large reserves of both metals and was easily able to absorb silver at the expense of gold without actually moving to a silver standard. The United States was also legally on a bimetallic standard for most of the nineteenth century. Until the 1830s, however, the country really operated on a silver standard, because at 15 to 1 the American mint ratio of silver to gold under-valued gold and led to its disappearance from circulation. But a *de facto* silver standard was inconvenient for a country which traded primarily with another, Britain, which was on a gold standard. It was probably for this reason that the Coinage Acts of 1834 and 1837 reduced the gold content of the dollar and established a new mint ratio of 16 to 1. Since this ratio was above the free market ratio, which generally settled around the French mint ratio of 15½ to 1, the previous trend towards a silver standard was replaced by a movement to a *de facto* gold standard similar to that found in Britain during the eighteenth century.

The pressures on the bimetallic standard mounted after 1850, when the discovery of substantial gold deposits in California and Australia produced dramatic changes in currency dealings and metal markets. The relative price of gold fell and the French mint ratio of 15½ to 1 proved to be inappropriate to the new world market situation for it overvalued gold. As silver appreciated relative to gold, France absorbed large quantities of gold and the French franc became a gold unit as Gresham's Law became operable. In an effort to stabilize the situation and promote an international bimetallic system, France summoned a meeting of the franc-using nations in 1865. As a result of this meeting, France, Belgium, Switzerland and Italy (often referred to as the Latin Monetary Union) agreed to regulate their currencies jointly. The agreement, however, did little to alleviate the monetary pressures exerted on the bimetallic countries.

As for the other European countries, by 1870 they were either on a silver standard—the Germanic States, Holland and Scandinavia—or, like Russia, Austro-Hungary, Italy, Greece, and more recently France, had been forced by wars and revolutions to issue inconvertible paper money, which, with the exception of the French issues, were depreciated paper.[1] Outside Europe, the Orient and Latin America were on silver, and the United States had inconvertible and depreciated notes, issued during the Civil War, still in circulation. By 1870, therefore, the gold standard was far from being internationally adopted. Britain alone operated on a legal gold standard. Bimetallism existed legally in the United States and the Latin Monetary Union, and Germany, Holland, Scandinavia, Latin America and the Orient adhered to the silver standard.

THE SPREAD OF THE GOLD STANDARD

During the 1870s the movement towards gold accelerated, and silver declined rapidly in importance as an international standard. This sudden change in the international monetary situation was brought about by two developments, each of which drastically affected the relative prices of the two main monetary metals. First, Germany transferred from a silver to a gold standard. It did this for a number of reasons. To begin with, several east European countries with which Germany had important trading relations had abandoned a silver standard for inconvertible paper so that Germany no longer derived any advantage from adherence to the silver standard in its commercial relations with these countries. Moreover, most of Germany's commercial relations with non-European countries tended to be financed through Britain where a gold standard operated. Finally, delegates from a number of European countries to an international monetary congress held in Paris in 1867 had overwhelmingly favoured the adoption of a universal gold standard. Given these arguments in favour of a changeover to gold, the large war indemnity extracted from France by Germany in 1871–2 provided the means for bringing it about. In 1872 a new currency unit, the mark, was adopted to replace the silver thaler and silver was

---

[1] 'Irredeemable' or 'inconvertible' legal tender notes cannot be converted into gold on demand, but only when the government is willing to allow it. Normally, of course, in a gold standard country, bank notes are convertible into gold on demand. An inconvertible currency may depreciate in value relative to gold, if the quantity issued tends to be excessive, and relative to convertible currencies if the excessive issue leads to, or is accompanied by, inflation.

relegated to subsidiary coins of limited legal tender. Surplus silver bullion and coins of large denominations were used to buy gold in the bullion markets to overcome the domestic shortage of gold for coinage purposes. In two years Germany acquired £50m. ($243m.) of gold, and so great were the pressures exerted on the markets that the price of silver in terms of gold commenced to decline dramatically.

The fall in the price of silver, and hence its demise as an international monetary standard, was also brought about by the sharp increase in the world output of silver that followed the discovery of large deposits of the metal in Nevada and elsewhere. In the face of the glut of silver in the world market, which was aggravated by the suspension of the minting of silver coins in the United States in 1873, the price of silver in terms of gold dropped below 16 to 1, and countries on a silver or bimetallic standard faced the possibility of substantial monetary inflation. As a result the demonetization of silver became general after the mid-seventies. Holland, crushed in between a gold-using Britain and a gold-using Germany, was the first to go. In 1874 it ceased coining silver and not long afterwards adopted gold as its unit of account. Norway, Sweden and Denmark quickly followed suit. The Latin Monetary Union, under pressure from its inception, encountered extreme difficulties in the early seventies and its members were compelled in January, 1874, to limit their coinage of five-franc pieces. In 1878 they suspended the minting of silver coins altogether, and from that time onwards France and her colleagues operated on the so-called 'limping' (or 'lame') gold standard. Silver was still legal tender, but it was neither coined nor used to any significant extent in commercial transactions, though banks continued to hold large quantities of the metal. Effectively, however, these countries adhered in all other ways to the gold standard. By 1878, therefore, Britain, Belgium, Holland, France, Germany, Switzerland and the Scandinavian countries were operating on gold, and, since most other continental countries were using irredeemable depreciated paper money, silver was no longer an international standard of value in Europe.

The movement to gold was completed by the end of the century. In the United States bimetallism was not legally abandoned until 1900, but the country was effectively operating on the gold standard once convertibility of paper notes was restored in 1879. Austria moved to gold in 1892, and Russia and Japan in 1897, the year in which India adopted a gold exchange standard by pegging the rupee to sterling. A year later the Philippine peso likewise became tied to the American dollar. After 1900, other countries, including Siam and Ceylon in Asia, and Argentina, Mexico, Peru and

Uruguay in Latin America, eventually adopted the gold standard, while others were, by the outbreak of World War I, proceeding in that direction. By 1914 China was alone among major countries in still clinging to a silver standard.

This brief description of the pre-1914 gold standard brings out one of its most striking features, namely, its relatively short duration as an international monetary system. Whereas it is not possible to date precisely its beginnings—it did not exist in 1870, but it did in 1900—World War I certainly marks its end, for, as we shall see, the post-war restoration of the system was short-lived. In short, the international gold standard was in full sway only from perhaps 1897 (some would argue 1880) to 1914, less than twenty (or just over forty) years.

THE ROLE OF STERLING AS AN INTERNATIONAL CURRENCY AND THE IMPORTANCE OF THE LONDON CAPITAL MARKET

In the institutional field, the developments in the London capital market were of paramount importance for the efficient functioning of the international gold standard. With Britain's increasing importance in world trade, organized markets were established in London for many types of commodities, a move which was greatly enhanced in the early years by the continued growth of the British re-export trade and later by the adoption of free trade. These markets in turn acted as a stimulus to British shipping and created a growing need for insurance facilities to cover transport risks. As a result of these developments, London grew in importance as a centre of international commerce and finance, and various institutions, such as discount houses, merchants banks, insurance companies, and other specialist financial organizations, which were later to provide the essential services for a rapidly expanding international economy, began to increase in numbers. From the beginning of the nineteenth century, therefore, London forged ahead of Amsterdam, Hamburg, and Paris as the leading financial centre of Europe and thus of the world.

While these developments were taking place, a growing proportion of world trade was being financed by short-term credit in the form of foreign bills of exchange. Under these arrangements, by accepting a bill an importer guaranteed payment within (say) three months of acceptance. The foreign exporter, on the other hand, if he required ready cash before the bill matured, could discount it with a bank (or other financial institution willing to do so) for something less than the face value of the bill, thus allowing interest to the discounter for holding the bill between the date of discounting and maturity and for accepting the risk against default. It was not until the early nineteenth century that these financial arrangements were perfected in Britain by the merchant banks and bill brokers, each of which came to perform a specialized function. The merchant banks, which were well known and respected for their integrity, then began to accept bills on behalf of reliable businessmen and firms whose names were less familiar than theirs. In other words, for the payment of a small commission, the merchant banks, by endorsing a bill of exchange, would guarantee that it would not be dishonoured on maturity. In this way the merchants banks ensured that a large number of bills would be available for discounting. The discounting function was performed initially by the bill-broker—a financial go-between who accumulated bills of exchange and sought out banks with surplus funds, with a view to persuading them to invest in the bills in his care. For his trouble and his knowledge, he charged a small commission. Some years later, the bill-broker began to give way to the dealer, who was himself a principal and not merely a commission agent. Supplementing his own sizeable funds with money borrowed on call or short notice from the large London banks, he used the money to discount bills on his own account. Still later came the discount houses, which were little more than large-scale dealers. They had more capital to invest; they took deposits from the public and paid interest on them; and they did a much greater volume of business.

The acceptance houses did not restrict their business activities to the market for short-term credit. With the growth of British investment abroad after 1820, they came to specialize in foreign security issues as well, and before 1850 they were also important dealers in foreign exchange and bullion. Later, however, the various merchant houses came to specialize either in the acceptance business or in the issue of securities, and foreign exchange dealings came to be concentrated in the hands of the branches of foreign banks in London. These branches increased rapidly in number after 1870, when the growth of the London capital market and the extent of Britain's foreign trade made it essential for many foreign banks to establish branches in the centre. Increasingly, in the years up to 1914, the operations of these foreign branch banks presented a growing challenge to the supremacy of the bill on London as an instrument of international payments. For, through the use of the telegraphic process, the accumulated sterling reserves in these foreign branches tended to replace the bill on London as a method of payment across the exchanges.

The growing importance of the London capital market, especially after 1870, was associated with the increasing use of sterling as an international currency. Throughout the nineteenth century Britain, on the whole, maintained a continuous surplus on current account in its dealings with the rest of the world. But she did not amass large gold reserves chiefly because of her willingness to invest the surplus abroad. Yet, from experience over a number of decades, foreign institutions and traders confidently accepted the ability of Britain to maintain the convertibility of sterling into gold. The stability of sterling was unrivalled, and the possibility of its devaluation never even considered. Sterling was as good as gold, and in some respects even better, because it was more convenient, in the sense that British exporters and importers, who dominated world trade, preferred to draw and to be drawn on in pounds sterling, and because it brought in an income, for holders of sterling received interest payments, whereas gold holdings earned nothing.

Given the general acceptability of sterling throughout the international economy, it is not surprising to find that gold played only a minor role in settling international debts. The vast majority of payments were made either by the transfer of bills payable in sterling, or by the purchase and sale of bills payable in foreign currencies, or simply by the transfer of credits in the books of banks, although the volume of business conducted under the latter two heads was never large before 1914. Hence sterling bills of exchange were used not only to finance the exports and imports of Britain, but also those of a large part of the rest of the world as well. The reasons for this world-wide preference for the pound sterling as a medium of international payments were numerous. It came about partly because Britain was the world's largest trader, the dominant carrier in world trade, and the largest single source of foreign capital. In part also, it was because the value of the pound sterling was kept stable throughout the period 1821 to 1914 by rigorous adherence to the gold standard. But equally important was the high standing of the British acceptance houses and the assurance that any bill receiving their endorsement could be readily discounted, at the world's most favourable rates, in the London discount market. Combined together, these forces turned London into the financial centre of the world, and the pound sterling into an internationally acceptable currency.

THE WORKING OF THE GOLD STANDARD

Whereas sterling was used to finance the bulk of international financial transactions in the nineteenth century, gold remained the ultimate means of settling balances which could not be adjusted in any other way. Moreover, the international acceptability of sterling in settlement of debts depended in the final analysis on its ready convertibility into gold. For these reasons, it is necessary to examine in some detail the working of the gold standard in the period before 1914.

Under the gold standard, because the basic monetary unit of each country on the gold standard had a fixed gold content, the value of each country's currency was fixed in terms of all other currencies at the 'mint parity' or 'par' value. But if the par rate of exchange between two currencies, say the pound sterling and the dollar, was fixed by the gold content of each currency, the market rate of exchange was determined by the forces of demand and supply. In the market, if the demand for dollars rose relative to their supply, the market rate of the dollar in terms of sterling would rise; if the demand declined, the market rate would fall. Under the gold standard, however, the fact that residents in member countries could export or import gold freely placed limits on the extent to which the market rate could rise above or fall below the par rate. If the demand for dollars in London increased so much relative to the supply that the market rate of exchange (dollars per pound sterling) rose above the mint parity rate by more than the cost of exporting gold, it would have been profitable for those demanding dollars to buy gold in London, ship it to New York, and sell it for dollars in that market. Similarly, if the demand for dollars had fallen relative to the supply forthcoming so that the market rate of the dollar had declined below the mint parity by more than the cost of shipping gold, those willing to supply dollars (and thus demanding sterling) would have profited by shipping gold from the United States to London and selling it for sterling.

The cost of shifting gold from one financial centre to another allowed a certain degree of flexibility in foreign exchange rates. Consequently, the market rate could fluctuate according to the forces of supply and demand between two values, termed the 'gold export' and 'gold import' points. These limiting rates of exchange were established at values above and below the par value determined by the cost of transporting gold. The distance between the gold points could change over a time if transport and other costs altered. Similarly, the distance between the two points was relatively large or small depending on the distance between the two countries whose currencies were linked together. In general, the spot rate of the dollar in London would move towards the gold export point when Britain experienced a deficit in its balance of payments with the United States (an excess demand for dollars and an excess supply of sterling in the exchange market). Similarly, a British surplus with the United States would produce an excess supply of dollars (demand for sterling) and a decline in the market rate of the dollar towards the gold import point.

Normally, most transactions would have been conducted in foreign exchange, and only large and persistent imbalances between the two countries would have produced gold flows. But while gold flows produced short-run balancing of the supply of and demand for foreign exchange, they obviously could not be continued indefinitely, for a country could not sustain gold exports forever without running out of the metal. Gold imports could go on somewhat longer perhaps, but eventually the importing country's trading partners would exhaust their supplies of gold. What then was the nature of the longer-run mechanism of adjustment under the gold standard which prevented these situations from arising?

One answer to the question was given by the classical economists, such as David Hume, Adam Smith, and J. S. Mill, who worked out the 'price-specie-flow' mechanism. According to this explanation, price changes induced by gold flows were supposed to bring about the adjustment. Suppose a country develops a balance of payments deficit because of excessive imports and proceeds to export gold to cover this excess. This loss of gold will reduce the domestic money supply, since either gold circulates as money in the country or the banking system keeps the country's internal supply of money adjusted to the quantity of its gold reserves. A decrease in the domestic money supply will lead to a decline in commodity prices, since less spending with output unchanged means lower prices. Lower prices for goods will in turn increase exports, as foreigners find the country a cheaper place in which to buy. Lower domestic prices will also reduce imports, since domestic substitutes for foreign goods become cheaper relative to foreign supplies. In the gold-receiving country the process is reversed. The inflow of gold increases the domestic money supply and raises commodity prices, which makes exporting more difficult and the importing of cheaper foreign supplies more attractive. These changes in the export and import capacities of the two countries will alter the supply and demand conditions in the foreign exchange market and bring about adjustments in exchange rates until a new equilibrium is established.

Late in the nineteenth century this price-specie-flow mechanism was elaborated in a number of ways, the most important of which concerned the effects of gold movements on the monetary policy of the central banks. In Britain, in particular, it was argued that gold flows led to changes in Bank Rate—the Bank of England's discount rate—which were in themselves automatic and which formed part of the adjustment mechanism. Thus it was argued that, as gold exporters obtained gold from the Bank of England, the Bank's ratio of reserves to liabilities would decline. If this decline persisted, the Bank would eventually raise its discount rate (Bank Rate) automatically to prevent further depletion of its gold reserves. Such action would produce increased interest rates generally and a restriction of credit. This would have an adverse effect on business activity and employment and lead to a fall in prices and wages, which would reinforce the direct effects of the price-specie-flow mechanism. On the other hand, when a gold inflow took place, the increased money supply would mean an abundance of credit and interest rates would fall. Declining interest rates would stimulate domestic activity and generate an upward pressure on wages and prices. If interest rate policy was, in this way, a 'rule of the game' requiring strict observance by monetary authorities, the gold standard mechanism would truly have been an automatic system. The combination of specie flows and interest rate changes would have produced an era of stable exchange rates, and, given a moderately large stock of monetary gold in each country, although its size was subject to fluctuation, it would not be in danger of permanent depletion, since a loss of gold would be automatically corrected by the operation of the adjustment mechanism.

DIVERGENCE BETWEEN CLASSICAL THEORY AND EMPIRICAL EVIDENCE

The weakness of the price-specie-flow theory of adjustment is that it fails to conform to the available empirical evidence on the functioning of the pre-1913 gold standard. Thus, contrary to the classical theory's prediction of divergences between the movements of exports and imports both within countries and between countries on the gold standard, we find a high degree of parallelism of movements in these trade flows.[1] Second, export prices in a number of countries moved together over time, although the classical theory would have called for more frequent divergences. Third, there is evidence to suggest that prices and especially wages were rather more inflexible in a downward direction than was implied in the classical theory and thus other forces would have been required to supplement any downward pressures which may have occurred when efforts were being made to restore a country's balance of

---

[1] The price-specie-flow theory predicts that a deficit country's exports would rise and its imports fall during the adjustment period. Conversely, a surplus country would experience opposite changes in the volume of its import and export trade.

payments to equilibrium. Fourth, major central banks often ignored the rules of the game and neutralized the foreign payments imbalance by refraining from using discount rate policy when such use would adversely affect the domestic economy. If, for example, it became necessary to increase interest rates to reinforce the deflationary tendencies required to improve the competitiveness of domestic industries and thus ensure that the trade balance became more favourable, central banks often allowed interest rates to decline in an endeavour to avoid the deflationary situation created by the outflow of gold. Fifth, the importance of capital movements was entirely neglected in the price-specie-flow theory, despite the fact that the current account of the lending countries remained for many years in continuous surplus, and the recipient countries continuously experienced an unfavourable balance on current account. In short, classical theory tended to be too preoccupied with the trade account and industrial competitiveness.

Since international capital flows depended to a large degree on economic conditions in the lending countries, it was the recipient countries which suffered most from changes in the level of foreign lending, particularly by way of instability in their exchange rates and their external balances. Finally, the discount rates of the major central banks in surplus and deficit countries tended to move together as the automatic adjustment mechanism came into action, and not, as one would expect from classical theory, in a divergent manner.[1]

OTHER FEATURES OF THE ADJUSTMENT MECHANISM

As noted above, the classical theory was over-simplified to the extent that it concentrated on the current account balance and neglected capital movements, the existence of which allowed the current account to remain unbalanced for a number of years. Later theorists supplemented classical theory by including capital movements, but early in the twentieth century economists were still at a loss to explain the rapidity with which the gold standard adjustment mechanism had in many cases produced external balance. The answer was eventually found in the changes in incomes which accompanied the price movements. Thus a fall in a country's exports reduces the income of its export industry and through multiplier effects brings about a reduction in spending on wages, salaries, raw materials, consumption goods, and savings. There will also be

[1] See R. Triffin, *Our International Monetary System: Yesterday, Today, and Tomorrow*, and W. M. Scammell, 'The Working of the Gold Standard', *Yorkshire Bulletin of Economic and Social Research* (May, 1965). This section and the one that follows lean heavily on these two sources.

a decline in the country's demand for imports, which, by offsetting the fall in its exports, will tend to bring about balance in the country's external payments position. On the other hand, a rise in exports, by increasing domestic incomes will tend to work in the opposite direction, reducing the payments surplus generated by expanding exports by encouraging a greater volume of imports. As Scammell points out: 'the potency of income adjustment can be judged from the fact that, on certain occasions, balance of payments adjustment has taken place in spite of simultaneous neutralising action by the central bank to offset the effects of gold flows'.[1] In other words, there is a strong case for arguing that the major burden of adjustment in the gold standard was carried by changes in income.

Another feature of the adjustment mechanism overlooked by the classical economists was the role played by international flows of short-term capital, which grew in importance as communications between nations were improved. Thus a deficit country experiencing downward pressure on its exchange rate was likely to receive an inflow of foreign short-term capital. This would come about for two reasons: first, because foreign speculators would be attracted by the profits to be made from purchasing a currency whose price (in terms of other foreign currencies) was likely to rise once the central bank adopted monetary policies aimed at correcting the balance of payments deficit; and second, because the higher interest rates associated with these monetary policies provided an added incentive to capital inflow, by offering it a higher return than could be obtained in its country of origin. By providing a partial cover for the receiving country's balance of payments deficit, the inflow of short-term capital would tend to reverse the downward movement of the exchange rate, help to minimize gold outflows, and speed up the adjustment process. One must be careful, however, not to exaggerate the importance of these capital flows, for, despite the unlikelihood of a devaluation, some short-term capital outflow may have occurred. Moreover, other countries may have responded to the new situation by increasing their interest rates in order to minimize the outflow of short-term capital from their money markets.

In one respect at least the classical theory was correct—it predicted few international monetary problems. One cannot help being impressed by the relatively smooth functioning of the nineteenth-century gold standard, more especially when we contemplate the difficulties experienced in the international monetary sphere during the present century. Despite the relatively rudimentary state of

[1] Scammell, op. cit., p. 43.

E

economic knowledge concerning internal and external balance and the relative ineffectiveness of government fiscal policy as a weapon for maintaining such a balance, the external adjustment mechanism of the gold standard worked with a higher degree of efficiency than that of any subsequent international monetary system. Trade and capital movements proceeded smoothly over the gold standard period (1880–1913), exchange rates, especially among major trading countries, remained comparatively stable and quantitative restrictions on trade and other payments were remarkably absent. What made this efficient functioning possible? Perhaps the chief reasons accounting for the successful working of the gold standard are to be found in the position of the United Kingdom in the international economy, the growth and strength of sterling as an international currency, and the working of the multilateral settlements network. Britain remained the major trading country throughout the century and the most important source of investible funds. Although it acquired and maintained a persistent trade deficit, it experienced a continuous current account surplus through its large 'invisibles' earnings from shipping and foreign investments. Nevertheless Britain's gold reserves remained relatively low throughout most of the period, for the current account surplus tended to be offset to a large extent by the capital outflow which occurred during the period. To a more limited extent, other western European countries tended to follow this pattern when they, too, became major lenders. Moreover, there was complete confidence in sterling as an international currency. Sterling balances tended rarely to become too small or too large chiefly because of the structure of the British balance of payments. 'Britain's inelastic demand for imports and the elastic nature of the demand for her exports ensured that in times of depression Britain ran a deficit in her balance of payments. Thus, if during a slump British capital exports declined, the deficit on current account compensated for this; while in times of boom the situation was reversed.'[1]

The gold standard period was an era of rapid industrial growth in the world economy, and in the circumstances it was possible to achieve adjustment without the appearance of deflationary tendencies. Changes in demand could readily be met by alterations in industrial structures, and if the adjustment process demanded price changes, these could be accomplished without widespread unemployment and reduced profits. In other words, the international economy was to a large extent dynamic and flexible in its operation. Often, too, an adverse payments situation did not lead to large reductions in international reserves because of the

[1] Ibid., pp. 44–5.

cushioning effect provided by the longer-term credit facilities which increasingly became available during these years. Furthermore, there was a greater degree of discretion exercised by central banks in the implementation of their policy than the classical theory admitted. This was true even of the Bank of England, for adjustments of Bank Rate were never completely 'automatic'. While protection of its gold reserves remained of paramount importance in determining the Bank of England's monetary policy, it nevertheless exercised considerable discretion in the choice and timing of its actions and was always aware of the need to achieve external balance with a minimum of interference with the level of domestic business activity. Finally, the growth of a complex multilateral settlements network by providing a variety of ways of offsetting payments between countries considerably reduced the need for gold flows to balance international accounts. This reduced the need for countries to hold large stocks of gold for balancing purposes and thus helped to prevent a shortage of gold from developing as more and more countries came to adopt the gold standard in the years after 1870.

CONCLUSION

During its relatively brief existence, the gold standard was not the standardized or automatic international monetary system it was widely believed to be in the 1930s. There were various versions of the gold standard, including the gold exchange standard, and the discretionary monetary policies of governments exerted some influence on the automatic functioning of the mechanism. Even so, the system worked smoothly, without large and frequent lapses of confidence in the parities of major currencies. This success was due in part to the growth of a multilateral settlements network, and in part to the predominance of Britain in the international economy, which led to the increasing use of sterling as a supplement to gold in the settlement of international commerical transactions. Indeed it is the growing use of sterling as an international currency and the declining use of gold in domestic money supply which give support to Triffin's argument that 'the nineteenth century could be far more accurately described as the century of an emerging and growing credit-money standard, and of the euthanasia of gold and silver moneys, rather than as the century of the gold standard'.[1]

[1] Triffin, op. cit., p. 21. Gold was becoming less important as a domestic currency towards the end of the nineteenth century due to the increasing use of credit money (paper currency and bank deposits), which perhaps accounted for over 90 per cent of the total expansion of money from the 1870s to 1913.

SELECTED REFERENCES

Beach, W. E., *British International Gold Movements and Banking Policy, 1881–1913* (Cambridge, Mass., 1935).

Bloomfield, A. I., *Monetary Policy under the International Gold Standard 1880–1914* (New York, 1959).

Bloomfield, A. I., *Short-term Capital Movements under the Pre-1914 Gold Standard* (Princeton, 1963).

Feavearyear, *Sir* Albert, *The Pound Sterling*, revised by E. Victor Morgan (Oxford, 1963).

Haberler, G., *The Theory of International Trade* (London, 1936).

Hawtrey, R. G., *The Gold Standard in Theory and Practice* (London, 1927).

Morgan, E. Victor, *A History of Money* (Harmondsworth, 1965).

Nurkse, Ragnar, *International Currency Experience* (Princeton, 1944).

Rostow, W. W., *British Economy of the Nineteenth Century* (Oxford, 1948).

Scammell, W. M., 'The Working of the Gold Standard', *Yorkshire Bulletin of Economic and Social Research*, Vol.17, No.1 (May, 1965).

Triffin, R., *Our International Monetary System: Yesterday, Today and To-morrow* (New York, 1968).

Viner, Jacob, *Studies in the Theory of International Trade* (New York, 1937).

Yeager, Leland B., *International Monetary Relations* (New York, 1966).

Chapter 8

INTERNATIONAL ASPECTS OF ECONOMIC GROWTH IN THE NINETEENTH CENTURY: THE SPREAD OF INDUSTRIALIZATION

INTRODUCTION

The international economy played a major role in promoting the spread of economic growth in the nineteenth century. The flows of trade, capital, and labour which linked countries together economically not only provided the means whereby the benefits of economic growth, in the form of higher real incomes, could be transmitted from country to country, but they were also the mechanism through which the technological and social innovations that are the essence of modern economic growth could be diffused. As a result, the economic growth of most countries came to depend as much on their ability to take advantage of the opportunities for trade and for the acquisition of new knowledge and additional factors of production presented by the international economy as on the quantity and quality of the economic resources domestically available to them. It is for this reason that any discussion of the nineteenth century international economy must include an examination of its function as an 'engine of growth'.

Obviously the international diffusion of modern technology and the stimulation of economic growth through an expansion of foreign trade are economic processes that are not independent of each other, if only because export-led growth implies some measure of technological and social change. Nevertheless, it does simplify our discussion of the international economy as a mechanism for transmitting economic growth and technical change between countries in the nineteenth century if we treat the two processes separately. Separate treatment is further justified by the fact that the spread of industrialization throughout Europe and North America, and the export-led growth characteristic of primary producing countries, represented significantly different responses to the economic opportunities presented by the emergence of an international economy in the century or so before 1913. Although a great deal of detailed work remains to be done in this relatively neglected field of historical research before a satisfactory account of the functioning of the international economy as a growth mechanism is possible, the general nature of its operation in the period before 1913 is readily apparent.

The nineteenth century world economy is best viewed as being composed of a centre and a periphery, with growth at the centre building up economic pressures tending to diffuse the development process to the periphery. Initially, Britain stood at the centre of this growth process, but as the century progressed, Europe, and in particular north-west Europe, came to play a larger part in fostering the spread of economic development overseas. Britain's central role in the world economy during these years rested on a technological revolution that began in the second half of the eighteenth century, and continued between 1820 and 1880 to transform a predominantly agrarian economy into the world's first industrial nation. But imitators were not lacking and, partly through a flow of capital and skilled labour from Britain, the new industrial technology spread first to Europe and then to the United States, so that by the 1870s, when Britain's rate of industrial growth began to slow down, these other countries began to play their part in the process of transmitting growth to the less developed regions of the world.

The peripheral regions were incorporated in this international growth process through a steady and persistent increase in the demand for primary products which many of these areas were well able to produce. Industrialization in Britain soon exposed her limited range of natural resources and her growing inability to feed a rapidly growing population. Increasingly Britain was forced to rely on other countries to supply her mounting needs for foodstuffs and industrial raw materials. To a lesser extent the other industrializing countries of Europe also came to depend on overseas sources of supply of primary products. The growing pressure of industrial demand on the centre's natural resources and supplies of foodstuffs and raw materials, and the resulting tendency towards rising prices, prompted a search for cheaper supplies in the periphery and an outflow of capital and skilled labour to develop peripheral sources of supply. In this way a cumulative process of growth was initiated in a number of countries overseas by the relation between the export demand for primary products and the inflow of foreign capital and labour that was associated with the expansion of the export sector. Particularly favoured by these developments were the United States and, later, the regions of recent settlement, including Canada, Argentina, Uruguay, South Africa, Australia and New Zealand, each of which, at different times and to varying degrees, came to depend on growth through primary product exports and the inflows of foreign capital and labour associated with it. At the other end of the spectrum were those peripheral countries which remained largely unaffected by these revolutionary changes, or those which became 'enclave economies', that is, countries in which foreign demand and the new technology served to revolutionize the export sector while leaving the rest of the economy virtually unchanged.

The failure of the expansion and modernization of the export sector of the enclave economy to spark off growth in the rest of the economy is only one of the problems arising out of the international record of economic growth in the nineteenth century. There are many others. Why, for example, did economic growth spread to only a limited proportion of the total world population? What accounts for the slow spread of industrialization? For even in Europe and the United States, rapid industrialization occurred only after 1870, more than a century after the new technology had emerged in Britain. More pertinent to the present discussion is the question whether these 'failures' in the diffusion of economic growth reflected weaknesses in the functioning of the international economy or whether they were the result of the existence of other obstacles to the spread of economic development. These questions, and many others like them, are the subject of a continuing and lively debate, for they are matters of enormous importance to the study of the economic problem of under-development, and to cover adequately the issues they raise would require another and much longer book than this. All that is possible here is for us to offer a few general observations on these issues so that the broad nature of the problems they raise and their relevance to the functioning of the international economy are more easily appreciated.

THE SPREAD OF INDUSTRIALIZATION

It is a matter of general observation that the diffusion of technology is closely related to the problem of mobility—of goods, people, ideas and behaviour. It is also apparent from what has been said so far in this book, that mobility in this sense was greatly enhanced during the nineteenth century by innovations in transportation and communications and in the field of international finance which greatly facilitated the large-scale movement of goods, men and capital between countries. These flows of economic resources were in turn important channels for the diffusion of the new industrial technology, since physical capital embodied it, immigrant artisans and entrepreneurs possessed the required technical skills, and imported goods provided opportunities for adaptive imitation.

Given the opportunity for adopting new methods of production presented by the international economy, the spread of technical innovation also required an economic incentive. Probably the most effective stimulus to innovation is the market to be supplied: both its size and the rate at which it is growing. A large and rapidly expanding market creates an environment that is highly conducive to technological advance and to all forms of innovation, including the adoption and adaptation of foreign techniques.

THE CONTRIBUTION OF THE INTERNATIONAL ECONOMY

The emerging international economy was itself an important form of market expansion in the nineteenth century, Foreign trade is simply an extension of domestic trade, and expanding opportunities for the international exchange of commodities did encourage the spread of industrialization. In Britain, industrialization was initially based on a rapidly expanding export of cotton textiles, and later it came to depend increasingly on exports of iron manufactures and coal. In the United States before 1860 raw cotton exports played an important role in supporting early industrial development in the country, and industrialization in Germany late in the nineteenth century was also closely tied up with an expansion of manufactured exports. Even in Russia and Japan, where governments created domestic markets for industrial goods through their own demands for military and railway equipment, the ability to develop an export trade, in wheat for Russia, and in cotton textiles for Japan, was necessary to provide the foreign exchange needed to service the inflow of foreign capital or to purchase the foreign machinery essential to industrialization. Whether the demand for industrial goods was satisfied directly through an expansion of manufactured exports, or whether it was created indirectly, through the growth of primary products exports leading to a rise in domestic real incomes, expanding foreign markets created an environment highly favourable to technological diffusion.

The growth of markets, both at home and abroad, is closely related to improvements in transportation, since poor transport facilities automatically restrict the size of the market thus limiting the scope for the use of modern technology. For this reason, good transport is perhaps the most powerful single weapon for accelerating the importation of modern industrial techniques. In this respect foreign investment was often of vital significance, since much of it in the nineteenth century went into railway building on the Continent and in North and South America and Australasia. Some of this capital also went into the development of shipping lines, the construction of docks and harbours, improvements in communications, and the provision of other ancillary services necessary for an expanding foreign trade.

The size of the domestic markets of some countries was also increased by immigration, which allowed population to grow faster than it would have done if dependent only on natural increase. Moreover, where the immigrant population could be used in combination with unexploited or unused economic resources, *per capita* real incomes often rose (thus further increasing market size) because a larger workforce permitted greater specialization and the use of more productive techniques. Furthermore, as in the United States and elsewhere, part of the immigrant workforce could be utilized in constructing the transport network so important for the growth and exploitation of domestic and foreign markets.

Finally, for a number of countries within Europe the movement towards larger domestic markets was aided by the gradual reduction of internal barriers to trade, by such trade liberalizing measures as the freeing of the Rhine to all shipping, and by the setting up of customs unions, such as the German *Zollverein*. At the same time the spread of free trade policies after 1850 provided most countries with expanding opportunities for the international exchange of goods and services. Later in the nineteenth century, however, the widespread adoption of protectionist policies, while reducing the size of foreign markets, encouraged industrialization in some countries by preserving the domestic market for local producers.

On the supply side, a country's rate of capital accumulation is obviously a major determinant of its capacity to absorb new ideas and new methods of production. Where, for example, technical change is embodied in capital equipment, a country's rate of capital investment is all important, since, in general, the more investment the greater the degree of technological progress. Capital shortage therefore may hinder technological diffusion in a number of ways. For example, it will place limits on a country's stock of social overhead capital, especially transport facilities, with all that that implies for the growth of the market. The need for relatively abundant supplies of capital is also stressed where innovations in techniques cannot be made singly but require simultaneous development in a number of industries. Moreover, the fact that techniques can rarely be borrowed without adaptation further adds to the capital cost of introducing the new methods of production. Finally, the fact that industrialization in the nineteenth century was accompanied by population growth and urban development meant that there were heavy demands on capital in the form of housing, public utilities and the additional tools and machines needed to equip an expanding workforce. While in most countries the bulk of their capital needs were satisfied out of domestic savings, the availability of foreign funds to finance the construction of social overhead capital, especially transport facilities, communications and public utilities (the demand for which was particularly heavy in the new countries overseas), meant that domestic savings could be used largely to finance the growth of primary production and manufacturing industry in borrowing countries without this expansion being threatened by inadequate transport or the lack of other ancillary services.

For many countries foreign trade and immigration flows also partly overcame the obstacles to industrialization caused by lack of natural resources, skilled labour and enterprise. In so far as the adoption of modern industrial techniques is dependent on natural resources, geographical location or some other unequally distributed endowment, growth opportunities are not likely to be equally available to all countries. Limited natural resources was probably an important factor restricting industrialization in many of the smaller countries of Europe. French economic development, it has been argued, suffered from a shortage of coal. But, whatever the relevance of scarcity of natural resources as an obstacle to technological diffusion, it must have become less important with time as progress during the nineteenth century began to make alternative processes possible, or to make imported resources effective substitutes for inefficient, highly-priced domestic supplies. Moreover, if the raw materials necessary for industrial development could be imported from abroad, so too could the necessary skills and entrepreneurial ability. Historically, the trader from abroad and the immigrant artisan have long been the main channel for the importation of foreign techniques; where the nineteenth century differed from earlier times was in the scale on which these movements of labour occurred and in the wider range of skills that people carried with them when they moved from country to country.

International Transfer Mechanisms

What prompted the greater part of the flow of labour, capital and trade between countries were differences in the relative prices of these resources in different countries. In the case of both labour and capital, non-economic considerations exerted some influence on their movement internationally, but for the most part it was differences in wage rates and the rates of return on investment that prompted the flow of factors of production from regions where earnings were low to those where they were higher. With commodity trade too, the exchange was prompted by differences in the relative prices of the goods traded, which reflected in turn differences in the costs of production in the various countries engaged in foreign trade. In so far as the flows of goods, capital and labour took place in response to differential economic advantages of this kind, they acted as spontaneous or 'natural' carriers of modern technology and ideas. On the other hand, specific and direct attempts were often made by governments and other interested bodies to transfer technologies internationally. In addition to sending students abroad to study the new techniques, governments also encouraged the inflow of foreign skills and capital through the use of subventions to immigrant entrepreneurs and guarantees of dividends on foreign loans. Implicit in such policies was the assumption that the diffusion of the new knowledge, either nationally or internationally, was likely to be slow in the absence of conscious efforts to encourage technological change.[1]

CAUSES OF THE LIMITED SPREAD OF INDUSTRIALIZATION

International

Yet despite the existence of these natural carriers of technology on a scale previously unmatched in history, and despite the efforts made by some governments to reinforce the market influences determining the volume of direction of these trade and factor flows, the rate at which the new technology was diffused was slow, and the spread of modern industry limited. Thus even in Europe and the United States, rapid industrialization occurred only after 1870, more than a century after the new technology had emerged in Britain. Even more striking is the fact that by 1913 the spread of industrialization was limited largely to western Europe, North America and Japan. While questions concerning the slow spread of industrialization in the period before 1913 can be answered only by a more detailed analysis of the problem than can be attempted here, a question more pertinent to the present discussion is whether 'failure' in the diffusion of modern industrial growth reflected weaknesses in the functioning of the international economy as a mechanism for trans-

[1] These two methods of transmitting technical knowledge enable us to draw a distinction between technological diffusion on the one hand and technological transfer on the other. Whereas the former term can be used to describe a natural spontaneous process of knowledge transmission, technological transfer incorporates 'an additional specific element, namely, planned and purposive type of action. It implies a conscious, predeterminate effort and commitment of resources to transplant technology from one country to another, and from one use to another'. (D. L. Spencer and A. Woroniak (eds.), *The Transfer of Technology to Developing Countries* (New York, 1967), p. 186.) Both mechanisms played their part in the process of economic development in the nineteenth century.

mitting growth between countries, or whether it was largely the result of the existence of other obstacles to the spread of modern techno- logy. Unfortunately we are still far from fully understanding the detailed working of the international economy as an 'engine of growth' in the nineteenth century, and much research remains to be done to fill the gaps in our knowledge. We are, for example, still limited in our knowledge concerning the extent to which the econo- mic growth of individual countries was dependent on the existence of the international economy, or how a country's dependence on the international economy may have changed over time, answers to which questions are obviously needed if we are to be able to weigh the relative importance of domestic and international obstacles to the spread of industrialization. Because of our lack of knowledge in these matters, comment on the problem just raised is necessarily limited, but nevertheless a few general observations on it can be offered.

To begin with, if the diffusion of modern industrial technology was limited before 1913, it was partly because the supply of capital and labour available for international transfer was limited, and be- cause not all of the countries desiring to import these productive resources were equally well-placed to attract them. For a number of reasons North America, and especially the United States, was parti- cularly attractive for foreign investors and migrant labour, and wes- tern Europe, because of its compactness and its proximity to Britain, the seat of the industrial revolution, was also conveniently placed to take advantage of the new technology. The fact that these two regions received the lion's share of the economic resources that did shift internationally during these years meant simply that there were fewer of these resources available for other capital and labour- importing countries, and their prospects for industrial development suffered correspondingly.

Moreover, in some countries primary production continued to be more profitable than manufacturing activities, in the sense that these countries' real income could be increased more rapidly by their specializing in agricultural and mining production and exchanging their surpluses of primary products for manufactures produced elsewhere. As long as the real incomes of primary producers were sustained by the mounting demand for foodstuffs and raw materials of the industrializing regions at the centre of the international econo- my, the spread of industrialization to peripheral countries was limi- ted by the economic advantages accruing to them from the growing territorial division of labour which formed the basis of the expanding international economy of the nineteenth century. When, however, changing demand and supply conditions in the post-World War I period resulted in a downward pressure on primary product prices which reduced the real incomes of countries supplying these commodities, industrialization programmes became a feature of many of these countries, as their governments endeavoured to diversify domestic economic activity by encouraging the production of manufactured goods previously purchased out of the export earnings of primary producers.

National

While the international economy may have functioned in such a way as to limit the spread of industrialization in the nineteenth century, for the most part the major obstacles to the diffusion of modern technology were to be found within countries rather than between them. The available evidence for this period suggests that the diffusion of modern industrial technology between countries was much faster than its diffusion within countries. Thus Watt's steam engine, first brought out in England in 1776, was introduced into France in 1779, into Germany in 1788, and into Italy in 1816. On the other hand, within Britain the steam engine did not come into general use until after 1850. In the other European countries, however, the lag was even greater, and in Italy the steam engine was still far from widely used even in 1913. A similar situation developed in the United States where the steam engine was introduced towards the end of the eighteenth century and quickly adopted for use in river boats. But it was not widely used in American industry until after the Civil War. Another example is to be found in the spread of the idea of interchangeable parts and standardized production. Developed in the United States well before 1850, and introduced into the British government's arms factory at Enfield in the 1850s, these innovations were adopted only very slowly by British manufacturers. While further evidence of disparate rates of technological diffusion between and within countries exists, for example, in the spread of new textile machinery and modern metallurgical processes during the nineteenth century, what obviously needs explanation is the cause of this disparity. In particular we need to know why, with easy international movement of inventions, a country's capacity to adopt new techniques on a wide scale should be so difficult to foster or to impart.

As we have already indicated, the adoption of modern technology is partly dependent on the availability of markets, capital, natural resources, and the necessary labour skills and entrepreneurial ability. But while limited markets and shortages of productive resources could be partially overcome with the help of foreign trade, capital and labour, in the final analysis the available domestic supplies of capital and entrepreneurship were often crucial in bringing about successful industrialization. Moreover, non-economic influences, particularly social attitudes, customs and beliefs are important determinants of the rate at which new techniques are diffused throughout an economy. The incompatibility of the new industrial technology with existing institutional arrangements, the reactions of merchants and businessmen to the uncertainty and risks attached to new ways of doing things, and the concern for social and political stability are only a few examples of the forces generating the social rigidities and resistance to change likely to be encountered in an industrializing society. Their existence serves to remind us that technological change is a cultural, social, psychological, and political process, as well as the imitation and adoption of techniques. Yet on the question of whether major structural shifts in the socio-political fabric must precede or accompany the adoption of industrial technology, the facts, such as they are, are not unambiguous. In France, for example, a very strong concern for continuity in the social and cultural sphere meant that technical change was relatively slow and that the government did not play a major role in promoting economic development. Germany, on the other hand, achieved rapid industrialization despite the fact that the old order retained much of its force. Denmark and Sweden also appear to have created expansionary economies as much by changing the direction of their economic efforts as by altering the structure of their institutions or the habits of their peoples. In south and east Europe, however, the existence of an essentially feudal system, and the rigid social stratification which accompanied it, as well as the low social value attached to industry and profit in the culture of some of these countries, constituted insurmountable barriers to the adoption of the new industrial technology, backed up as they were by deficiencies of resources, scale of markets, and education. Only Russia, in this part of the continent, succeeded in industrializing to any significant extent, and then only after the resistance of the government and other conservative forces had been overcome, largely by outside events.

Outside Europe the spread of industrialization to the United States, Canada, and, to a lesser extent, the other regions of European settlement overseas was helped by a level of receptivity to the new technology that was at least as high as that in Britain and the more industrially advanced countries in Europe, with which countries they shared a common social, economic and cultural background. These ties were also useful in fostering periodic inflows of European capital and labour which considerably assisted the diffusion of industrial techniques within the countries concerned.

High receptivity to the new technology was not confined to European countries or their offshoots overseas however. In Asia, Japan began industrializing rapidly towards the end of the nineteenth century and in this respect it is interesting to contrast the experiences of Japan and China before 1914 when confronted by Western technology and economic intervention. Displaying a common policy of exclusiveness and virtual absence of contracts with foreign countries, as well as a social structure and system of land ownership that acted as a barrier to industrialization, their responses to Western intervention in their affairs were totally different. Whereas Japan adopted Western industrial techniques rapidly and succeeded in achieving economic 'take-off' seemingly without any major social or cultural changes, the Chinese government remained contemptuous of Western civilization and opposed to all forms of social and economic change.

CONCLUSION

The spread of industrialization from Britain to the continents of Europe and North America was assisted by the functioning of the international economy. The flows of capital, labour and trade, which linked together the countries of the world, provided the channels through which modern industrial technology could be diffused between nations. If the extent of this technological diffusion was limited in the nineteenth century, it was partly because the stock of capital and labour available for international transfer was limited and partly because not all of the countries desiring to import these extra productive resources were equally well-placed to attract them. But what was an even greater obstacle to the spread of industrialization was the fact that many countries, even when they received inflows of foreign labour and capital, lacked the internal flexibility necessary for them to take advantage of the changing technological opportunities that presented themselves. It was this weakness rather than any fundamental deficiency in the functioning of the international economy as an 'engine of growth' that accounts for the limited industrialization before 1914. To industrialize successfully, there had to be capital formation, technical change, reallocation of resources, as well as changes in social, political and cultural attitudes to economic activity. Since in most countries the forces of inertia were strong and deeply entrenched, the spread of industrialization was necessarily a slow process.

SELECTED REFERENCES   See Chapter 9.

Chapter 9

INTERNATIONAL ASPECTS OF ECONOMIC GROWTH IN THE NINETEENTH CENTURY: THE EXPORT ECONOMIES

INTRODUCTION

Outside the industrializing countries economic growth was primarily a reflex action to the steady and persistent rise in the world demand for primary products. In these peripheral countries, economic growth took place for two reasons. First, trade was the means whereby the benefits of technological progress in Europe could be passed on to the rest of the world, mainly through the exchange of manufactured goods for foodstuffs and raw materials. At the same time, specialization in the production of those primary products most suited to the economic resources of these countries tended to raise the general level of their skills and productivity. Moreover, this increased productivity, along with the continued growth of exports and the accompanying rise in real incomes, provided an incentive to the establishment and expansion of other forms of economic activity and paved the way for further economic development. In this way an expansion of primary product exports could induce growth in the rest of the economy.

Faith in the transmission of development through trade was not too difficult to justify in the light of what was happening during the nineteenth century. Great Britain, for example, was developing successfully, first on the basis of textile exports, and later by expanding her exports of coal and iron. More relevant for primary producing countries, however, was the experience of the United States, which grew impressively before 1860, largely as a result of a rapid expansion in her raw cotton exports. Other nineteenth century examples of successful development based on primary product exports include Denmark, Sweden, Australia, Canada, New Zealand, South Africa and, to a lesser extent, Argentina and Brazil. In certain other countries, the export trade, if not a leading sector, was still a most valuable support to economic development. In Russia, for example, wheat exports provided the foreign exchange needed to service the inflow of foreign capital essential to industrialization, whereas in Japan, where the creation of a domestic mass market was precluded by the low income condition of the peasants and workers, the expansion of foreign markets was imperative as an outlet for the products of the country's new manufacturing industries.

Yet, if, during the nineteenth century, there were many countries in which exports played an important part in inducing growth in the rest of the domestic economy, there were many others, accounting between them for the bulk of the world's population, in which foreign trade failed to generate conditions conducive to self-sustaining growth. Broadly speaking, two explanations have been advanced to account for this breakdown in the transmission of growth through trade. The first explanation emphasizes the drawbacks and disadvantages of dependence on exports of primary products for promoting economic growth, while the second attempts to explain why growth in the export sector fails to carry over to the other sectors of the economy and cause a general expansion of the economy. The first approach concentrates on the drawbacks to a country's specializing in primary production. In particular, the disadvantages arising out of a country's dependence on a single export product are stressed, with all that this means for the country's future development should the world demand for the product fall, or should superior sources of supply be discovered elsewhere. Other disadvantages to primary production include the excessive price fluctuations displayed in the markets for primary products and their influence, through a country's foreign exchange earnings, on its financing of economic development. Finally, there is the declining terms of trade argument which runs to the effect that specialization in primary production is an undesirable policy in the long-run, since it condemns primary producers to ever-declining terms of trade.[1] While each of these arguments has some relevance in explaining the growth experiences of the export economies during the past hundred years or so, what is of immediate interest is the second explanation of the phenomenon,

---

[1] According to this argument, while the gains of technological progress in industrial countries are distributed to producers in the form of higher incomes—because of the existence of industrial monopolies and upward pressures exerted on wages by well-organized trade unions—in the primary producing countries competitive pressures ensure that the gains from technical improvements in agriculture and mining are passed on in the form of lower prices. Consequently, it has been claimed that in the long run the prices of manufactured goods (the imports of primary producers) have tended to rise relative to the prices of primary products (the exports of these countries). This, in turn, has meant that primary producing countries were able to purchase fewer and fewer manufactured goods with a given quantity of primary product exports.

which concentrates attention on the factors limiting the carry-over of growth from the export sector to the rest of the economy. It is this carry-over problem which lies at the centre of the successful or unsuccessful transmission of growth through trade.[1]

REGIONS OF RECENT SETTLEMENT

In discussing the carry-over problem it is useful to draw the distinction between those countries in which, despite immigration, labour was scarce but land abundant, and the overcrowded countries of Asia. The former group of countries, often described collectively as the regions of recent settlement, include Canada, the United States, Australia, New Zealand, South Africa and Argentina, and they constitute for the nineteenth century the outstanding example of growth through trade in primary products. In them, a large inflow of European labour and capital supplied the factors needed for export industry production, with the immigrant workers and entrepreneurs making up a rapidly integrated and largely homogeneous society, conversant with European needs and markets and receptive to the forces of innovation and change. In some of these countries, such as the United States and, to a lesser extent, Canada and Australia, the large size of the country could give rise to internal economic development independent of any significant impetus from the export sector, while in all of them, abundant and readily accessible natural resources attracted foreign capital with the profits to be made from their exploitation.

Moreover, with the exception of Argentina, these were high-wage economies. Generally speaking, we should expect to find higher wage levels in sparsely populated countries than in densely populated ones, as well as a tendency for wage levels to show a rising trend over periods of rapid expansion of output requiring more (scarce) labour. These expectations are broadly borne out by experience in the newly settled regions of North America and Australasia. What is even more important, however is that high wages assisted economic development in two ways. First, they provided buoyant markets, even in countries with relatively small populations. Second, through the efforts of entrepreneurs to counteract high wage costs and overcome labour scarcity they generated technical progress, which in turn supported and enhanced the high productivity which came in time to provide the basis upon which these high wages were paid. This inter-

---

[1] A country's ability to overcome the difficulties inherent in monoculture and unstable primary product prices depends very much on the flexibility of its economic structure. This question of flexibility is closely connected with the problem of the carry-over in export-led growth.

action between rising productivity, high wage levels and expanding domestic markets was not experienced by all labour-scarce countries. In the Argentine, for reasons shortly to be discussed, the high-wage/ low-rent economy never materialized in the nineteenth century, and the opportunities for the further development of the economy were correspondingly reduced despite very high rates of growth in the country's export sector. It is for this reason that we include the Argentine in the following discussion of those countries in which export expansion was unsuccessful or only partially successful in generating self-sustaining growth.

THE EXPORT ECONOMIES

Owing to the steady growth in the world demand for primary products characteristic of the period, the demand side can be neglected in attempting to explain the breakdown in the transmission of growth through trade that occurred in a large number of countries during the nineteenth century. To explain the phenomenon we have to concentrate on the supply side, where two major problems presented themselves to peripheral countries desiring to benefit from the growth forces generated by European industrialization. First, these countries had to integrate themselves into the expanding lines of trade created by the rising European demand for foodstuffs and raw materials. When this was achieved, the expansionary forces generated within the export sector of these integrating economies had then to be diffused throughout the rest of the economy. In other words, the lack of successful economic growth in underdeveloped countries during the nineteenth century can be explained either by inadequate or late integration into the world economy, or by the obstacles which prevented the growth forces originating in the export sector from transmitting themselves to the rest of the economy.

Late integration into the world economy partly explains the relative backwardness of many African economies. Although there was a rapid expansion of African exports in the late nineteenth century, the extent of the continent's integration into the international economy was seriously limited by transport difficulties. In a continent with few navigable rivers, where the ravages of the tse-tse fly restricted the use of animal power, and where, as a result, porterage was the chief means of transport, the transition from an economic system based on slave labour to one based on wage labour tended to have a paralysing effect on transport and through it on internal trade. Apart from gold and ivory, there were few commodities that could bear the high cost of porterage from the interior. When it arrived, even the railway could provide only a limited system of communications in the absence of animal-drawn wheeled transport and feeder roads. As far as low-value bulky commodities were concerned, a radius of 30–40 miles from a railway, or a navigable river for that matter, was the extreme limit of profitable production for export under conditions of porterage. This transport deficiency blunted the impact of world demand on the African economy and accounts for the persistence of a substantial African subsistence economy which, through its low productivity and lack of monetization, slowed down the overall economic growth of the continent.

In those regions and countries which did achieve relatively early and successful integration into the world economy, the problem is one of explaining the lack of successful export-led growth. Here two broad categories of explanations have been put forward, the one economic, the other political and socio-cultural. The economic explanations tend to concentrate on the differential effects on economic growth of the various export commodities according to their production characteristics. In particular this approach singles out for attention the export sectors' demand for inputs, its effects on income distribution and the creation of markets, and the opportunities it provides for the diffusion of technical, organizational and administrative skills. The second approach stresses such factors as land tenure systems, the basic values and attitudes of the indigenous population, political conditions, including the effects of colonialism, and other largely non-economic considerations. In actual fact, neither set of explanations is completely independent of the other, and in discussing the failure of export-led growth to materialize in any given country both must be taken into account, although the weights to be allocated to each will obviously vary from one country to another.

The economic explanations centre on the different types of productive activity to be found in the primary producing countries and their differential effects on income distribution and the opportunities for long-term development. In particular, the distinction is drawn between peasant export economies, on the one hand, and those economies primarily dependent on exporting the products of mines and plantations on the other. These basically different patterns of productive activity are important because they generate different export-income distributions between foreign and domestic producers, and because they provide differing opportunities for improving the skills and productivity of the indigenous population.

Peasant exports, which include such commodities as rice, palm-oil, cocoa, cotton, rubber and copra and other coconut products, are important in Africa and a number of Asian countries. Apart from land, peasant production typically requires very little durable capital equipment, since it amounts to little more than an extension of the traditional economic organization and technology of the subsistence sector. It is also a form of production which has little need of outside capital and labour. In fact, where the peasant combines the growing of cash crops with other crops intended for his own personal consumption, export production is largely self-financing. Typically, too, peasant production draws little or no labour from outside the household. Two links, outside the peasant's control, are needed, however, to connect him to the world markets for which he produces. Improvements in transport and communications can help open up new areas of production, and a middleman is often necessary to collect, process and convey the peasant's produce to foreign buyers as well as supply the imported goods that act as an inducement to increased export production, since by stimulating new wants among the peasants, the expansion of imports can act as a major dynamic force encouraging the expansion of exports.

In the last quarter of the nineteenth century the output of many peasant economies increased substantially in response to a growing world demand for their products. Between 1870 and 1913 peasant rice exports from Burma and Thailand grew some 10 to 13 times. Egyptian cotton production rose from 500,000 kantars in 1860 to 3·1m. in 1879 and 7·7m. in 1913. On the west coast of Africa palm oil and oil-seed accounted for over three-quarters of the total value of Nigerian exports in 1913, and cocoa contributed 80 per cent to the value of the Gold Coast's total exports in the same year.

Despite these impressive export performances, in most countries their impact on the rest of the economy was either limited or insignificant. There were a number of reasons why this should be so. The partial commitment to export production implicit in an economic set-up where the peasant household continued to produce all its own subsistence requirements in addition to growing cash crops, limited the spread of a money economy. If, in addition, market transactions were restricted largely to an exchange of exports for imports, then the monetized sector obviously had little impact on the rest of the economy. On the other hand, complete export specialization, while more conducive to the development of the domestic market—since peasant families producing for export would set up a cash demand for locally produced foodstuffs and other locally-produced goods and services—was not without its drawbacks.[1] The peasant was now completely at the mercy of an often unstable export market. More

[1] The extreme situation was reached in Malaya during the rubber boom at the start of this century, when so much rubber was planted by Malayans and to a lesser extent by Chinese and Indian smallholders that the country came to depend upon imports for much of its staple food supply.

important, his activities ceased to be self-financing so that in the event of drought, plant disease, or a fall in world prices, he might be forced to fall back on outside sources of credit, including money-lenders who charged high rates of interest. In these circumstances, partial specialization often represented a rational response to the prevailing set of economic conditions under which the peasant operated.

The spread of a money economy was also restricted by lack of transport which, as we have already seen, accounted for the persistence of a subsistence sector in large areas of Africa. Limited technical knowledge, primitive methods of production, and poor quality produce also reduced the level of peasant income, either by keeping productivity low or by influencing the prices received for peasant produce on world markets. In some countries the increase in production and exports achieved during these years was absorbed partly by an increase in population and partly by a rise in the level of living of the upper and middle classes and by a much smaller rise in that of the mass of the population. This appears to have been the case in Egypt in the half century before 1913.[1] There was also the possibility of a part, and often a substantial part, of the peasant's income passing into the hands of some person or group in the export sector, especially in those situations where the middleman handling the peasant's crops could exercise monopoly power. Thus a few foreign import–export firms could combine to purchase the peasant's output at low prices while selling him imports at highly inflated prices. Alternatively, this monopoly power could be exercised by a government agency, such as the Nederlandse Handel Maatschappy, which was set up in the Dutch East Indies in the 1820s to purchase peasant produce at low fixed prices or to acquire it as taxes in kind. Exploitation of the peasant could also occur when the peasant's crops had to be processed at a company factory possessing a local monopoly. This appears to have happened in Cuba, where improvements in sugar technology and an influx of foreign capital led to a reduction in the number of sugar mills and an increase in the manufacturing capacity of those that survived. At first competition between the mills worked in favour of the sugar farmers. But later, when, in order to ensure adequate supplies of sugar cane, the mill companies created territorial monopolies by purchasing plantations and by building private railways to transport the cane to the mill, the surviving farmers found themselves completely at the mercy of one or other of the large companies.[2]

[1] C. Issawi, 'Egypt since 1800: a study in lop-sided development', *The Journal of Economic History*, Vol. XXI (March, 1961), p. 11.

[2] Ramiro Guerray Sanchez, *Sugar and Society in the Caribbean. An Economic History of Cuban Agriculture* (London, 1964).

While peasant export economies have certain features that are potentially highly favourable to the spread of economic growth, from its very beginnings plantation-type production displayed characteristics highly inimical to successful economic development. This type of agriculture predominated in Latin America and the Central American and Caribbean regions where sugar, bananas, coffee and cotton were the major plantation crops grown. It was also to be found in Ceylon, parts of India and in south-east Asia, where the emphasis was on tea, coffee, and rubber. In Africa, plantations developed relatively late. By the 1890s cocoa, coffee, and tobacco plantations had been established in the German Cameroons, and sisal was first introduced into Tanganyika in 1892. Banana plantations in the Cameroons, tea plantations in Nyasaland and East Africa, and oil-palm plantations in the Belgian Congo, were not established until the start of this century.

Originally based on the use of slave labour, in the nineteenth century plantation production was characterized by a high degree of foreign ownership and control; the provision of finance by foreign banks and agency houses; large-scale, factory-style operation of the plantations using large amounts of labour specially imported from abroad for these purposes; control of the import–export trade by foreigners; and virtually complete reliance on imported supplies of capital equipment, estate supplies and, often, even food for the workforce. These key characteristics of plantation production had important consequences for the working of the export sector and its capacity to transmit growth to the rest of the economy.

Where the export sector consisted almost wholly of foreign-owned plantations employing foreign capital and imported labour, it constituted an enclave economy which, because the income it generated was largely remitted abroad, contributed little to the formation of the domestic market and the promotion of local economic growth. Low wages with no rising trend (despite rapid growth of output) was also characteristic of those export economies where use was made of indigenous labour. In some countries, such as the Central American republics, where the coffee and banana plantations has to depend on the local population for their workforce, money wages, plus a variety of devices designed to cut off the peasant from free access to land, were used to force the local population into employment at low wages. When these methods proved insufficient, the governments often resorted to more direct, coercive measures in an effort to meet the labour requirements of the rapidly growing export sector. Similar policies, including the imposition of money taxes on the indigenous population, were used in Africa to drive the natives into paid employment in the mines and plantations. In other plantation economies, the relatively abundant supply of cheap labour imported from India and China tended to depress wages in the export sector as well as in the economy generally. In so far as the local population was deterred from entering employment in the export sector by the prevailing low level of wages, they tended to crowd into alternative paid occupations, thus depressing wages in those industries as well. Alternatively, the local population was forced to fall back on the subsistence sector, with its associated low productivity and lack of market contact.

The outcome of this situation was a high concentration of a country's income and wealth in the hands of a small group of people, whether of local or foreign origin, and, as a consequence, an underdeveloped domestic market. Foreign ownership also meant leakage of export income overseas, but even when the plantation owners were local entrepreneurs employing local capital, their contribution to local economic growth, either through their consumption or their investment expenditures, was often minimal. In some economies the local entrepreneurs formed too small a group to permit economic production for their demand domestically; in others, contact with Western culture and consumption patterns turned them into large-scale importers of foreign goods and services. In both situations the end result was the same, the creation of a group of 'luxury importers' who contributed little to the promotion of a domestic market, either by way of consumption or of investment. Indeed, it was much more profitable to invest in export production, and where the concentration of income generated substantial local saving, it was channelled almost wholly into the further expansion of the export sector.

If the market contribution of the export sector to domestic economic growth was small, so, too, was the technological contribution, in the sense of improvement in the quality of the workforce. Since there was little pressure from labour for higher wages, the entrepreneur had no interest in replacing his labour by capital or in improving the skills of his workforce. The same arguments applied to land where it was in abundant supply. Lacking any incentive for improvements in methods of cultivation or of labour skills, the tendency for the entrepreneur to invest new capital in the simple extension of his plantation was reinforced. Given the prevailing pattern of resource availability, with capital scarce and land and labour abundant, the method of production used and the form investment took were rational ones, although their capacity for promoting growth in the rest of the economy was limited. Potentially, mining was the most effective form of production for diffusing technical skills and raising the level of labour productivity. In fact, its potential was rarely ever realized. Initially, the use of modern mining techniques inevitably

meant that foreign skills had to be imported as well, and the indigenous workers could find employment only as unskilled labourers.
Over time the structure of the mining labour force changed very
little, either because of discrimination against local workers, which
prevented them from gaining promotion and the opportunity to
acquire new skills, or because the nature of the local workforce gave
the employer no incentive to impart new skills to it.[1] The outcome
of all this was a tendency for the low wages paid to the local workforce to persist, along with relatively little improvement in its average
level of skill.

Whether in plantation or mining economies, these low wages eventually became institutionalized in a cheap labour policy which was
justified on a number of grounds, including the low productivity of
the workforce, its customarily low material standard of living, its
lack of response to the incentive of high wages, and the belief that,
in general, indigenous labour not only had low productivity but that
it also had limited capacity for improvement. Since low wages meant
low productivity, the cheap labour policy became self-justifying, and
through the vicious circle of low wages and low productivity, the
productivity of the indigenous workforce even in thinly populated
countries was fossilized at its very low initial level. It was the pattern
of low wages and productivity perpetuated by the cheap labour policy
of the mines and plantations, rather than primary production as
such, which accounted for the failure of exports in underdeveloped
countries to be a leading sector initiating growth in the rest of the
economy.

The other set of factors relevant to this discussion is comprised
of the social, political, cultural and legal constraints on the propagation of export-led growth. These constraints largely reflected the
psychological and ideological attitudes generated by the export
economy's one-sided orientation, wherein agricultural production
for export was what really counted. Change in the existing socio-
political system, in so far as it occurred, was effected only to the
extent required for the realization of this objective. This fact is seen
all too clearly in the land tenure system that developed in the plantation economies. Where property in land became economically
meaningful only when coupled with technical and commercial know-
how and easy access to finance, the resulting system of land ownership was rapidly structured around the plantation as the central
type of organization in agricultural export sectors. This structuring
of the export sector was often brought about by deliberate govern-

---

[1] For example, the unskilled workforce in African mining consisted largely of
migrant African workers who spent only a limited time in paid employment
before returning to their tribal areas.

ment policy. In the Central American republics, for example, the inability of the respective governments to raise capital on international markets made them dependent upon foreign firms, particularly banana producers, for the building of railways and the improvement of port facilities. In return these plantation companies received generous land grants and other government incentives, including exemption from taxes. In other countries, what government policy failed to do in the way of discriminating between those who could and those who could not own land, the market did through unequal access to financial and commercial processes and institutions and through differences in technical knowledge. Whatever the forces at work, be they government or free market inspired, the outcome was almost always the same, a bimodal property distribution, with a few enormous plantations at one end of the scale and many very small farms at the other.

Although it was not a plantation export economy, a similar state of affairs developed in the Argentine. Here, the early growth of an export economy based on cattle-raising led to the fertile areas of the Pampas passing into the hands of a few large cattle ranchers. Later, when new export lines were developed, particularly wheat, the lack of readily accessible land for occupation by immigrant farmers seriously impeded the growth of output and employment in the rural sector.

The tendency toward concentration of land ownership affected the development of agriculture and of the economy as a whole in a number of different ways. First, it restricted the growth of rural output and employment as well as the growth of domestic markets. The lack of available agricultural land held back rural output by discouraging immigration, since the immigrant was obliged to work as a tenant farmer or as a low paid field hand. Alternatively, immigrants were forced into the towns, thus swelling the supply of manpower for urban employment and forcing down wages in these labour markets. Second, the concentration of land ownership led to a stratified society in which the bulk of the country's income and wealth went to a few people. while the mass of the population lived on incomes barely above the subsistence level. With income concentrated in a few hands, there was a disproportionate demand for luxury consumption and investment, usually met out of imports, whereas the low income level of the mass of the population restricted the latter's demand for manufactured goods and was therefore an obstacle to industrial development. Industrial growth was also limited by the free trade policy adopted by nearly all of these countries. The landowning class constituted the ruling political group and, mindful of its own interests and those of foreign circles to which it was linked in a variety of ways, it advocated a free trade policy which, by allowing the unrestricted entry of foreign manufactures, limited the development of the basic industries needed to integrate the whole economy.

ECONOMIC IMPERIALISM AND COLONIALISM

Economic development was also hindered for various reasons in those territories which became colonized following the burst of imperialist expansion that occurred in the late nineteenth century. Beginning in the 1880s, a wave of 'colony grabbing' began that continued until the outbreak of war in 1914. Africa was divided among the European powers, British control was extended over Burma and Malaya. France consolidated its Indo-Chinese empire. Even the United States was not free from this desire for political and economic expansion. The Philippine Islands were seized during a war with Spain, a republic was established in Hawaii, and political intervention occurred in Mexico, Costa Rica, Dominica, Colombia and Nicaragua.

The root causes of this burst of imperialism in the late nineteenth century are extremely complex, as the numerous theories put forward to explain the phenomenon indicate. Some explain the acquisition of colonies in these years in purely political terms, seeing the colonies either in strategic terms or as political bargaining counters for use in the game of international diplomacy. Still others see the new imperialism as a manifestation of a popular and emotional concern for national prestige and power. Economic explanations of the phenomenon abound. The commercial needs of Europe, in particular, are stressed, including the growing need for new markets fostered by the spread of protection and the growth of industry; the desire to gain control over supplies of raw material, particularly tropical products; and the need to find alternative outlets for surplus capital for which domestic investment opportunities did not exist. Providing an additional pretext for intervention in the affairs of other countries and possibly leading to their eventual acquisition as colonies, were the missionaries, planters, labour recruiters and traders of the colonizing countries. These people, who through their activities (usually quite unwittingly) undermining the established order in the foreign territory, often forced their country's government to step in to protect their lives and property and to restore political stability.

The need for colonies has often been argued in purely economic terms, yet the available evidence suggests that the colonial annexations of the late nineteenth century were of limited economic benefit to the colonizing powers. Most of these tropical colonies were too poor to provide valuable markets for manufactured exports, and while some of them were suppliers of important industrial raw materials, for example metals and crude rubber, the combined share of the colonies in the raw material markets of the world was relatively small. Consequently, with the exception of Britain, whose empire was by far the largest and provided uniquely favourable markets and a wide variety of raw materials, trade with the tropical dependencies was only a small fraction of the total trade of their owners. Moreover, even when the trend towards protectionism became intense, the fact that up to World War I and beyond, Britain, Holland, Belgium and Germany retained liberal commercial policies in their dealings with their colonies meant that non-colonial nations generally had easy access to the colonial markets of these states.

If tropical colonies were not acquired to provide exclusive markets and sources of raw materials and foodstuffs for the metropolitan country, neither were they an important outlet for the surplus capital of that country. Indeed there is very little geographical correlation between capital exports and the acquisition of new colonies after 1880, and compared with foreign investment in Europe and the regions of recent settlement, the funds invested in Africa and southeast Asia were relatively insignificant. Thus, whereas by 1914 almost $11,000m. of British investments were to be found in the United States and the British Dominions, only some $600m. was invested in West Africa, the Straits Settlements and the rest of Britain's recent overseas acquisitions. Furthermore, many imperialist powers—notably Russia, Italy, Portugal and Spain—far from having an embarrassing surplus of capital, were net importers of capital and must therefore have had other motives for making annexations. Nor, when it was undertaken, was investment in the tropics always highly profitable. Studies of the type of loans issued in the heyday of colonial expansion reveal that the greater part was in fixed interest government securities; that the profitability of this investment was only marginally higher than that of domestic investment; and that in the end some European investors lost their money through defaults. On the other hand, the return on some risk capital (equities) was often high, and probably higher than could be obtained at most times on industrial investments in Europe or America. Yet the high profits earned on colonial equity investment were more the result of the heavy industrial demand for particular products, for example metals and rubber, the scarcity of local capital, and the superior bargaining position of Western countries in their dealings with politically and economically weaker societies, than the outcome of the exercise of formal imperial power as such.

In fact, to assume that political control is necessary if one country is to exercise economic domination over another is to forget that this end can be achieved just as well through the use of diplomatic and economic advantage as through direct colonial rule. Some historians argue, for example, that Europeans by using their easy access to the financial and technical resources of the West were able to skim the most readily available profit opportunities in the underdeveloped continents, thus making the job of indigenous economic development extremely difficult. This is the thesis of 'informal imperialism', whose nature and functioning have been amply illustrated in the earlier pages of this chapter.

Whatever the nature and extent of the benefits accruing to the metropolitan powers from the possession of colonies, however, there can be little doubt that colonization placed severe limits on the economic development of the annexed territories. In these countries the indigenous population could not resist penetration by Westerners into the heart of their economy, or the reorganization of their laws and institutions according to the interests of Western entrepreneurs and governments. Changes in the system of land tenure, the conditions of labour supply and the nature of the economic activities of large populations were introduced by colonizing governments. At the same time, the setting up of an orderly framework of government administration and the introduction of sanitation and other public health measures caused a rapid growth of population in many colonies. The result was a disruption of the traditional balance between population, natural resources and technology.

The case of India may be cited by way of illustration. Here the British need of an efficient and simple method of raising land revenues resulted in two systems of land tenure being introduced. In the Presidency of Bengal the land was concentrated in the hands of a group of great landlords who were expected to remain strongly pro-British, since their income and security depended, in the last analysis, upon the strength of the British regime. Elsewhere in India, the British made land settlements on a field-by-field basis with the individual cultivating peasants, as in southern Madras, or on an estate basis with groups of leading families in the villages, as in the central parts of India. Where peasant farming predominated, the nature of the revenue and land tenure systems—annual payment of taxes in money and in full, plus the private property structure of landholding which permitted mortgaging, transference, alienation—meant that in time of drought or other financial difficulty, the peasant was forced to turn to the moneylender and merchant for credit. Whichever land tenure system operated, however, it afforded to the landlord and moneylender a means for drawing away from the peasant everything but the mere minimum required to keep cultivation going.

Another result of British rule which served to undermine the position of the peasantry was the increase in population. Political stability and improvements in sanitation and other public health measures served to reduce the death rate while leaving the birth rate unchanged. Population rose exerting pressure on the available supply of land. Industrialization could have provided the answer to the population pressure in rural areas by taking up the surplus labour, but so long as India remained a major market for British manufactures, a full-blooded industrial policy was out of the question. When industrialization did get under way in India towards the end of the nineteenth century, its scale was inadequate to deal with the emerging population problem. The net effect of population increase, therefore, was rural overcrowding which, in the absence of any attempt to improve agricultural techniques, placed severe limits upon the ability of the agricultural sector to generate surpluses of crops for sale and for export. In short, the overall nature of the economic situation in India was much the same as that described earlier for the plantation economy: a concentration of income and wealth in a few hands; the vast mass of the indigenous population subsisting at a low level; and a commercial policy which hindered the spread of industrialization within the economy.

It is not possible in the compass of one short chapter to deal adequately with all aspects of the economic impact of nineteenth century European industrialization and imperial expansion on the underdeveloped regions of the world. Rather what we have endeavoured to show here is how the characteristic features of export production in these countries, along with the existence of certain legal, political and cultural institutions and processes, hindered the spread of growth throughout their economies even when export expansion did occur. In doing this, we are not arguing that the integration of these countries into the international economy was not beneficial to them. Living standards did rise in these countries, even if, for the bulk of the population, the improvement was small. Moreover, in many underdeveloped countries the choice was not between foreign-inspired development and indigenously stimulated growth, but rather between what happened and nothing. In short, European economic expansion in the nineteenth century, despite its various destructive elements, was a powerful agent of modernization, and colonial status was often the price that had to be paid to gain admission to the industrial age. Whether, for the countries colonized, the benefits of colonialism and imperialism outweighed the costs of political and economic subservience to another country, however, is still an open question.

SELECTED REFERENCES

Cairncross, A. K., *Factors in Economic Development* (London, 1962), especially Chaps. 11 and 12.

Falkus, M. E., *Readings in the History of Economic Growth* (London, 1968).

Kindleberger, C. P., *Foreign Trade and the National Economy* (New Haven, 1962).

Landes, D. S., *The Unbound Prometheus* (Cambridge, 1969).

Myint, H., *The Economics of Developing Countries* (London, 1964), especially Chaps 3, 4, and 9.

Nurkse, R., 'Patterns of Trade and Development' (Wicksell Lecture, April 1959). Reprinted in *International Trade and Finance. A Collected Volume of Lectures 1958–1964* (Stockholm, 1965).

Spender, D. L., *and* Woroniak, A., *The Transfer of Technology to Developing Countries* (New York, 1968).

Supple, B. E., *The Experience of Economic Growth* (New York, 1963).

Chapter 10

TRENDS AND FLUCTUATIONS IN THE INTERNATIONAL ECONOMY BEFORE 1913

Along with economic growth, fluctuations in economic activity may be transmitted from country to country through the operation of the international economy. Since economic fluctuations appear to be a characteristic feature of industrial economies, and since the nineteenth century saw the emergence of a number of these economies closely linked with each other through trade, labour and capital flows, it is not surprising to find evidence of a tendency for economic expansion and contraction in one industrial country to spill over into other industrial countries. But the spill-over effects of these fluctuations did not stop there. They also spread to primary producing countries, producing excessive fluctuations in the prices and volume of their exports which, through their influence on these countries' foreign exchange earnings, placed severe constraints on their capacity to generate sustained economic growth. Potentially more damaging to the long-term prospects of growth in these countries, however, is the claim that the spread of modern technology has been associated with a secular tendency for primary product prices to decline relative to the prices of manufactured goods. If true, this movement of the terms of trade against primary producers meant that they were, and are, faced with the possibility of a long-run decline in their export real incomes.

THE INTERNATIONAL TRANSMISSION OF BUSINESS CYCLES

The available historical evidence suggests that in the past there has been a substantial degree of business cycle conformity between countries, especially when the fluctuations have been violent ones. The international impact of the great financial crises of the nineteenth century has long been recognized and is amply borne out by an examination of the business annals of numerous countries for the period.[1] But while it is true that the importing of an erratic shock, such as a financial panic, by one country from another represents one type of transmission of economic fluctuations, studies of such phenomena are only the first step in a full-scale investigation into the possibility that complete cycles are transmitted between countries. Even when countries are found to conform over the full cyclical expansion and contraction, this is not sufficient in itself to justify the conclusion that business cycles are regularly and immediately transmitted from country to country. Indeed, as some economists have noted, the conspectus of trade cycles to be found in the business annals may point only to the necessity of fluctuations in capitalist economies rather than to the existence of the international transmission of business cycles. Moreover, even if transmission did take place in the nineteenth century, the annals tell us little about the mechanism by which it was affected or the predominant direction of these effects.

An important hypothesis concerning the functioning of the international economy in the nineteenth century has served only to emphasize the need for more detailed investigations of the nature of cycle propagation during these years. S. B. Saul has argued recently that whereas before 1890 Britain was able, through the export of capital, to lessen the impact of slumps on the international economy, after that date, because of the spread of industrialization and the growth of a more closely integrated system of multilateral trade, she was less able to perform this 'buffer' function. In the earlier period the international economy consisted of a number of self-contained trading networks, with little economic contact between the countries in each network, except through Britain, which stood at the centre linking them together. Thus a slump in the United States would affect, say, Australia only indirectly through its impact on the British economy, where the consequent fall in the American demand for British exports, by reducing the level of economic activity in Britain, would lead eventually to a decline in the British demand for Australian exports. This decline in Australian export income, however, could be offset to some degree by the export of British capital to Australia, so that that country was able to maintain or even raise its level of imports and economic activity despite the American recession. But after 1890, because of the spread of industry and the accompanying growth in the world demand for industrial raw materials and foodstuffs, direct trading relations between continental Europe and the United States and the primary

[1] See W. L. Thorp, *Business Annals* (New York, 1926); especially useful is Section VI of the Introduction which deals with international relationships between business cycles.

F

producing countries overseas, especially those in the British Empire, became more common. The system of separate trading blocs gradually coalesced into a single network of world trade and the possibility of fluctuations being transmitted directly from one part of the international economy to another became more and more real. In this new situation British capital exports were called upon to nullify not only the decline in the British demand for colonial produce brought about by a slump, but also the equally great, if not greater, direct fall of demand for these goods from other countries as well. In so far as economic expansion in one region offsets economic decline in another, the British task of acting as a stabilizer of the world economy was made that much easier. When, however, decline was general, her efforts to act as a buffer were largely inadequate. Indeed, the generally depressed economic conditions then existing could constitute a major deterrent to the international flow of capital.[1]

It should be noted that Saul implicitly assumes the transmission of cyclical influences, although the statistical data he uses in support of his hypothesis do not in themselves tell us much about the workings of the mechanism of transmission. Moreover, no attempt has yet been made to test the relationship between cyclical activity in the various trading countries for conformity with Saul's hypothesis. Much more research is obviously necessary before the validity of this hypothesis concerning the changing structure of world trade and its impact on the international transmission of business cycles in the nineteenth century is fully established. In the meantime, his work remains an outstanding contribution in this largely neglected field of historical research.

LONG SWINGS AND THE INTERNATIONAL ECONOMY

While a greater knowledge of the nature of international business cycle transmission will obviously help us better to understand the functioning of the international economy as a mechanism of growth during the nineteenth century, what is perhaps of even greater relevance in this connection are the longer fluctuations in economic activity to be observed in both North American and European economies after 1870, and probably before, for it has been argued that these fluctuations exhibit an inverse relationship which is suggestive of a pattern of alternating growth between the different parts of what has come to be called the Atlantic economy.

The existence of long swings in economic activity, averaging

[1] S. B. Saul, *Studies in British Overseas Trade 1870–1914*, (Liverpool, 1960) Chap. 5., especially pp. 111–6.

between 15 and 25 years' duration is now an undisputed fact. Investigations have revealed such fluctuations in building activity, where the phenomenon has long been recognized, railway construction, public utilities, and migration. They are also evident in the merchandise imports and exports of a number of countries, as well as in the flows of capital between countries. Given the existence of these long swings in economic activity in a number of countries, two questions immediately pose themselves. The first concerns the nature and internal logic of the long swing in economic activity. This matter is currently under investigation, and much more work, both of a theoretical and an empirical nature, needs to be done before a clear understanding of the mechanism of the long swing is possible.[1] More immediately relevant, however, is the second question which is concerned with the nature of the international relationship between the long fluctuations in economic activity in different countries. Of particular importance in this context is the evidence of long-term inverse movements in British home and foreign investment and the related tendency, at least in the period after 1870, for general long swing movements in economic activity in the United States and Canada to vary inversely with swings in British building and domestic investment generally.

Table 11 illustrates the nature of this inversion. The figures in columns 1 and 2 describe the opposing movements in Britain's home and foreign investment. Domestic investment rose in the 1870s and 1890s and early years of the present century, and declined in the 1880s and in the years after 1906. Foreign investment, on the other hand, moved in the opposite direction, falling in the 1870s and 1890s and rising in the 1880s and 1900s. Outflows of population from Britain[2] move parallel to the outflow of capital. Since a large part of both flows of men and money went to the United States and Canada after 1870, these countries received substantial injections of population and capital from Britain, as well as from other European countries, in the 1880s and 1900s. These were periods when domestic investment and economic activity were running at high levels in the North American economy. In other words, in those periods when domestic investment and business activity were depressed in Britain, the United States and Canadian economies

[1] For a discussion of this problem see M. Abramovitz, 'The Nature and Significance of Kuznets Cycles', *Economic Development and Cultural Change* (April, 1961), pp. 225–48.

[2] The immigration figures in col. 3 of Table 11 refer only to British immigration into the United States, but total British migration to all countries during these years followed a similar pattern—falling in the 1870s and 1890s, and rising in the 1880s and 1900s.

TABLE 11. *Great Britain, the United States, and Canada: Inverse Long Swings in Economic Activity, 1871–1913*

Period	BRITAIN		UNITED STATES			CANADA		
	Net domestic Fixed capital formation £m.	Capital outflow £m.	British immigration (000s)	Net capital inflow $m.	Net capital expenditures railways $m.	Immigrant arrivals (000s)	Net capital inflow* $m.	Total fixed capital formation $m.
	(1)	(2)	(3)	(4)	(5)	(6)	(7)	(8)
1871–75	358	373	370	896	940	181	166	n.a.
1876–80	382	124	178	−348	383	162	93	n.a.
1881–85	297	309	385	258	996	477	167	n.a.
1886–90	174	438	423	1,045	642	409	242	n.a.
1891–95	289	260	195	392	726	182	202	n.a.
1896–1900	540	202	76	−807	−130	157	124	n.a.
1901–05	686	245	201	−730	328	556	317	1,061
1906–10	446	729	325	238	1,808	1,088	830	2,025
1911–13	267	618	191	−66	1,126	1,108	1,156	2,919†

* Excluding net short-term capital flows. † For the years 1911–15. n.a. not available.

Sources: Col. 1 B. R. Mitchell and P. Deane, *Abstract of British Historical Statistics* (Cambridge, 1962), Table, pp. 373–4.
Col. 2 A. H. Imlah, *Economic Elements in the Pax Britannica* (Cambridge, 1958), pp. 72–5.
Col. 3 U.S. Bureau of Census and Statistics, *Historical Statistics of the U.S. Colonial Times to 1957* (Washington, 1960), Table, pp. 56–7.
Col. 4 J. G. Williamson, *American Growth and the Balance of Payments 1820–1913* (Chapel Hill, 1964), Table B–19, pp. 280–1.
Col. 5 M. J. Ulmer, *Capital in Transportation, Communications and Public Utilities: Its Formation and Financing* (Princeton, 1960), Table C–1, pp. 256–7.
Cols. 6 and 8 M. C. Urquhart and K. A. H. Buckley, *Historical Statistics of Canada* (Cambridge, 1965), Tables, pp. 23, 138.
Col. 7 A. I. Bloomfield, *Patterns of Fluctuation in International Investment before 1914* (Princeton, 1968), Appendix 1, pp. 42–4.

were growing rapidly, and this economic growth was sustained partly by the outflow of population and capital from Britain to these countries. On the other hand, in those periods when the British economy was growing rapidly, the outflow of capital and population slowed up, and the growth of the North American economy was correspondingly reduced.

It is, however, the explanation of this pattern of fluctuations rather than the existence of the phenomena, which is presently the subject of argument. According to Cairncross, for example, the explanation is to be found in the behaviour of the terms of trade, since British foreign investment generally varied with Britain's terms of trade, increasing when the terms of trade worsened and decreasing when they improved. Since a worsening in Britain's terms of trade meant a rise in import prices relative to export prices, investment opportunities in those countries supplying Britain's imports—mainly primary producers—became more attractive. Moreover, changes in the terms of trade would also affect real wages, with a movement unfavourable to Britain lowering British real wages, since the cost of living of the working classes was highly dependent on import prices, especially of foodstuffs. Consequently, as well as stimulating an outflow of British capital, a deterioration in the terms of trade would also exert some push on emigration. Moreover, a pull on emigration would develop in overseas countries, as the inflow of capital made settlement in them more attractive through the employment opportunities that it created. Thus, there was a close and consistent interrelationship between a deterioration in Britain's terms of trade, falling real wages, rising emigration and rising foreign investment. Finally, given the existence of certain types of population-sensitive capital formation, emigration resulted in a decline of domestic investment in Britain for emigration left houses empty, and this depressed house building and investment in public utility services and other public works which are closely dependent upon the rate of growth of population and urbanization. This, in turn, led to a general fall in home investment, a rise in unemployment, and therefore increased pressure to emigrate.[1]

When the terms of trade moved in Britain's favour, the opposite sequence of events took place. Import prices fell relative to the prices of British exports discouraging foreign investment and resulting in a rise in British real wages which served to reduce the desire to migrate overseas. The decline in the level of economic activity overseas, which was partly the result of the cessation of British capital exports, also served to deter emigration from Britain. The

---

[1] A. K. Cairncross, *Home and Foreign Investment 1870–1913*, (Cambridge, 1953).

increased availability of capital in the home market, along with a fall in interest rates, and a rising demand for new houses to accommodate a relatively faster growing population, served, on the other hand, to bring about an upsurge in domestic investment.

While broadly accepting the Cairncross position, Brinley Thomas prefers to give much greater weight to the causal role of migration. He sees these population movements as the main influence producing the cycles in building activity which he considers to lie at the core of the inverse movements in British home and foreign investment. He also argues that up to the 1860s the pace of economic activity in the United States was conditioned by the inflow of migrants and capital from Britain and Europe. After that decade, however, the immigration waves were largely determined by the course of American domestic investment in producer durables, with American building activity continuing to lag behind immigration.[1]

Whereas Thomas favours a shift over time in the locus of the economic stimulus generating long cycle interactions, other economists and economic historians have tended to argue in favour of one centre to the exclusion of all others. Thus some economic historians have emphasized the central role of the United States in this inter-actionary process, while others have reacted to the American pull hypothesis by directing attention to changes in Britain's willingness to lend abroad or to the domestic ingredients in Britain's bursts of home investment as important determinants of these alternating fluctuations in economic activity. One weakness of this debate is that it is centred almost exclusively on economic interactions within a region often referred to as the Atlantic economy. It is true that Brinley Thomas has claimed that the inverse cyclical relationship to be found within the Atlantic economy before 1914 can also be extended to take in the remaining countries comprising the regions of recent settlement. Such an extension appears questionable, however, especially as the experiences of some of these other countries fit rather uneasily into the framework of inverse cycles. The Australian experience, for example, does not seem to fall within the Atlantic economy hypothesis, since the Australian long swings appear to be longer (some 30 years in duration) and consequently fewer in number than those recorded in other countries. As a result the Australian long swing pattern differs in many notable respects from that of the United States and Canada on the one hand, and that of Britain on the other. The part played by continental Europe in the international long swing mechanism also remains obscure. Thus long swings are not apparent in French net capital exports, and some economists have also argued that, in contrast to the British

[1] B. Thomas, *Migration and Economic Growth* (Cambridge, 1954).

experience, high rates of French capital exports tended to coincide with high rates of domestic growth, although this conclusion is not based on a long swing analysis. Furthermore, since a not inconsiderable part of the capital exports of European countries went to tropical regions and since the export trade of these regions was highly dependent on the demand for tropical products in industrial countries, the role of the tropics in the interactionary process needs to be examined. Preliminary investigations reveal that long swings in American demand appear to have been of some significance in accounting for secular fluctuations in the growth of rubber exports and for those found in the series of sugar exports from Hawaii and Puerto Rico. On the other hand, Cuban sugar exports and world sugar exports moved in response to world demand and long swings are not apparent in these series.

The conflicting opinions on the causes of the inverse long swing mechanism and its centre of origin, and the gaps in our knowledge concerning the part played by countries and regions outside the Atlantic economy in the interactionary process, serve only to underline the considerable amount of research still needed in this field. What is already apparent, however, is that the long-cycle mechanism offers an attractive framework within which to study the growth process associated with the functioning of the international economy in the years before 1913. That these long fluctuations are to be observed in the international flows of capital, population and trade emphasizes this fact, for these flows represented some of the real forces at work influencing changes in the level of economic activity in different parts of the world at this time. It should also be obvious from our brief review of the subject, that the economic phenomenon under investigation is too complicated and far-reaching for it to be encompassed by uni-causal explanations or for it to be viewed as an economic stimulus to growth continuously located in any one country or region. Whatever the true nature of the mechanism generating these inverse long swings in economic activity, its functioning obviously depended on the complicated interplay of many variables, including immigration, the terms of trade, lenders' preferences, and so on, as well as on numerous other factors whose importance have yet to be assessed.[1]

LONG-RUN TRENDS IN THE TERMS OF TRADE

Before commencing a description of trends in the terms of trade for a number of countries during the nineteenth century it is necessary

[1] For a fuller discussion of some of the problems raised in this section see A. R. Hall, *The Export of Capital from Britain 1870–1914* (London, 1968).

to consider briefly the nature and significance of the terms of trade concept. The commodity (or net barter) terms of trade compare the changing relationship between export and import prices for a particular country over a number of years. A weighted index is usually constructed for both export and import prices in terms of base year prices and from these two indexes the terms of trade index is derived by calculating the export price index as a percentage of the import price index. The main use of the terms of trade index is to determine (purely on the basis of relative price changes), whether over a number of years a country gains additional real income (or loses it). If, for instance, a particular country's export volume remains unchanged in two successive years, but export prices increase by 10 per cent on the average, the money incomes of exporters will increase by 10 per cent despite the fact that total production remains unchanged. If, at the same time import prices are constant, the country is able to obtain a greater volume of imports for the same volume of exports. In other words, the country experiences a gain in terms of real income. On the other hand, if export prices declined by 10 per cent, other things remaining the same, a reduction in real income would eventuate. To summarize: a net gain will always accrue to a country so long as its import prices increase at a slower rate, or decline faster, than its export prices. On the other hand, if import prices increase faster, or decline more slowly, than export prices, the country will tend to lose real income purely from changes in international prices.[1] On the production side, increased export prices, especially if the trend is sustained for a period of several years would tend to produce a transfer of factors from other sectors into export industries, thus altering the country's distribution of productive factors. In this way, long-run trends in the terms of trade can have an important effect on the economic growth path of a country whose development is highly dependent on its export income.

When we come to examine the long-run trends in the terms of trade during the nineteenth century we find that reasonably accurate information exists for only a handful of countries, and that for most

[1] The terms of trade argument should not be restricted to changes in prices alone, since other factors are also important in determining the gains from trade over time. For example, improvements in productivity in export industries may reduce the costs of producing exports faster than the fall in their prices, thus nullifying the loss of real income implied in a deterioration of a country's commodity terms of trade. To take these factors into account, a number of other terms of trade concepts have been developed, some of which can, and some of which cannot, be measured statistically. For practical purposes, however, the commodity terms of trade provide the easiest way in which to use the available data, despite the difficulties that inevitably arise in constructing such an index.

of them the data relate only to the period after 1870. The longest terms of trade series available are those for the United Kingdom and the United States, both of which cover the period 1800–1913. Taking the British estimates first, these reveal a general long-run decline in the commodity terms of trade during the period from 1802 until the mid-1850s, followed by a sustained upward trend over the rest of the period. The tendency for the United Kingdom terms of trade to deteriorate over the first half of the nineteenth century arose because British cotton export prices fell faster than raw cotton import prices. Between 1814 and 1843 the prices of raw cotton imports fell by almost 80 per cent, while cotton textile prices declined even more sharply, partly because of the fall in raw cotton prices, and partly because of the technological advances occurring in the production of cotton textiles. The heavy weighting of cotton textiles in British exports and the precipitate fall in cotton textile prices led to a decline in the weighted average of British export prices that was greater than that of import prices with a consequent deterioration in the British commodity terms of trade. Indeed, if textile manufactures in general are removed from the terms of trade series, the residual series exhibits a fluctuating pattern with no long-run tendency to deteriorate.

Between 1857 and 1873 there was a decided improvement in Britain's commodity terms of trade as export prices rose while import prices fell. Thereafter, up to 1881, a deterioration set in caused by a heavy fall in export prices. From 1882 to 1913 both export and import prices moved together, declining in the years up to the mid-nineties and rising in the remainder of the period up to 1913. As the result of the relative movements of the two series, the British terms of trade tended to become progressively more favourable, initially because import prices were falling generally faster than export prices, and later because export prices tended on the whole to rise faster than import prices. Thus, except for the trough in the series between 1873 and 1884, the terms of trade index moved in such a way as to allow Britain to experience considerable gains from trade as the result of price changes for more than half a century.

The American terms of trade improved substantially during the second half of the 1790s, and then deteriorated sharply in the years up to the end of the Napoleonic Wars, when wartime shortages brought about a sharp rise in import prices. This was followed by a period of generally improving terms of trade between 1815 and 1860, the most favourable periods being 1816–19, the mid-thirties, and 1849–60. Import prices followed a general downward trend until the late 1840s after which they tended to rise. On the other hand, export prices fluctuated more widely with the most favourable improvements occurring during the thirties. Over the twenty years after 1860 the American commodity terms of trade appear to have continued an upward trend, although there was some deterioration in the early 1870s. In the remaining years up to 1913 there is little apparent upward or downward trend in the United States terms of trade. Thus from the end of the Napoleonic Wars until World War I, movements in international prices tended on the whole to benefit the United States economy, with perhaps the most unfavourable effects of price movements occurring during the late eighties and the 1890s.

Terms of trade estimates are available for a few European countries after 1870. What is most striking about the German series, especially after 1880, is its exceptional stability, for even during the one period of marked change—the years of deteriorating terms of trade between 1901 and 1913—the index fell only 12 per cent. It is therefore highly unlikely that Germany either lost or gained real income during these years as a result of changes in international trade prices. French experience was very similar to that of Germany. Like Germany, with the possible exception of the last decade before World War I, when a deterioration of approximately 20 per cent is apparent in the French terms of trade, the French economy tended not to be too greatly disturbed by movements in the relative prices of its imports or exports.

The only other countries for which reasonably acceptable statistical series have been constructed for periods of thirty or more years before 1914 are India, Japan, New Zealand, and Australia. Despite the violent fluctuations exhibited by the Indian series, it has a definite upward trend over the period 1861 to the mid-1890s, followed by a general levelling out during the remainder of the period. On the other hand, the Japanese terms of trade rose in the years up to 1900 and then displayed a tendency to fall thereafter. Despite the deterioration in the Japanese terms of trade in the 1900s, however, the available evidence suggests that neither Japan nor India experienced any significant loss of real income because of relative movements in international trade prices. The New Zealand data suggest that the terms of trade deteriorated throughout the 1860s, recovered in the early seventies and followed a sustained upward movement over the remainder of the period. Contrary to expectations the Australian data exhibit different characteristics from those of New Zealand. There appear to have been favourable terms of trade for Australia during the 1870s, an adverse movement during the 1880s and the first half of the nineties, and then a sustained improvement over the remainder of the period. Although it can be reasonably concluded that New Zealand received fairly substantial increases in real income from international price movements, such a conclusion is harder to sustain in the case of Australia, given the economic difficulties experienced by that country during the 1880s and the early 1890s.

Thus, an analysis of the available data on the terms of trade suggests that only in a relatively few periods did any country experience a long-run loss of real income because of sustained adverse movements in world prices, for example, Britain between 1800 and 1850, the United States in the 1820s and in the 1890s, and Australia between 1880 and 1895. Generally speaking, however, these losses in real income resulting from deteriorating commodity terms of trade were offset by other changes, such as increased productivity reducing costs of production in export industries, so that any net loss of real income, if it occurred, was unlikely to have been very large. Even more interesting is the conclusion that primary producing countries, such as Australia, New Zealand and India, all of which traded extensively with the United Kingdom, could experience improving terms of trade at the same time as Britain did. This could happen because of the effect of falling freight rates on the prices of internationally-traded goods. Thus the price of a primary product could fall in the country importing it despite increased production costs in the exporting country, if a reduction in transport costs more than offset the rise in production costs. It could also come about because of the different product mixes of the exports and imports of the different countries involved in trade with each other. It is noticeable, for instance, that because of the similar commodity composition of the two indexes, the Australian import price index follows fairly closely the trend in the British export price index from 1870 to 1913. On the other hand, great divergences exist between the Australian export price index, which was heavily influenced by the prices of a few products of major importance, such as wool, and the British import price index which incorporated a much wider range of commodities. Given the different commodity composition of imports and exports and variations in the movement of the prices of individual commodities, the possibility of the import and export price indexes of different countries, and consequently their commodity terms of trade, moving together are greatly enhanced. It therefore does not follow that an improvement in the terms of trade of an industrial country must lead inevitably to a deterioration in the terms of trade of the primary producing country.

SELECTED REFERENCES

Beckford, G. L. F., 'Secular Fluctuations in the Growth of Tropical Agricultural Trade', *Economic Development and Cultural Change* (October 1964).

Bloomfield, A. I., *Patterns of Fluctuation in International Investment before 1914* (Princeton, 1968).

Cairncross, A. K., *Home and Foreign Investment, 1870–1913* (Cambridge 1953).

Hall, A. R., *The Export of Capital from Britain 1870–1914* (London, 1968).

Imlah, A. H., *Economic Elements in the Pax Brittanica* (Cambridge Mass., 1958).

Kindleberger, C. P., *The Terms of Trade: A European Case Study* (New York, 1956).

Morgan T., 'The Long-Run Terms of Trade between Agriculture and Manufacturing', *Economic Development and Cultural Change* (October, 1959).

North, D. C., *The Economic Growth of the United States, 1790–1860* (Englewood Cliffs, 1961).

Saul, S. B., *Studies in British Overseas Trade 1870–1914* (Liverpool, 1960), especially Chap 5.

Thomas, B., *Migration and Economic Growth* (Cambridge, 1954).

Thorp, W. L., *Business Annals* (New York 1926), especially Section VI of the Introduction.

Part II
THE INTERWAR YEARS

Chapter 11

THE INTERNATIONAL ECONOMY IN THE INTERWAR YEARS

The international economy which had grown up during the nineteenth century came to an end with the outbreak of war in 1914. Four years of armed conflict involving all the great industrial nations left a legacy of problems to the international economy that were never completely solved in the economic reconstruction that followed the end of the war. Consequently, the post-war international economic system was ill-prepared to withstand the shock of a world-wide depression in the early 1930s, and a rapid break-up of the world economy inevitably followed. Five more years of war were to elapse before another attempt at restoring the international economy could be undertaken.

World War I affected the whole structure of the international economy. Trade patterns altered significantly, as the diversion of productive resources in Europe from manufacturing for export to turning out war materials led to the emergence of alternative sources of supply overseas. With the coming of peace, most of this trade returned to its normal channels, but some of the changes persisted, creating difficult problems of economic adjustment for a number of countries, including Britain. The gold standard was another casualty of the war years, when most countries went off gold. Although restored in a modified form by the late 1920s, it never again functioned as effectively as it had done before 1913, and by the early 1930s it had been reduced to a state of near collapse by a series of financial crises. In only one important respect did pre-war trends continue into the interwar period. In the field of commercial policy the movement towards protectionism became more marked, as international considerations were increasingly subordinated to national monetary and employment policies made necessary by post-war reconstruction and, later, by the onset of a world depression.

Associated with these monetary and trade problems was a tendency for the rate of growth of the world supply of primary products and manufactures to outstrip the rate of growth of demand for these commodities. This came about largely because of techno-logical progress and the continued spread of industrialization, which, along with population changes and rising real incomes, led to significant adjustments in the structure of world output and demand. How these real changes affected the orderly functioning of the international economy is the subject of this chapter, while the international monetary problems created by the first World War are discussed in the one that follows.

PRIMARY PRODUCTION

Technological progress was particularly rapid in agriculture during the interwar years. In temperate latitudes improvements continued to be made in the breeding of plants and animals, and the use of artificial fertilizers became widespread. Mechanized agriculture was also spreading, with improvements in the efficiency of tractors and the introduction of a growing range of ancillary equipment. Many new developments were also evident in tropical and sub-tropical agriculture. Particularly important were the selective breeding of plants, the increased use of fertilizers, the greater attention paid to the control of plant diseases and pests, and the growing use of selective weed-killers. There was also considerable progress in mining operations and in the initial processing of minerals during these years. The mechanization of mining proceeded rapidly in many countries. There was even more rapid progress in the processing of metallic ores, where flotation techniques developed in the early years of this century made possible the exploitation of low grade ores and complex ores containing several metals. Their use in working the low grade ores of Chile, for example, made that country one of the world's largest producers of copper. Even more striking has been the rapid development of the world's petroleum resources during this century. Along with the opening up of the oilfields and the advances made in drilling and refining techniques went the growth and spread of the world's oil-refining industry. Activity was particularly marked in the Middle East, where oil-refineries were established in Bahrein and Saudi-Arabia by American engineers, and in Iraq and Lebanon by British and joint European enterprises.

The widespread adoption of new techniques in agriculture and mining during the 1920s led to a substantial rise in the output of primary products that was added to by the appearance of new sources of supply, many of which had been brought into being by wartime demand and post-war shortages. Consequently, there appeared in the late twenties a rather general tendency for supply to outrun demand, and there was an appreciable fall in prices as a result. While there were considerable differences in commodity price movements, some rising and others falling or remaining stationary, when it occurred, the fall in prices was mainly in raw materials, though the prices of certain foodstuffs, particularly sugar and wheat, also declined heavily. Even when substantial price falls occurred, however, they did not always reflect the true extent of the changes in market forces, since the sale of some primary products was subject to monopolistic influences with the result that their prices were often higher than they would have been had competitive conditions prevailed. Thus commodity control schemes existed for varying periods in the 1920s for products such as rubber, coffee, sugar, wheat, and copper, and during 1927 and 1928 attempts were made to establish partial restriction of output schemes for petroleum, lead and zinc, though without any really significant effect on prices.

The downward pressure on primary product prices was not due solely to increased productivity and the opening up of new areas of production. Other forces were also at work. The speedy revival of Europe's sugar-beet industry was certainly a more important cause of excessive world sugar supplies than the rapid technical progress achieved in Cuba and Java during these years. Weaknesses in the management of the industry's commodity control scheme, which by holding prices at too attractive levels tended to induce further plantings, were as much a cause of the overproduction of coffee in Brazil as the opening up within the country of new, rich coffee lands. In explaining the overproduction of wheat during these years, the decline in *per capita* consumption owing to a shift to more expensive foods as living standards rose needs to be taken into account, along with the increased acreage under cultivation, greater mechanization, and the increased yields due to the application of scientific methods in the selection of seeds and plants. Indeed, as real incomes grew, changes in demand pervaded the world economy. Thus there was a relative decline in the world consumption of cereals and a substantial growth in that of fruit, dairy products and certain tropical foodstuffs. Canned products, ready-cooked meats and vegetables were eaten far more than pre-war. The consumption of cigarettes increased enormously all over the world, while the demand for cigars and pipe tobacco in general declined. Cotton and wool gave place to silk and artificial silk, as lighter and finer clothing increased in demand. Overall, however, rising incomes were associated with a declining percentage spent on food and an increasing proportion spent on other commodities, especially manufactures. Of course, these shifts in demand were not universal, but where they did occur they were sufficiently strong enough to call for marginal adjustments in production which became more difficult to bring about as economic conditions deteriorated.

POPULATION GROWTH AND MIGRATION

The difficulties facing primary producers may also have been due partly to the slowing up of the rate of growth of Europe's population, which reached its peak during the 1920s. Thereafter it declined, largely because of a fall in the birth rate that had begun in north-western Europe and then spread gradually to the east and south. Even more striking was the decline in North America where, under the influence of the depression, the annual rate of growth of population per 1,000 persons fell from 14·4 in the 1920s to 7·9 in the 1930s. In Asia and Africa, on the other hand, population began to increase more rapidly than in Europe. In India, for example, the first clear signs of a rise in the expectations of life appeared in 1921–31, when a significant fall in the death rate took place. The result of all these demographic changes was a slight decline in the relative importance of European populations. If the combined populations of Africa and Asia are taken as a rough measure of the world population of non-European stock, it accounted for 75 per cent of the world total in 1800, had fallen to 61 per cent in the 1920s, but then recovered slightly to 62 per cent of the total by 1940.

Despite the slowing up in the rate of growth of Europe's population, the pressure to migrate continued high. But with few great fertile and readily accessible areas of the world remaining unoccupied, and with the United States in particular showing less willingness to absorb immigrants than it had done in the past, the outflow of population from Europe fell heavily. It declined even further with the onset of the depression, and for a short time in the 1930s Europe became an area of immigration rather than of emigration. Thus, compared with an annual outflow of 1½m. between 1909 and 1914, European emigration declined to around 700,000 annually in the 1920s, and to 130,000 in the 1930s. Britain remained the most important single source of migrants, and southern and eastern Europe continued to provide well over half of the total outflow of population from Europe (Table 12b and Diagram 12).

Even though direct restriction of immigration into America was inaugurated by the Quota Act of 1921, which set an upper limit on the number allowed into the country during one year, the United States still took the largest share of gross immigration during the interwar years. Compared with the pre-war period, however, there was a substantial drop in American immigration in the twenties and thirties, when the annual average intake fell to less than a quarter of

TABLE 12A. *Growth and Percentage Distribution of World Population, 1920–40*

| | Number (m.) | | Distribution (per cent) | |
Region	1920	1940	1920	1940
Europe (including U.S.S.R.)	487	573	26·9	25·5
North America	117	146	6·5	6·5
Latin America	91	131	5·0	5·8
Asia	966	1,213	53·4	54·0
Africa	140	172	7·7	7·7
Oceania	9	11	0·5	0·5
Total	1,810	2,246	100·0	100·0

TABLE 12B. *European Emigration, 1921–1940*

| | Number (thousands) | | Distribution (per cent) | |
Country/Region	1921–30	1931–40	1921–30	1931–40
N.W. Europe	*3·11*	*0·53*	*45·4*	*43·1*
Britain	2·15	0·26	31·3	21·1
Germany	0·56	0·12	8·2	9·8
S.E. Europe	*3·76*	*0·70*	*54·6*	*56·9*
Spain and Portugal	1·56	0·24	22·7	19·5
Italy	1·37	0·24	19·9	19·5
Poland	0.63	0.16	9·2	13·0
Total	6·87	1·23	100·0	100·0

TABLE 12C. *Gross Immigration into Selected Countries, 1921–40*

| | Number (thousands) | | Distribution (per cent) | |
Country	1921–30	1931–40	1921–30	1931–40
U.S.A.	2·72	0·44	37·5	31·9
Canada	0·99	0·08	13·7	5·8
Argentina	1·40	0·31	19·3	22·5
Brazil	0.84	0.24	11·6	17·4
Australia	0·95	0·14	13·1	10·1
Others	0·35	0·17	4·8	12·3
Total	7·25	1·38	100·0	100·0

Sources: *U.N. Demographic Yearbook* (various); Woytinsky, W. S. and E. S., *World Population and Production* (New York, 1953); Woodruff, W., *Impact of Western Man* (New York, 1966), Tables III/4 and 5.

Diagram 12: Emigration from Europe, 1921–40

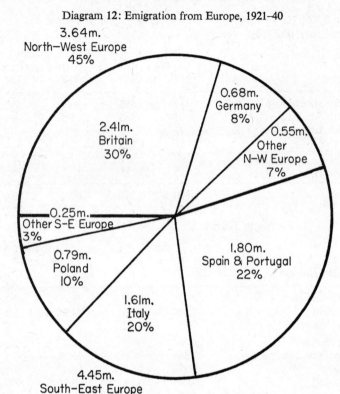

3.64m.
North–West Europe
45%

2.41m.
Britain
30%

0.68m.
Germany
8%

0.55m.
Other
N–W Europe
7%

0.25m.
Other S–E Europe
3%

0.79m.
Poland
10%

1.80m.
Spain & Portugal
22%

1.61m.
Italy
20%

4.45m.
South–East Europe
55%

Total: 8·10 m.
Sources: See Table 12

a million compared with an annual average of nearly one million in the nine years before 1914 (see Table 12c and Diagram 13).

Of the other countries of immigration, Canada and Australia continued to absorb large numbers of British migrants, as well as a smaller number of migrants from other European countries. Much of Canada's ability to attract and absorb immigrants came from the rapid expansion of its manufacturing and construction industries, and from the 1920s onwards the country showed a preference for the skilled industrial workers essential to its industrial progress. In Australia, where rapid industrialization also set up a growing demand for labour, the Empire Settlement Act of 1922 and the '£34 million agreement' reached between Great Britain and the Australian government in 1925 provided for government loans to assist migra-

Diagram 13: International Immigration, 1921–40

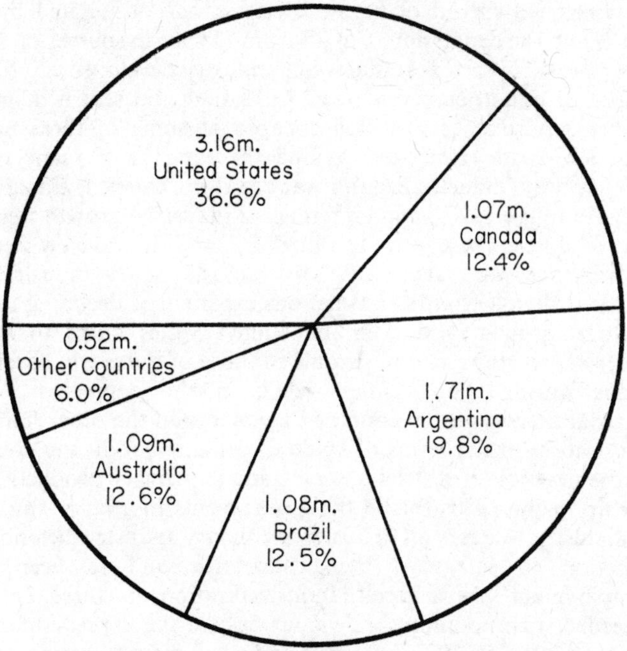

Total: 8·63 m.
Sources: As for Table 12

tion to Australia. Planning for some 500,000 migrants in ten years, the project proved to be over-ambitious. All the same, there was a net inflow of over 300,000 migrants in the twenties, of whom two-thirds were assisted.

Large numbers of European migrants also went to Brazil and Argentina during these years. In Brazil, where the World War I had provided the initial stimulus for industrialization, the immigrants came mainly from Italy and Germany in the twenties, and there was also a record inflow of Japanese in the thirties. In Argentina, the immigrants came overwhelmingly from Latin Europe, mainly Spain and Italy. As with all other countries of immigration, the Argentinian population inflow, which was substantial in the 1920s, fell heavily in the 1930s, when a catastrophic fall in agricultural prices and land values reduced the flow of immigration and encouraged the Argentinian government to introduce restrictive legislation.

MANUFACTURING PRODUCTION

The continued spread of industrialization was stimulated by both the war and the depression. Cut off from European sources of supply during the war years, manufacturing industry developed rapidly in a number of countries overseas, and although the return of normal peacetime production saw the collapse of some of these nascent industries, tariff protection ensured the survival of many others. After the war, industrialization was rapid in America, Canada and Australia in the 1920s, and high rates of industrial growth were also achieved during these years in Brazil, Finland, India, New Zealand, South Africa, and Japan. Relative to the newly industrializing countries, the older industrial nations experienced declining rates of industrial growth, and even the United States failed to achieve industrial growth rates comparable to those of the newly developing nations during the twenties, while in the depressed thirties, industrial activity in the country stagnated. On the other hand, the deterioration in the terms of trade of primary producing countries and the network of restrictions on trade in primary products which grew up in the 1930s forced the governments in a large number of non-industrial countries to foster secondary industry behind tariff protection to safeguard living standards and to keep down unemployment. As a result, industrialization in these countries proceeded with undiminished vigour despite the depression.

Taking 1913 as 100, the world index of manufacturing activity averaged 185 in the years 1936–8, whereas the index for the United States stood at 167, Germany 138, Britain 122, and France 118, all well below the world average. In contrast, many new countries had industrialized at an enormous pace: the Soviet Union's index rose to 774, Japan 529, Finland 289, India 230, and Sweden 223. Over the whole period, therefore, the slower growth of the old countries was largely offset by the rapid progress of the new industrial nations and, as Table 13 clearly shows, significant changes in the distribution of the world's manufacturing production occurred as a result. The notable features of this table include the dominant position of the United States in world manufacturing during the late 1920s and its subsequent decline during the depression years; the increased shares in world manufacturing activity of the Soviet Union and Japan; and the decline in the relative shares of the old-established European industrial powers, Britain, France and Germany.

Too much should not be read into these production figures, however. To begin with, the statistics themselves are open to some questioning, especially those for Russia. More important still, the figures tell us nothing about the significant differences in the nature

TABLE 13. *Percentage Distribution of the World's Manufacturing Production, 1913–38*

Period	U.S.	Germany	U.K.	France	Russia	Sweden	Japan	India	Rest of world	World
1913	35·8	14·3	14·1	7·0	4·4	1·0	1·2	1·1	21·1	100·0
1926–29	42·2	11·6	9·4	6·6	4·3	1·0	2·5	1·2	21·2	100·0
1936–38	32·2	10·7	9·2	4·5	18·5	1·3	3·5	1·4	18·7	100·0

Note: The 1913 percentages represent the distribution according to the frontier established after the 1914–18 war.
Source: League of Nations, *Industrialization and Foreign Trade* (Geneva, 1945). Table 1, p. 13.

of the industrial growth being experienced by the various countries concerned. In the new countries, growth took the form of the expansion of textile manufactures and other types of fabrication typical of a country in the early stages of industrialization. On the other hand, in the United States, and to a lesser extent in some of the old industrial countries, industrialization during these years involved the rapid growth of new industries, such as motor-cars, household appliances, and chemicals, as well as the increasing use of new methods of production, such as the assembly line. These new industrial techniques involved a considerable increase in the use of capital and of power. They also brought about significant changes in the composition of world manufacturing output.

As the American experience suggests, the interwar period was marked not so much by startling new inventions as by remarkable advances in the efficiency of already familiar techniques. Fuel economies were achieved in iron and steel production and in the generation of electricity, with the best power stations halving fuel consumption between 1918 and 1939. The variety of materials available for engineering was greatly extended with the introduction after the war of new alloys, especially the light alloys based on aluminium. There was also an increasing use of plastics. Few radical improvements were made in machine tools, although the use of tungsten carbide as a tool material after 1926 was a significant advance. Refrigeration techniques improved greatly, and substantial increases in the efficiency of gas engines, petrol and oil engines, including the diesel, and steam turbines were also achieved during these years. But with the exception of the gas turbine, which passed through the critical stages of development shortly before the outbreak of the second World War, the twenty years between the two wars were not remarkable for the invention of prime movers.

By far the most important development in production methods during these years was the widespread adoption of the assembly line. Initially developed by Henry Ford as the key to the efficient, large-scale, and therefore cheap, production of motor-cars, the assembly line system was widely used in the United States after World War I to mass-produce such items as washing machines, radios and refrigerators. In addition, many other products, including shoes, stockings, glassware and chinaware, were passed through factories from operation to operation in a continuous process from raw material to finished product. By enormously increasing the volume of output, and thereby reducing costs, the assembly line led to a marked rise in productivity and a consequent increase in real incomes, which was partly used to purchase the growing output of consumer goods made possible by the new industrial techniques.

Indeed this emphasis on durable consumption goods is only one of a number of ways in which the new industrial technology was marked off from that of the nineteenth century, for the new industries were as much concerned with mechanizing the home as they were with mechanizing production. This trend, which began around 1900 with the introduction of the telephone, the gramophone, the bicycle and the motor-car, was continued after the war when, with the development of the vacuum-cleaner, the washing-machine, the refrigerator and the radio, machines became familiar in the home. Moreover, the growing range of household electrical appliances and the increasing use of electricity for domestic lighting and cooking, along with the rising industrial consumption of electrical power, enormously increased investment in electrical generating capacity during these years and created a growing demand for electrical plant and equipment of all kinds.

Apart from the rapid development of the aeroplane, the interwar years did not witness many new revolutionary changes in the means of transportation. Railway mileage continued to grow, particularly in the less-developed continents, where the railway mileage increased from 152,000 miles in 1920 to 184,000 in 1940. Railway construction was especially heavy in the Soviet Union where the railway mileage increased by one-half between the wars. On the railways, locomotive performance continued to improve, and the first diesel-electric locomotive appeared in the United States in 1924. Other railway improvements introduced during these years related to traffic control systems, the air-conditioning of trains, and better communication systems for trains. Many of these innovations were the result of efforts to increase railway efficiency in the face of the growing competition of motor transport. This competition was most apparent in the United States where, despite the efforts of the railway companies to counter road competition, the railway mileage in operation in the country declined by almost 19,000 miles between 1920 and 1940. At sea oil-burning ships were gradually replacing the coal-burner, while improvements in the design of ships led to substantial reductions in fuel consumption. Here, too, competition was beginning to make itself felt, at least for the ocean passenger trade, as air travel became faster, safer, and more regular.

Rapid technological change and the spread of industrialization to new regions brought with them the problem of economic adjustment in established industrial economies. In no country was this more important during these years than in Britain, where the coal and cotton industries declined absolutely in the face of competition from new producers and the development of substitutes for their products. Other British industries in trouble during these years included ship-building, which lost ground because of the world-wide excess capacity created by the war, the failure of foreign trade to grow as rapidly as industrial production, and the continuous growth of overseas ship-building. While the great staple industries of Britain stagnated and their trade declined, her iron and steel and engineering industries continued to expand, and new industries, notably motor-cars, electrical goods, chemicals, rayon, and various other manufactures underwent a vigorous expansion. Even so, the growth of these industries and the support they gave to British exports failed to offset the decline in Britain's traditional industries. The consequent stagnation of the British economy and the associated decline in Britain's international commercial and financial position goes a long way towards explaining the failure of the international economy to function as smoothly during the 1920s as it had before 1914.

THE INTENSIFICATION OF PROTECTIONISM

Within the world markets for primary products and manufactures, adjustments in supply and demand to take into account the changed economic conditions of the interwar years were made difficult by the spread of restrictions on foreign trade. The war itself was responsible in a number of ways for the intensification of protectionism. In Japan, India, Australia, and some Latin American countries, the disappearance of European competition in many lines of manufacturing for four years called forth considerable local production. Some of these 'war babies' died a natural death with the return of peacetime trading conditions, but many others, inspired by motives of self-interest and national security, clamoured for and obtained the support of tariffs. In Australia, iron and steel, machinery, railway materials and chemicals were given protection; in India, iron and steel, cotton textiles, paper and chemicals; in Argentina, pharmaceutical manufactures.

Protection also flourished in Europe, where the post-war creation of entirely new nations in central and eastern Europe lengthened Europe's tariff frontiers by some 12,000 miles. Behind these barriers, new governments, faced with economic dislocation and production shortages of all kinds, endeavoured to achieve some measure of economic stability. Currency disorders were an added problem in many countries encouraging the use of tariffs and the introduction of many direct restrictions on trade, such as import and export licensing, quotas, prohibitions and exchange controls. France, Germany (after 1925), Italy, Spain, Belgium and the Netherlands were among the many European countries that introduced tariffs for the first time or revised existing tariffs upwards during the 1920s. These tariffs were not restricted to manufacturing industry or to the control of balance of payments problems created by currency disorders and production difficulties. Agricultural protection also became more widespread and severe in Europe. It played its greatest role in Italy, where, behind high protection, the 'Battle for Wheat' was launched in 1925, to reduce the country's heavy dependence on outside sources of supply. But the movement towards agricultural self-sufficiency was general throughout Europe at this time, and its consequences for the growth of world trade in primary products were grave.

In Britain, the McKenna Act of 1915, which imposed duties of $33\frac{1}{3}$ per cent on cars, motor-cycles and certain other manufactures in an effort to save wartime shipping space and foreign exchange, laid the foundations for a return to protection after the war, when the Act remained in force and was extended to commercial vehicles and tyres. Further protection to British industry was afforded by the Safe-guarding of Industries Act and the Dyestuffs Importation Act, both passed in 1921, which placed duties on the products of a number of key industries, including optical glass and instruments, considered to be vital for national security, and prohibited the importation of all synthetic dyestuffs and intermediate products. Even more crucial for the well-being of the international economy was the introduction by the United States of the Fordney–McCumber Tariff of 1922. This Act, which raised American tariffs to the highest level in the country's history up to that time, was utterly inconsistent with the new-found role of the United States as the world's most important creditor nation. Since high tariffs made it difficult for the debtor nations to earn dollars with which to make interest payments on American loans and to repay war debts, and since gold was in short supply, the difficulties of America's debtors were prevented from becoming glaringly obvious only by the willingness of the Americans to lend capital abroad.

Protection also became a feature of many primary producing countries, where the desire to support war-induced manufacturing industries was supplemented by the need to reduce dependence on foreign manufactures in the face of deteriorating terms of trade. Whatever the reason for introducing protection in these countries, however, one feature of the international economic situation in the 1920s is perfectly clear: the growing range of restrictions placed on trade between nations reflected an enlargement of the objectives of protectionist policy. In particular, the use of commercial policy during these years came to be extended from the protection of certain industries to the protection of a country's balance of payments against declining export prices and the effects of the prevailing currency disorders of the 1920s. Later, during the depression years, commercial policy developed another function, that of creating employment through the setting up of domestic manufacturing industries to cater for demands formerly satisfied by imports which were denied access to the domestic market by the use of tariffs or other restrictive measures.

The spread of protection, the frequent adoption of deliberately high duties for bargaining purposes, and the introduction of quantitative restrictions on trade imposed a severe handicap on the recovery of world commerce in the 1920s, and in an attempt to remedy the situation, the League of Nations called a World Economic Conference in 1927 which had an immediate, though short-lived, effect on trade relations. Through autonomous measures and bilateral agreements, such as the Franco-German Commercial Treaty of August, 1927, which laid the basis for an integrated European treaty system, the rising trend in tariffs was temporarily checked. Another conference summoned in the same year tried to deal with the problem of quantitative restrictions on trade, but it dragged on until 1930 without achieving anything of real value. What finally defeated the efforts of both conferences, however, was the onset of depression and the threat of even higher tariffs in the United States.

This failure of international policy making highlights a fundamental weakness in the international economy during the interwar years. Whereas the major economic problems of the day demanded solution at the international level, the authorities through which existing regulation was exercised were, with few and partial exceptions, national. International attempts to produce solutions to the world's economic problems were made, but they were rare and largely unsuccessful. The League of Nations, which played a useful constructive role in the early twenties, particularly in negotiating international loans for countries wishing to stabilize their currencies, had a less active role in the 1930s. It produced a large number of reports and inquiries on both international and national affairs, but their effect on policy appears to have been minimal.

This lack of determined international policy making is, of course, easily explained. It was difficult to convince people who remembered the free operation of the international economy during the pre-war years of the necessity for a greater degree of international control in the changed conditions of the interwar period. The post-war difficulties would soon be overcome, it was felt, once the pre-war international monetary mechanism had been restored to full working order. Even more of an obstacle to international co-operation was the decline of economic liberalism which became such a marked feature of the interwar years. If the exigencies of war forced most governments to become more involved in economic affairs, the political changes and economic difficulties of the interwar period ensured that this involvement would continue and even intensify. The spread of new political faiths, such as communism and fascism, the powerful stimulus given to economic nationalism by the war, the economic and financial difficulties of the twenties, and the depression of the thirties made it inevitable that the government would play a larger role in the economic life of the nation than formerly. This increasing dependence on purely national solutions to economic problems made international co-operation difficult, if not impossible.

This economic nationalism even spread to the field of monetary policy, where, despite the professed reverence for the gold standard mechanism, the independent national control of the domestic supply of money came to supplant the pre-war principle of the international gold standard, according to which any nation's stock of money was dependent upon the ebb and flow of gold. By giving to the central bank the power to influence strongly the supply of money inside the country, the government tended to insulate the national monetary system from international forces and in doing so it impaired the very mechanism upon which so much faith in future economic progress rested.

SELECTED REFERENCES

Ellsworth, P. T., *The International Economy*, 3rd edn. (New York, 1964).

International Institute of Agriculture, *World Trade in Agriculture* (Rome, 1940).

Kahn, A. E., *Great Britain in the World Economy* (London, 1946).

League of Nations, *Quantitative Trade Controls. Their Causes and Nature* (Geneva, 1943).

League of Nations, *International Currency Experience* (Geneva, 1944), especially Chap. 8.

League of Nations, *Industrialization and Foreign Trade* (Geneva, 1945).

Lewis, W. A., *Economic Survey 1919–1939* (London, 1949), especially Part III.

Lilley, S., *Men, Machines and History* (revised edn, London, 1965).

Tracy, M., *Agriculture in Western Europe* (New York, 1964).

Woytinsky, W. S. *and* E. S., *World Production and Population* (New York, 1953)

Chapter 12

THE RESTORATION OF THE GOLD STANDARD AND THE ECONOMIC RECOVERY OF THE TWENTIES

The war years saw the end of the gold standard when its two basic requirements, interconvertibility between paper money and gold and the free export of gold, were suspended. Initially, most of the belligerent countries were able to maintain adequate gold reserves and familiar exchange rates, chiefly by taking gold coins out of domestic circulation and concentrating them in official hands. As the years passed, however, it became increasingly difficult for the warring nations to support the pre-war pattern of exchange rates. For Britain and France the difficulty was overcome finally by the receipt of American loans, following that country's entry into the war early in 1917. Lacking such support, the German and Austrian exchanges were in state of collapse by 1918. But for most countries, including the United States, Britain and the Empire, France, Italy, the Netherlands, Spain, Sweden, Japan, Argentina, and Brazil, exchange rates at the end of the war diverged remarkably little from the pre-war pattern despite the upheaval of the previous four years.

POST-WAR INFLATION AND THE RESTORATION OF THE GOLD STANDARD

This apparent normalcy in the pattern of exchange rates cloaked the profound changes that war had brought. In particular, the war economies had all experienced varying degrees of price inflation, the true extent of which had been disguised by price controls and rationing. In the immediate post-war years, a reconstruction boom plus the wide-spread dislocation of trade and production in central Europe caused a further inflationary rise in prices, which reached a peak in most countries in 1920, and then gave way to a couple of years of business depression and heavy price declines. In Germany, France and central and eastern Europe, however, inflation continued for several more years, and in the process the old money units of

Austria, Hungary, Poland, Germany and Russia were practically destroyed.[1]

In an effort to achieve monetary stability, international financial conferences were held in Brussels (1920) and Genoa (1922). Shortly afterwards, with the help of large international loans from the United States and Britain, financial reorganizations were carried out in Austria (1922) and Hungary (1924). In 1925 further loans for stabilization purposes were made to Poland and Czechoslovakia, followed by similar arrangements with Bulgaria, Italy and Rumania. The outstanding event in post-war financial progress, however, was the stabilization of the German mark in 1923–4, which was accompanied by the drawing up of the Dawes Plan for the settlement of the German war debt.

The post-war inflation in Germany was due mainly to the government's refusal to balance its budget. The resulting government deficits were financed initially by borrowing, but when the deficits persisted and even increased in size because of rising prices, the German public refused to take up more government securities and the government was forced to issue treasury bills to cover its excess expenditure. These only added to the quantity of money in circulation and led to a further rise in prices. Eventually, the expanding money supply and rising prices by depreciating the value of the mark caused it to be spent more rapidly. From the combined force of large quantities of money being spent faster and faster a runaway inflation inevitably developed.

In the final stages of this hyper-inflation the rise in domestic prices left the increase in the quantity of money far behind, and it was the consequent acute shortage of money which eventually provided the government with the opportunity to bring the inflation under control. A new Rentenmark introduced late in 1923 was quickly taken up by a public long inconvenienced by the lack of a stable currency. This enabled the government to cover its expenditures with new issues of money while taking steps to balance its budget through spending cuts and tax increases. A decline in the velocity of circulation of money as inflationary pressures abated sufficed to offset any further monetary expansion. Stabilization of the mark was completed with the receipt of an international loan of 800 million marks (£40m.) under the Dawes Plan of 1924.

The Dawes Plan was the outcome of a reconsideration of the

[1] By the end of their respective inflations, pre-war price levels had been multiplied by roughly 14,000 in Austria, 23,000 in Hungary, 2½ million in Poland, 4,000 million in Russia, and a million million in Germany. (W. A. Lewis, *Economic Survey 1919–1939* [London, 1949], p. 23.)

whole German reparations problems that had inevitably followed the financial collapse of the mark. The Treaty of Versailles (1919) had established the principle that Germany should indemnify the Allies for their war losses, and had created a Reparations Commission to assess the amount. In 1921 the Commission assessed the war damage at 132 billion gold marks (equal to £6,600m.) and laid down a time schedule of payments. It soon became obvious, however, that Germany, already in the grip of inflation, was in no position to meet her obligations. Under the Dawes arrangements, Germany was required to make reparations payments rising in five years from £50m. to £125m. per annum, the number of years of payments being left undetermined.[1] The first payment was made possible by the floating of an international loan (the Dawes loan), which also enabled Germany to return to the gold standard in 1924 with the introduction of a new currency, the Reichsmark, at the old pre-war gold parity of 23.8 cents. Foreign countries now became interested in the reconstruction of Germany, and for the rest of the 1920s both the government and private firms were able to borrow large sums abroad. The German economic situation was stabilized.

Linked with the problem of German reparations was the question of the repayment of inter-allied war debts. Italy, France, and Belgium had emerged from the war in debt to one another and to Britain, while all of them, together with several other countries, had received loans totalling $7,700m. from the United States by the end of 1918. Post-war lending for relief and reconstruction added to these debts, until by the end of 1922, the debt owing to America stood at $9,400m., of which the share of Britain was $4,100m., France $2,900m., Italy $1,600m., with the remainder divided among Belgium, Cuba, Czechoslovakia, Greece, Rumania, Russia and Yugoslavia.[2] Since many of the allied countries came to regard German reparations payments as a means of liquidating their American debts, there developed a chain of debt payments commencing in Germany and ending in the United States.

For these debt repayments to proceed smoothly, two requirements had to be met: large sums of marks had to be extracted annually from the German people, and these sums had to be transferred regularly into other currencies—ultimately a large proportion into dollars. These requirements could be met by increasing German taxes sufficiently to release a flow of goods and

---

[1] The total reparations figure and period of repayment was fixed later under the Young Plan (1929), which scaled down the annual payments to £100m. and envisaged the termination of payments in 1987–8.

[2] Cleona Lewis, *America's Stake in International Investments* (Washington, 1938), p. 362.

services for export large enough to earn the foreign exchange
needed for reparations payments. But because the German government lacked the gold and foreign exchange necessary to make the
initial reparations payment and was also never able to achieve a
budget surplus, and because the creditor countries were opposed to
accepting the large inflow of German goods needed if the country
was to earn the foreign exchange with which to make reparations
payments, the transfer process was never able to function effectively.
In the event, the problem of reparations and inter-allied war debts
was not settled until the mid-twenties, when Germany began
receiving large loans of foreign capital, mainly from the United
States. Then the chain of debt repayments began to function
smoothly, but when this foreign lending to Germany ceased in the
late twenties, the transfer of reparations also stopped, and with it
the repayment of the related war debts.

Germany's return to the gold standard, following the floating of
the Dawes loan in 1924, was the start of a general return to the gold
standard in the next few years. In Britain the wartime peg of the
pound/dollar rate had been abandoned in March 1919 so that a
temporarily fluctuating rate could be used to measure progress in
deflating British prices enough relative to American prices to make
pre-war parity workable again. It was not until April, 1925, however, that the pound rose near enough to parity with the dollar for a
return to gold to be announced. This decision was made legal
shortly afterwards by the Gold Standard Act passed on May 13,
1925. The French inflation, on the other hand, continued until
mid-1926 and went far enough to prevent a return to pre-war parity.
When, at the end of 1926, the franc was eventually stabilized *de
facto* by official dealings on the foreign exchange market, it stood at
about one-fifth of its pre-war parity. *De jure* ratification of this
80 per cent depreciation followed in June, 1928, when a law was
passed re-defining the gold content of the franc in line with the
prevailing exchange rate.

Between 1925 and 1928, the reconstruction of the international
monetary mechanism was substantially completed. By early 1926
some thirty-nine countries had returned to gold, either at their
pre-war parity or at a devalued level, or had displayed exchange
rate stability for a full year. This list included Great Britain, the
Netherlands, Sweden, Denmark, Switzerland, Germany, Austria,
Hungary, Finland, Czechoslovakia, Yugoslavia, Bulgaria, Russia,
the British Dominions, twelve Latin American countries, and the
United States, which had returned with ease to the full gold standard
in 1919, and thereafter had been the guidepost for the realignment
of other currencies. During the next two years most of the countries

G

which had not already done so returned to gold, the most notable being France, Italy and Argentina.

WEAKNESSES IN THE POST-WAR GOLD STANDARD: INTERNATIONAL INVESTMENT

With the restoration of the gold standard it was widely assumed that the most essential aspect of post-war economic reconstruction had been achieved. As it turned out, these hopes were largely illusory. The belief that a familiar and highly efficient international monetary mechanism had been restored to full working order overlooked the fact that to function successfully the pre-war gold standard had required a special kind of environment which no longer existed, and that the pre-war machinery was in many essential respects quite different from that which had now replaced it.

Nowhere were the changes so marked compared with the pre-war period than in the field of international investment, for the war had brought about shifts of unprecedented magnitude in the structure of international debt. America had emerged from the war as the principal creditor on private account, whereas Germany had been transformed from a major creditor country to a debtor. The war had also weakened Britain's international lending position, by forcing her to liquidate part of her long-term assets, while further losses arose because of the confiscation of British assets in enemy countries and in Russia. French and German losses on these accounts were relatively greater even than those of Britain. On the other hand, the United States had not only repatriated American securities held by British and French investors during the war years, but she had also invested heavily in foreign securities, while granting considerable war credits to the allies.

Britain's efforts to re-establish her international financial position in the post-war years were complicated by her poor export performance. Her problem of expanding exports in the 1920s on the basis of a stagnant economy and in the face of growing foreign competition was aggravated after 1925 by a return to the gold standard at an exchange rate which it is now generally agreed was overvalued by some 10 per cent. This made Britain's exports relatively more expensive in world markets and therefore more difficult to sell, while imports, becoming relatively cheaper, were encouraged to grow. With imports growing faster than exports, the resulting trade gap absorbed a steadily increasing proportion of Britain's invisible earnings. The result was small current account surpluses, seldom reaching one-third or one-half of the pre-war real size (allowing for price rises), which failed to cover the long-term foreign security issues floated in the highly developed London capital market.

In these changed circumstances, the United States became the chief source of international loans, followed by Britain and France. American lending was concentrated largely in the 1920s, when the total of all American foreign investments grew from $7,000m. in 1919 to $17,000m. in 1930.[1] Just over one-half of the long-term investments were direct investments, almost one-half of which went to underdeveloped countries, mostly in Latin America. Of the portfolio investment, some 40 per cent went to Europe, 29 per cent to Canada, 22 per cent to Latin America, and the other 9 per cent to Asia. In the London capital market new overseas issues averaged £125m. per annum from 1921 to 1930, or about £80m. to £90m. ($390–440m.) after allowing for loan repayments and foreign participation in the new issues. Loans were extended to a number of European countries, including Germany, Austria and Belgium, and to government and public authorities in the Empire. There was also much investment in primary production, including rubber, coffee and oil. Other fields of direct investment included railways, public utilities, finance, mines, and metal smelting. By the end of 1930, British long-term investment showed a slight preponderance of direct over portfolio investment, and a geographical distribution in favour of the Empire, which accounted for 59 per cent of the total invested at that date. Within the Empire, Australia, India, Canada and South Africa were large borrowers in the 1920s; elsewhere, Argentina and Brazil.

Apart from the emergence of the United States as the world's principal creditor, the other striking feature of international investment activity during the interwar years was the large-scale borrowing of foreign capital by continental European countries in the years after 1924. Germany was the chief capital-importer, absorbing close to $4,000m. from 1924 to 1929, inclusive. Other European borrowers during these years included Austria, Bulgaria, Czechoslovakia, Greece, Hungary, Poland and Rumania. Elsewhere, Argentina and Australia, after having exported capital during certain of the early post-war years, returned to their traditional roles of heavy borrowers in the twenties. The Union of South Africa also raised loans during the middle and late 1920s. Canada, on the other hand, only began to borrow from 1929 onward, when the capital exports from the chief creditor countries were declining. Broadly speaking, London contributed relatively little to the European investments, but supplied a very large share of the money invested in the Empire, including a number of Asian and African countries.

[1] Including $2,000m. invested on short-term.

On the other hand, investments in Europe and Canada, and those in Latin American countries, were raised chiefly in the United States.

The pattern of foreign investment activity that emerged in the 1920s had a number of weaknesses which acted as powerful de-stabilizers during the early stages of the world-wide depression that developed after 1929. To begin with, in contrast to pre-1913, when European capital had gone to countries that supplied the foodstuffs and raw materials demanded by Europe's expanding markets, much of the American investment in the 1920s went to nations, particularly those in Europe, whose exports were competitive with rather than complementary to those of the United States. Moreover, trading relations between America and Europe had changed significantly. Largely as a result of American industrialization, Europe never regained its pre-war position as a supplier of American imports, averaging only about 30 per cent of the total in the twenties compared with over 50 per cent before 1913. The United States, however, had become an important market for raw materials and foodstuffs, and since several of these commodities were supplied by countries with whom European nations had export surpluses, America's growing export surplus with Europe depended in considerable measure upon the volume of American imports from these third-party countries. Thus the world pattern of settlements in the 1920s and, in particular, the growing American trade surplus with Europe depended upon American foreign investments in Europe and elsewhere, a high and stable American demand for the products of third countries, and the existence of a European surplus on current account with these latter areas which was settled in gold and dollars. When, therefore, along with a drastic decline in its imports of raw materials and foodstuffs, American international investment practically dried up in the early 1930s, a world payments crisis was inevitable.

Another source of weakness was to be found in the debtor countries, especially those primary producers faced with declining world prices for their exports. Apart from the possibility that some of the foreign lending of the period, by financing the further expansion of primary production, may have contributed indirectly to bringing about these price falls, the heavy demand for foreign capital in the 1920s was accompanied by a rise in the percentage return on the outstanding investments. Thus the annual net outward payments of interest and dividends by debtor countries (excluding regular amortization payments and reparations payments) rose from $1,400m. annually around 1920 to about $2,500m. in 1928. This increase in net payments of interest and dividends was not evenly distributed among debtor countries, however. Whereas

Canada's net outward payments during these years remained stable, others, such as Australia and Argentina, rose by between 50 and 100 per cent. But the heaviest increases occurred in central and eastern Europe. These rising debt charges came at a time when falling export prices made it increasingly difficult for some of these debtor countries to earn the foreign exchange necessary to finance needed imports and to meet the debt payments on heavy borrowings at high rates of interest. The effect on a country's balance of payments of these developments could be concealed only as long as creditor countries were prepared to fill the gap with new loans and thus give at least an appearance of equilibrium to a situation fraught with instability and danger.

One further threat to international economic stability came from the heavy and frequently unpredictable movements of short-term capital which became a feature of the interwar period. French foreign investment in the 1920s, particularly after 1924, was largely of the short-term kind, involving temporary investment on short-term account or in securities bought on foreign stock exchanges. Some of it also took the form of a flight of French capital for investment in stable foreign currencies, more especially the dollar and sterling, brought about by the instability of the French franc in the mid-twenties. However beneficial these capital inflows were to the receiving countries, they represented de-stabilizing capital flows, since their rapid withdrawal could easily bring about a major financial crisis in the centre experiencing the loss of funds. A difficult situation was made even worse by the practice that grew up of British and American financial institutions using these funds to lend, in their turn, on long and short-term. For this meant that a cessation of French lending, involving possibly the repatriation of French capital, could bring about a chain reaction in the sphere of international finance involving the whole community of international borrowers and lenders.

INSTITUTIONAL WEAKNESSES OF THE RESTORED GOLD STANDARD

The emergence of New York as a major international financial centre had important consequences for the functioning of the restored gold standard. In particular, it involved the de-centralization of the international clearing function. Whereas pre-war international transactions had been centralized in London, with payments typically being made in a relatively simple way, by transfer of bank balances held in London, the post-war system became de-centralized, with New York and Paris taking over a large part of the function hitherto performed by London. The existence of more than one major financial centre made international clearing more complex and less efficient, for the various centres now had to arrange for off-setting claims among themselves and to hold balances with one another for this purpose. Moreover, the existence of a number of financial centres created the conditions under which foreign-owned funds were liable to move erratically from one financial centre to another in response to changing interest rates, changes in confidence or distrust in currencies, and other developments besides deep-seated balance of payments disequilibrium. This 'hot-money' danger had been far less serious before 1914, when no centre rivalled London as a place where short-term funds might move and be profitably held.

These difficulties were added to by the institutional shortcomings of the new financial centres. New York not only lacked the experience of London in the role of distributing international securities to investors, but its money market was also less responsive to changes in the balance of payments which tended to make international investment attractive. The overwhelming importance of the financial requirements of the domestic market in American economic life (exemplified by the stock exchange boom of 1928–29), the small fraction that foreign trade constituted in gross national product, together with the slow development of international investment banking in the United States, prevented the establishment of any close connection between a surplus in the American balance of payments and its level of long-term international lending. Moreover, even when capital was lent abroad, American commercial policy placed major obstacles in the way of debt repayment, since the high tariff policy adopted by the United States during these years made it difficult for foreigners to earn dollars in the American market. Borrowers were thus able to make these payments temporarily only by further borrowing rather than by export expansion based on increased productivity associated with the investment of foreign capital and shifts in world production.

The functioning of the international monetary system was also hindered by a shortage of gold, and the rather uneven distribution of the existing gold stocks brought about by the war. The American holdings, as a proportion of the world's gold stock, had grown from 24 per cent in 1913 to 44 per cent at the end of 1923, while those of Britain had risen from 3 to 9 per cent. On the other hand, certain other countries, including Germany, Italy, Russia, India and Brazil, had suffered not only a relative but also an absolute loss of gold during these years. Given this shortage of world gold reserves, some other acceptable means of international payment had to be found to supplement gold. This was the significance of the widespread adoption of the gold exchange standard during the 1920s, which was officially recommended by the 1922 Geneva Conference as a means of alleviating the world shortage of gold. Under this system assets in the form of foreign currencies could be counted as part of a country's international monetary reserves. In other words, a country was allowed to stabilize its currency in terms of a foreign currency that was convertible into gold and to hold its reserves in the form of that currency. This system was not new. Before 1913 it had been adopted by Russia and Austro-Hungary among others in Europe, and overseas by India, Japan and Argentina, which tied their currencies to sterling, and by the Philippine Islands, which linked its currency to the dollar. During the 1920s, however, the spread of the gold exchange standard was largely a European phenomenon.

As it operated in the twenties, the gold exchange standard had a number of glaring weaknesses. The first concerned the manner in which some countries built up their reserves of convertible currencies. In the absence of a current account surplus in their balance of payments or of access to long-term borrowing, many countries acquired reserves by borrowing on short-term. Such reserves, however, were highly mobile and particularly vulnerable to changes in confidence. Faced with a foreign exchange crisis, a country was thus likely to find that its foreign reserves tended to disappear at the very moment they were most needed. The weakness of London as an international financial centre was another flaw in the system. Since exchange standard countries kept claims on sterling and dollars as reserves, both London and New York had to hold larger stocks of gold than were necessary simply to back their own trading transactions. New York had adequate gold reserves for this purpose, but London had not, and adequate stocks were never acquired. Indeed, London had difficulty preventing a loss of gold in the 1920s, largely because it was lending abroad more than its balance of payments permitted. One answer to the difficulty would have been to place a temporary ban on capital exports, but such a policy would have been inconsistent with London's claim to be a centre of international finance.

One further drawback to the gold exchange standard (and the one which eventually brought the system to an end) was that the most important countries on the exchange standard regarded their use of the system as a temporary expedient. Since the holding of foreign exchange instead of gold was considered by some of these countries as damaging to national prestige, transfer to the gold standard was for them only a matter of time. Of the countries on the exchange standard, France alone accounted for more than one-half of the total central bank foreign exchange holdings at the end of 1928.[1] When, in that year, France decided to take nothing but gold in settlement of the large surpluses accruing to her from the repatriation of French capital that followed the advent of financial stability at home and from the favourable trade balance generated by an undervalued franc, the end of the gold exchange standard was in sight.

Finally, because many central banks adopted policies of offsetting or neutralizing the domestic monetary effects of gold inflows and outflows, the traditional correctives to balance of payments disequilibria did not occur promptly and actively under the restored gold standard of the 1920s. While offsetting was not entirely absent from the pre-1913 system, it may often have been automatic rather than the result of deliberate official policy, as was frequently the case in the 1920s. Thus the United States pursued a policy of 'gold sterilization' during these years, the Federal Reserve Banks deliberately offsetting some of the country's gold receipts by reducing their holdings of government securities. A similar policy was followed by the Bank of England in the six years after the country's return to gold in 1925. In France, where post-war inflationary experiences may have influenced government policy, gold movements were also not allowed to have their traditional influence on domestic money supplies.

In summary, the gold standard of the late 1920s was little more than a façade. Gold disappeared from active domestic circulation, and the adoption of the gold bullion or gold exchange standards, with all their drawbacks, represented further attempts to economize on gold. Neutralization or offsetting of international influences on domestic money, incomes and prices was widespread so that gold standard methods of balance of payments equilibration were largely destroyed, but without being replaced by any alternative mechanism. Exchange rate adjustments had been carried out by many countries to take account of changed economic conditions, but some rates were clearly pegged at wrong levels. With both the prices and incomes and the exchange rate mechanisms of balance of payments adjustment inoperative, it was only the large injections of American capital into the world economy that prevented the system from collapsing.

THE ECONOMIC BOOM OF THE LATE TWENTIES

Despite its weaknesses, the restoration of the gold standard marked

---

[1] In 1926 and 1927 the Bank of France acquired the largest stock of foreign currencies—mainly sterling and dollars—of any central bank in the world. Its motive for doing this was to prevent an unwanted appreciation of the franc rather than to adopt the gold exchange standard. An undervalued franc was desired because it assisted French exports.

the beginning of a major industrial boom centred on Europe. After the economic collapse of 1920–1 and up to 1925, Europe suffered a relative decline in its economic standing in the world. Whereas European production did not regain pre-war levels until 1925, it increased by 20 per cent between 1913 and 1925 in Asia and Oceania, by 25 per cent in North America, and by even more in Latin America and Africa. But with the general improvements in economic and political conditions on the continent following the stabilization of inflated currencies and the settlement of the war debts, the stage was set for rapid economic development. Over the next five years the world experienced a construction boom based largely on the need for re-equipping the European countries. In the period after 1925, therefore, growth was much more vigorous in Europe than in the other continents.

The expansion of production that took place in the first post-war decade affected all sectors of the world economy. Food production increased by 10 per cent between 1913 and 1925, and grew by another 5 per cent by 1929 when compared with 1925. Over the same two periods, the production of raw materials grew by 25 per cent and 20 per cent, respectively, the much higher rate of growth in the latter period as compared with that for foodstuffs being the result of the high level of demand for raw materials generated by the European boom. In manufacturing, there was rapid growth in iron and steel production, engineering, and motor-car manufacture during these years. Shipbuilding was running at a high level, with motor-ships increasing as a proportion of total output from 14 per cent in 1923 to 44 per cent in 1929. The output of heavy chemicals grew by a third. Textile production expanded rapidly in Japan and certain other newly industrializing countries, but stagnated in Europe, although the output of artificial silk rose by 133 per cent between 1925 and 1929. By the end of 1929, however, there was much evidence that the boom had passed its peak. Stocks were accumulating and there was considerable surplus capacity evident in manufacturing production. The spread of commodity control schemes indicated the growing difficulties of primary producers. Indeed, in North and South America and in Oceania the peak of productive activity had been reached in 1928. To the effect of accumulating surpluses was added another adverse element—a tendency for imports of capital into these countries to decline. But it was when the outflow of gold from the United States reversed its direction as a result of the Wall Street boom that the true nature of the flaws in the international economy stood fully revealed.

SELECTED REFERENCES

Brown, W. A., Jr, *The International Gold Standard Re-interpreted* (New York, 1940).

Ellsworth, P. T., *The International Economy*, 3rd edn. (New York, 1964).

League of Nations, *The Course and Phases of the World Economic Depression* (Geneva, 1931).

League of Nations, *International Currency Experience* (1944).

Lewis, W. A., *Economic Survey 1919–1939* (London, 1949).

Royal Institute of International Affairs, *The Problem of International Investment* (London, 1937).

Triffin, R., *Our International Monetary System: Yesterday, Today, and Tomorrow* (New York, 1968).

United Nations, *International Capital Movements during the Inter-War Period* (New York, 1949).

Yeager, L. B., *International Monetary Relations* (New York, 1966).

Chapter 13

THE COLLAPSE OF THE GOLD STANDARD AND THE DISINTEGRATION OF THE INTERNATIONAL ECONOMY

The great depression of the 1930s had its origin in the United States. It is true that signs of declining production had already appeared at various times between late 1927 and mid-1929 in a number of countries, including Australia, Germany, Canada, and Argentina, and that commodity prices in the world as a whole began to fall in the second half of 1928. But the economic crisis did not become widespread and severe until after the industrial downturn in the United States in mid-1929 and the collapse of the security market in the October of that year. It is usual therefore to date the beginning of the world depression from the American stock market crash, for the subsequent collapse of the American economy not only intensified the economic difficulties of those countries already suffering from depression, but also brought about a rapid economic decline in most other parts of the world.

CRISIS IN AGRICULTURE

By the middle of 1929, many primary producers were experiencing financial stringency as falling export prices and declining capital inflows gave rise to acute balance of payments problems. Partly responsible for the decline in foreign lending, particularly by the United States, was the rise in interest rates in America during 1928 and 1929, as the stock market speculation intensified. Both the rise in interest rates and the prospect of earning speculative profits kept American funds at home and attracted substantial funds from abroad. This difficult international lending situation was further aggravated by the repatriation of French capital that followed the stabilization of the franc in 1928. The British money market, under pressure from these and other developments, was in no position to fill the gap created by the withdrawal of France and the United

States from foreign lending. The result was a general tightening of credit everywhere, and a lack of finance at the very time when the pressure of falling primary product prices was worsening the balance of payments position of the agricultural debtor countries.

When the American stock market crash finally came, it was followed by a virtual end to American lending abroad and a repatriation of American funds. As a result the economic difficulties in the agricultural debtor countries rapidly approached crisis proportions. In a desperate effort to balance their international accounts and obtain the foreign exchange needed to service their external debt these countries endeavoured to expand exports still further, which only added to the heavy surpluses of primary products thrown on the market. At the same time, the commodity control schemes, which had operated in the 1920s to maintain relatively high prices for some primary products, collapsed because of the lack of foreign capital to finance the withholding of stocks from the market, releasing a flood of accumulated stocks on to an already depressed market. The dominant feature in the deepening economic depression of 1930–1 therefore was the collapse of agricultural and raw materials prices, which strengthened the already existing depression in primary producing countries. In this rapidly deteriorating situation any improvement in the balance of payments of the debtor countries could only be temporary, since successful export expansion only depressed commodity prices further, thus making even greater export volume increases necessary in the future if the improved trade position was to be maintained. Furthermore, the restrictions on imports of manufactures imposed by some primary producers tended to spread the depression to industrial countries, which reduced their ability to import foodstuffs and raw materials. Moreover, the policy of expanding exports and restricting imports created a dangerous tariff situation. Thus a number of European governments reacted to the flood of cheap primary products from overseas by protecting peasant producers at home. Even more damaging for the debtor countries, however, was the Smoot–Hawley Act of June 1930, which substantially increased the American tariff level. Coming on top of the rapid decline in income and production in the United States, the tariff increase only served to reduce further American purchases of foreign goods.

The greatest number of the heavier duties included in the Smoot–Hawley Act was imposed upon manufactured articles, so that exports of European countries, and particularly of Germany, to the United States were most affected. Europe was, on balance, a large debtor to the United States, and in default of new loans being available or of ready access to the American market for its exports,

Europe had to seek to mobilize dollar resources by exporting to third countries earning dollar surpluses. But in 1929 and 1930 these raw material producing countries were in serious trouble, and it was not feasible to increase exports of manufactured goods to them. In any case, indirectly the American tariff made matters even worse for European countries, since many of the third countries retaliated by raising their duties, markedly on products of particular importance to the United States, chiefly manufactures, which were also their main imports from Europe.

The deepening of the economic crisis throughout the latter months of 1930, therefore, was due largely to the growing difficulties of the debtor countries, especially those among them which relied mainly upon exports of raw materials and foodstuffs. There were many other complications, perhaps the most important being the steady repatriation of French short-term balances and the imposition of the Smoot–Hawley tariff. The former was accompanied by a persistent drain of gold to France, that not only weakened the financial standing of sterling and the dollar, but also hindered the revival of large-scale long-term capital exports from the United States and Britain. The latter still further hampered the free exchange of commodities which alone could make possible the heavy payments on account of debt services.

FINANCIAL CRISIS IN EUROPE

Until the late spring of 1931, the depression in many respects appeared to be following the course of ordinary business slumps of the past. A number of primary producing countries had gone off gold, but no major international trading country had been involved, and the gold standard was still intact in western Europe and America. Moreover, there were some signs of a definite easing of the economic situation. Although the debtor countries continued to experience financial difficulties, all the changes in official bank rates were downward suggesting conditions of monetary ease in the chief creditor countries, and the accumulation of liquid capital funds. Steadiness or slight rises in seasonally adjusted figures of industrial production in Germany and the United States during the early months of the year even afforded some hope that the revival was not very far away.

This hesitant optimism was soon shattered by the outbreak of an international financial panic. It began in Austria, where a revaluation of the assets of the Credit-Anstalt of Vienna revealed the bank as insolvent. Despite quick action by the Austrian government to guarantee all deposits of the bank, this flaw in Austria's financial structure led to a heavy withdrawal of foreign short-term credits. This was stemmed only when loans by the Bank for International Settlements and the Bank of England to the Austrian government enabled it to guarantee the Credit-Anstalt's existing liabilities to foreign creditors, while, for their part, the foreign creditors of the bank undertook not to withdraw their advances for a period of two years.

Meanwhile the panic had spread to Germany, which had come under suspicion mainly because of its close commercial ties with Austria. A run on the Reichsbank developed, and attempts were made to end it by raising an international loan in support of the bank and by the announcement of a year's moratorium on reparations and war-debt payments. Withdrawals continued, however, and were accelerated when the disclosure of enormous losses by the North-German Wool Company, involving the shutdown of the Danat (Darmstädter und National Bank), converted a run mainly of Germany's foreign creditors into a flight from the mark into foreign exchange by Germans as well. The German government reacted to this new crisis by temporarily closing the banks and stock exchanges and by raising the discount rate from 7 to 10 per cent. Steps were also taken to introduce exchange controls and to place restrictions on bank payments. The international loan granted earlier was renewed, and, with the panic subsiding, the signing of a standstill agreement, immobilizing for six months the funds owed by Germans to foreign banks, consolidated the movement towards more normal conditions.

Britain, too, was now suffering a steady loss of gold, and throughout the summer months Bank Rate rose steadily until it reached $4\frac{1}{2}$ per cent at the end of July. Her difficulties were closely linked with those of Germany and Austria, for British bankers had advanced them a large amount of short-term credit which was rapidly becoming 'frozen' by the inability of the debtors to meet their foreign obligations. In Germany alone British short-term holdings amounting to $70m. were locked up under the standstill agreement. Unwanted attention was drawn to the volume of short-term claims in London by the publication on July 13th of the report of the MacMillan Committee, which revealed that London's short-term claims on foreigners, including those 'frozen' on the continent, amounted to only about £153m. whereas deposits and sterling bills held in London by foreigners amounted to some £407m. While there is nothing unusual about a banker having demand liabilities far in excess of immediately liquid assets, knowledge of the fact is inconvenient in time of crisis. Almost as damaging to Britain's international financial standing was the publication on July 31st of the May Committee report on the country's public finances. This revealed an impending deficit in the government budget and recommended cuts in government expenditure, as well as tax increases. In an age when the first canon of orthodox finance was a balanced budget, this report served only to convince foreigners of the waywardness of Britain.

With the withdrawal of short-term balances and the sale of British securities intensifying the strain on Britain's gold reserves, the Bank of England secured on August 1st a credit of £50m. from French and American banks. The run continued, however, despite the resignation of a Labour government unwilling to implement the May Committe recommendations on cuts in government expenditure, and the election of a coalition government pledged to put the economies into effect. On August 29th a further credit of £80m. was arranged, but the drain continued. The introduction by the government of a supplementary budget (September 10th) designed to balance the government's accounts failed to halt the run, which developed panic proportions following reports of an alleged naval mutiny at Invergordon on September 15th caused by proposed naval pay cuts. During the following three days, over £43m. was withdrawn from the London money market, making a total withdrawal of over £200m. in the preceding two months. On September 21st, therefore, legislation was passed suspending the Bank of England's obligation to sell gold. Bank Rate was raised to 6 per cent, and the Stock Exchange was closed for two days. Temporary restrictions were also imposed on all foreign exchange dealings.

Immediately after Britain suspended gold payments the pound sterling fell heavily in relation to currencies still on the gold standard.[1] In order not to be put at a trading disadvantage, many other countries quickly followed Britain off the gold standard. By the end of 1932, when thirty-two countries had suspended gold payments, Scandinavia, Portugal, Egypt, Latvia, most of Latin America, Japan, and all British territories and dominions except South Africa were also off gold. Only France and the United States among the big nations, and Belgium, the Netherlands and Switzerland among the smaller states remained on gold for the time being.

Britain's abandonment of gold in 1931 marks the beginning of the sterling area. A number of factors, both non-economic and economic in character, serve to explain why some countries sought to tie their currencies to the pound sterling. One non-economic consideration was the sentimental ties which existed between Great Britain and the other members of the British Commonwealth of Nations. Sentimen-

---

[1] Sterling fluctuated freely on the foreign exchange market up to April 1932 when the Exchange Equalization Account was established. Operated by the Bank of England under Treasury control, the Account's purchases and sales of sterling in the market were supposed to smooth out excessive short-run fluctuations. In particular, the Account operated to protect the domestic credit base from the effects of international short-term capital movements.

tality, although important, was definitely not the major reason for adherence to sterling, however, since a number of countries not members of the British Commonwealth joined the sterling area, and one of the more important British dominion countries, Canada, did not (Canada's economic ties being much stronger with the United States than with Great Britain). Fundamentally, three economic factors accounted for the willingness, and desire, of some countries to enter the sterling area. First, sterling was an important currency in the world, it was widely used, and its prestige was relatively high. As gold ceased to be an international standard of value, certain countries sought to tie their currencies to another standard of value, in this case the pound sterling. Second, Britain constituted the major market for the exports of many countries. These countries sought to promote a close currency link between Britain and themselves to protect this commercial relationship. In tying their currencies to sterling, the exporting countries were able to protect commodity prices and the competitive position of those producers dependent upon the British market. Third, a number of countries were debtors of Britain, and they accordingly fixed exchange rates between their currencies and the pound sterling in order to preserve a constancy of cost in servicing their debt obligations.

THE END OF THE GOLD STANDARD

After Britain left gold in September, 1931, the international panic centred on the United States, and nearly $2,000m. in gold left the country in the fiscal year ending June, 1932. To stop the drain the American monetary authorities were forced to adopt a savage deflationary policy to the accompaniment of rising unemployment and still deeper depression. When therefore the United States came to leave the gold standard, it was because of a deliberate act of policy aimed at relieving the desperate financial and economic conditions existing in the country rather than because of any external balance of payments difficulties as such. In its search for a policy of combatting the depression, the newly elected Roosevelt administration believed that a revival of the American economy could only follow from a general rise of domestic prices, and for this reason a number of government policies were initiated and aimed at bringing this about. Finally, on April 20, 1933, the United States suspended gold payments in the belief that if the price of gold was raised commodity prices would automatically rise in direct proportion, thus encouraging business expansion.

The abandonment of gold by America marked the virtual end of the gold standard. The next year or so saw the gradual polarization of countries around a few major industrial powers and the eventual emergence of a number of regional currency systems. At its peak this de-centralized currency mechanism consisted of the sterling area, centred on Britain, the dollar area, headed by the United States and composed chiefly of Latin American countries, the exchange control area of central and south-east Europe in which Germany played a leading role, the yen area dominated by Japan in the Far East, and the gold bloc in western Europe.[1] The remnant of the gold standard was not long in existence, however. As the depression continued, and balance of payments pressure mounted, doubts were entertained about the ability of the gold countries to resist devaluation. Consequently a speculative flight of capital developed in these countries, reinforced later by growing fears of war. Belgium was the first to go, devaluing its currency by 28 per cent in March, 1935. The other members of the gold bloc followed at the end of September, 1936. France devalued by 30 per cent and Switzerland by approximately the same amount. No definite margin of devaluation was set by the Dutch, but a newly established equalization fund kept the exchange rate against the dollar in the vicinity of 20 per cent below the old parity.

GROWTH OF RESTRICTIONS ON FINANCE AND TRADE

The widespread exchange and trade regulations which accompanied the collapse of the gold standard, while offering greater resistance to uncontrolled capital movements, prevented any return to a steady capital outflow from creditor to debtor countries during the 1930s. Exchange control hindered the repatriation of capital, while trade regulations eliminated a large portion of the multilateral trade through which returns on foreign direct investments as well as the service of foreign loans had been transferred. Moreover, the volume of lending inevitably declined during these years, and the direction of the loans became even more circumscribed than formerly because of the development of regional currency blocs. The loans floated in London were thus with few exceptions confined to members of the British Commonwealth and certain other countries within the sterling area. Countries with overseas territories confined themselves chiefly to supplying these territories with funds, and Japan invested largely in Manchuria. Other loans, based on geographical proximity or close economic relations, included those by the United States to Canada, by Sweden to other Scandinavian countries, and by Bel-

[1] A number of countries with diverse commercial and financial ties, such as Canada and Argentina, did not fit naturally into any one of these groups, and had to maintain an intermediate and precarious position in this system of group exchanges.

gium, the Netherlands and Switzerland to France. France and the other members of the gold bloc also recorded heavy capital exports during the middle and late 1930s. But only a small part of this capital went to debtor countries. The bulk represented capital seeking refuge in other creditor countries, particularly the United States, because of the menacing monetary instability in Europe, and after 1936, because of increasing political instability and the growing threat of war.

The depression of the 1930s and the financial difficulties associated with it also had a profound influence on commercial policy during these years. Confronted by a world-wide depression, no country escaped untouched, and there was consequently a reaction against international economic interdependence. Each national fell back on its own resources and pursued a policy of fostering internal recovery first and foremost. In such an atmosphere, the regulation of foreign trade and financial transactions was a natural and inevitable development. Broadly speaking, these controls took two main forms: those aimed directly at controlling the making of payments between countries, and those affecting in the first instance the movements of individual commodities between countries. The former group included exchange controls and all the various blends of clearing and payments agreements associated with it; the latter, tariffs, import quotas, prohibitions, and the like. While the distinction between the two types of trade controls is not completely clear cut, for in operation they overlapped at every stage, it does provide us with convenient headings under which to discuss the developments in commercial policy during the 1930s.

Exchange Control

Although any form of government intervention that affects the level of foreign exchange rates is, in a broad sense, exchange control, the narrower and more common interpretation of the term refers to various forms of official restrictions upon private transactions in foreign exchange. Where such restrictions were introduced during our period, governments, often through central banks, assumed control of foreign exchange by requiring exporters to surrender the foreign money received from sales abroad and by requiring importers to purchase foreign exchange from authorized sources, with both the buying and selling of foreign exchange taking place at official rates fixed arbitrarily by the government. Whereas few countries succeeded in passing through the depression without resort to some exchange restrictions, if only for a short period, severe and thoroughgoing systems of control were necessary in debtor countries faced with difficult payments problems and, sometimes, the danger of a simultaneous flight of both domestic and foreign capital.

In these countries, of which Germany is a leading example, the government attempted to control all transactions that affected the demand for and supply of foreign exchange. Inevitably the system of control grew more complex, as it became necessary to implement the overall regulations with a host of detailed provisions designed to eliminate evasion.

The increasing severity and persistence of exchange control policies in the 1930s was partly the result of a broadening in the objectives supporting its introduction and retention in the countries concerned. While the original object of exchange control was to curb the outflow of capital associated with the financial crises of the early thirties, with the deepening of the depression the objectives of such a policy soon multiplied. Thus the insulation given to an economy by exchange control afforded an opportunity to introduce domestic expansionary measures to raise incomes and increase employment. Exchange control was also necessary if a country wished to maintain an official rate of exchange higher than that dictated by the free interplay of market forces, either because it feared exchange depreciation would lead to inflation, or because depreciation would lead to subsequent increases in the burden of debt service.[1] It could also be used to protect domestic industries, since such a policy enabled a country to allocate foreign exchange for imports on a product by product basis, so that the exclusion, or carefully controlled admission, of particular imports brought about by the lack of foreign exchange also served to protect the home market for domestic producers. Finally, exchange control was used to acquire revenue for the government. By setting a higher rate (or rates) for selling than for buying foreign exchange, the difference accrued to the government as profit. A number of countries (e.g. Argentina and Chile) employed exchange control for this purpose, amongst others.

Bilateral Trading Agreements

As a matter of historical fact, however, the main change of emphasis that occurred in the use of exchange control during these years related to the control of trade. The shortage of foreign currency which made exchange control necessary was not merely general, but tended to be relatively greater for some currencies than for others. Moreover, the fact that some currencies were relatively more scarce than others led to bilateralism, that is, to a deliberate balancing of accounts between pairs of trading countries. Bilateral arrangements

[1] Since foreign loans are ordinarily expressed in the currency of the lending country, a rise in the exchange rate for the lender's currency increases the amount of domestic money that the debtor country must pay out to acquire the lender's currency necessary to service the foreign debt.

had advantages other than just that of overcoming the trading difficulties associated with shortages of foreign currencies. They were attractive in situations where the opportunities for trade discrimination afforded by exchange control enabled one country to gain from its monopoly control of the trade of other, often smaller, countries. Germany in particular was able to take advantage of this sort of situation in its trade with eastern and central European countries in the 1930s. They could also be used to settle the problem of blocked balances held by exchange control countries. These arrangements, however, included one significant new element. Whereas the bilateral trading arrangements for dealing with problems other than those of blocked balances almost invariably involved only exchange control countries, the problem of blocked balances often involved free exchange market countries as well.

What all these bilateral arrangements had in common was that they were agreements between pairs of trading countries designed to keep trade at a relatively high volume, but to do so without the accumulation of soft currencies, which could not be used to settle hard currency deficits, and without incurring deficits payable in hard currencies. In other words, these agreements sought to reduce the need for settlement in gold or scarce foreign exchange. Such agreements took three major forms: (*a*) private compensation agreements, (*b*) clearing agreements, and (*c*) payments agreements.

Compensation agreements, the simplest of the new trading devices, were merely a modern form of the age-old principle of barter. Obviously, no currency transactions were necessary when two countries could agree to an exchange of goods of equal value. Where governments were involved in such barter deals, the arrangements were described as a compensation agreement. More often, however, the the negotiations were conducted by private individuals or firms in which case the term private compensation was used to describe the transaction. A considerable volume of German trade came under these compensation deals in 1932 and 1933, including the exchange of some 9 million marks worth of German coal for Brazilian coffee, and the exchange of German fertilizer for Egyptian cotton. In some countries the growth of these trading practices was encouraged by the setting up of organizations to act as middlemen in these barter deals. The Polish Company for Compensation Trade, which began operations in November, 1932, was one of the more important of these organizations. In Germany, on the other hand, chambers of commerce established clearing information bureaux for this purpose, and in Copenhagen five importing firms organized in 1934 the Association for Commodity Exchange to arrange private compensation transactions with foreign firms.

Private compensation agreements, even when assisted by barter agencies, involved enormous difficulties, since they required the offsetting of individual exports and imports in each transaction. Clearing agreements, which were also entered into during these years, avoided these difficulties by providing a broader and more general procedure for offsetting claims. Under such arrangements each country agreed to establish, usually in its central bank, an account through which all payments for imports and exports were to be cleared. For example, under the German clearing arrangement with Yugoslavia, German importers of Yugoslavian goods would pay marks into an account at the Reichsbank, where they were credited to the account of the Yugoslav clearing agency. German exporters to Yugoslavia were then paid marks from this fund, debited to the Yugoslav account. In Belgrade, the opposite process took place. Yugoslav importers made payments into the clearing account in dinars and exporters received dinars from the account.

As with many developments in the exchange control field during these years, the Germans led the way with clearing agreements. The first was signed in 1932 with Hungary, and by 1937 Germany had negotiated clearing agreements with every European country except Britain and Albania, as well as with Argentina, Chile, Uruguay, and Colombia. The principal feature of these clearing procedures was that they covered not only payments arising from merchandise trade, but also various other payments, including the transfer of interest and dividends, travel expenditures, shipping services, remittances, and so on. In each case exchange clearing provided a way of settling individual transactions between two countries in terms of their respective domestic currencies. The necessity of dealing in foreign exchange was eliminated. Of course, strict bilateral balancing of accounts was very rare. Indeed, as Germany soon discovered, a lack of balance in its trade with other exchange control countries provided a means whereby it could take advantage of its buyer's position to exploit countries largely dependent on Germany for their export market.

If, for example, Yugoslavian exports to Germany exceeded its imports from that country, then in Yugoslavia outpayments of the clearing fund must exceed inpayments if the exporters were to be paid. But this could not occur automatically without limit, since the Yugoslavian currency in the clearing account was limited in amount. In this situation, either the Yugoslavian exporters had to wait for payment—that is, they had to wait until the clearing account favouring Germany had been built up again by importers making purchases in Germany—or the Yugoslavian central bank had to advance credit to the clearing account to enable it to pay the exporters. In either case Germany borrowed (via an import surplus) from Yugoslavia. During the 1930s Germany effectively exploited the bilateral clearing system to borrow from the poorer countries of south-eastern Europe in this way. She purchased large quantities of foodstuffs and raw materials from Bulgaria, Hungary, Rumania, and Yugoslavia amongst others, paying high prices in terms of the local currency, while the powerful exporting interests in these countries, succeeded in getting their governments to finance their export surpluses. Thus large claims on Germany were built up which could be used only as Germany reluctantly made goods available from its rearmament programme, at prices dictated by Germany.

Payments agreements differed from clearing agreements chiefly in that they covered a wider range of transactions and used the normal method of payment over the foreign exchanges rather than special clearing accounts. In addition, a payments agreement often linked an exchange control country with a free exchange country, whereas clearing agreements were negotiated only between exchange control countries. Consequently, most of the payments agreements in force in the summer of 1939 were between free exchange countries of western Europe, on the one hand, and exchange control countries in central and south-eastern Europe or Latin America on the other.

The chief reason for free exchange countries becoming involved in bilateral agreements during these years was the difficulty of realizing frozen debt and service payments in exchange control countries. A major item of frozen debt arose out of the standstill agreements negotiated during the financial crisis of 1931. Britain had been deeply involved in these developments and it is not surprising therefore to find that the first creditor country to make use of payments agreements in its relations with debtor countries was the United Kingdom. Thus the Anglo-German Agreement of November, 1934, is generally regarded as the model of subsequent payments agreements, although the British government had first employed the payments principle in the Runciman–Roca Agreement of May, 1933, with Argentina. The Anglo–German agreement limited Germany's imports from Britain in any month to 55 per cent of the value of its exports to Britain during the last month but one. Apart from a sum earmarked at the beginning to clear existing commercial debts, the surplus 45 per cent was partly used to service the Dawes and Young loans in Britain and to cover other charges, including the payment of freight expenses in sterling, the remainder being placed at the free disposal of the Reichsbank.

Confined to preventing capital movements, exchange control need not result in restrictions on trade, discrimination between countries, or protection of particular producers. Indeed, it was currency overvaluation rather than exchange control as such that was ultimately responsible for the contraction of trade that took place during the 1930s. Once exchange control is applied in support of currency overvaluation, payments made in the currencies of control countries lead inevitably toward the accumulation of blocked balances. Bilateral trading arrangements, which are themselves only instruments of policy, then become necessary to liquidate these frozen claims. In the process trade is distorted and discrimination against countries inevitably practised. It is then but a short step from this type of discrimination to discrimination with a view to economic domination. Throughout the process, however, exchange control and bilateral trading arrangements are essentially instruments or tools of policy.

Whatever the reason for adopting a policy of exchange control, however, its use led inevitably to a loss of world real income, because by distorting trade from its normal channels into bilateral grooves, the resultant trade represented less gain in welfare terms to its participants than trade carried out under full multilateral conditions. Yet given that the setting of equilibrium exchange rates and the liberalizing of international payments was impossible in the depressed conditions of the 1930s, bilateral trading arrangements did make possible trade in specialized commodities that would not otherwise have taken place. Both partners to clearing payments agreements gained. Exports to other exchange control countries increased, despite the economic difficulties of the early 1930s, and these additional exports made it possible to acquire useful imports. Moreover, exchange clearing made possible the liquidation of frozen balances, and permitted the maintenance of debt service owed to creditor countries.

Tariffs and Other Restrictions on Trade

Despite the spread of exchange control, tariffs remained the greatest single obstacle to the international movement of goods in the thirties. The upward movement of tariffs, which characterized the early depression years, continued well into the middle thirties, when there was some relaxation of restrictions from late 1936 onwards. But in 1938 the decline in world trade and a fall in primary product prices led to a resumption of the upward movement. By the end of the 1930s, therefore, close to half the world's trade was restricted by tariffs alone.

Britain's conversion to whole-hearted protectionism represents the outstanding single development in the tariff history of the period In practice, Britain was still predominantly free trading at the beginning of the thirties, for out of £1,030m. of imports, £138m. paid revenue duties, and only £13m. were subject to McKenna or Safeguarding Act duties. But the situation changed radically with the passing of the Import Duties Act of March, 1932. This Act imposed a general duty of 10 per cent *ad valorem* on all imports into the United Kingdom, except Empire goods and those named on a free list, which included most foodstuffs and raw materials. The Act also set up an Import Duties Advisory Committee to recommend additional duties. In April a 33⅓ per cent duty was placed on most kinds of steel; the general level of duties on manufactured goods was raised to 20 per cent, on luxury goods to 24–30 per cent, and on a few items (including some chemicals) to 33⅓ per cent. With a few exceptions, British Empire products again received exemption from these charges.

The other significant feature of commercial policy in these years was the spread of import quotas and other forms of quantitative controls over trade. France was the first country to adopt import quotas on a wide scale as a means of combatting the depression, and she was quickly followed by a number of other countries. By the end of 1932 eleven countries had fully fledged quota or licensing systems. Despite its further spread, import quotas remained primarily a European instrument of trade control. At the beginning of 1939, twenty-eight countries, nineteen of them European, operated quota or licensing systems applying to a substantial range of commodities.

There were various reasons for adopting quantitative import controls. They could be used to protect domestic manufacturing and, perhaps even more importantly, to protect domestic agriculture from the severe overseas competition that followed the violent fall in primary product prices in the early thirties. Import quotas were also of vital importance to the gold bloc countries after the abandonment of the gold standard by Britain and the United States. With their currencies becoming overvalued in the face of currency depreciation elsewhere, these countries experienced severe balance of payments pressures. Denied the use of exchange control by their adherence to the gold standard, they imposed severe control on imports to bring their foreign trade into balance. Moreover, import quotas often formed part of national recovery programmes. In 1933, for example, the United Kingdom introduced quotas on agricultural products in support of national marketing schemes aimed at reviving British agriculture and in favour of Empire producers. Import quotas were also used for purposes of retaliation and commercial bargaining.

Import quotas were even more damaging to international trade than tariffs, since a quota directly limits the level of permissible imports and thus operates independently of the price mechanism. Thus while it is always possible for the foreign exporter to beat the tariff by lowering his price sufficiently to make him competitive with domestic producers even when the tariff is added to his price, the quota limits the importation of a commodity to a fixed amount irrespective of supply and demand conditions (or prices) in the domestic or foreign markets. But while appreciating the additional restrictions placed on foreign trade by import quotas as compared with tariffs, the extraordinary difficulties of the 1930s should always be kept in mind when considering the welfare implications of these additional controls on international exchange. In the depression years tariffs proved completely inadequate in protecting domestic industry, whether agriculture or manufacturing, from distress sales of foreign goods induced by serious deflationary pressures abroad. Only import quotas could ensure the strict limitation of these imports, thus reducing the damage they inflicted on domestic production and employment. Moreover, where balance of payments difficulties called for the reduction of a country's imports, import quotas or the licensing of imports provided the only certain way of confining the total value of imports within predetermined limits. It is not surprising, therefore, to find that import licensing and other forms of quantitative restrictions on imports were often used in connection with systems of exchange control.

INTERNATIONAL FINANCIAL CO-OPERATION

By the middle of 1932 the opinion was widespread that international action was necessary to combat the breakdown of international trade and finance and to promote economic recovery. Consequently a World Economic Conference was held in London in June, 1933, to discuss among other things the question of currency stabilization. However, shortly before the meeting was convened, the dollar went off gold and was allowed to fluctuate freely without any immediate hope of stabilization. With the future of the dollar uncertain, international agreement on currency stabilization was impossible, and the Conference was adjourned without having achieved any worthwhile success.

The need for some measure of international financial co-operation arose again in 1936, when the abandonment of the gold standard by the gold block countries created problems for those countries operating exchange stabilization funds. Meanwhile all major obstacles to an agreement between the major financial powers in the world had been removed by the final collapse of the remnants of the gold standard and by the change in the American government's attitude to international currency stability following the stabilization of the dollar in 1934. The result was the Tripartite Monetary Agreement between France, Britain and the United States, which was concluded just before the French devaluation in September, 1936, and which was later joined by Belgium, Holland and Switzerland. While it would be a mistake to exaggerate the concrete accomplishments of this Agreement, which were largely in the field of technical co-operation, it was important, nevertheless, because it endorsed the principle of managed exchange rates which had come to replace the free exchange rates associated with the gold standard, and because it involved recognition of the need for effective international co-operation in a managed exchange rate system. In this sense the Tripartite Monetary Agreement of 1936 was a forerunner of the International Monetary Fund.

REGIONAL ECONOMIC CO-OPERATION

The failure to achieve international agreement on matters of trade and finance in the early 1930s led many nations to consider the alternative possibility of trade liberalizing agreements on a regional basis. An early example of this type of economic co-operation was that between the Danubian agricultural countries, Hungary, Romania, Yugoslavia and Bulgaria, which in the early thirties obtained tariff preferences for their chief exports in a number of individually negotiated bilateral agreements with European industrial countries. The regional economic pact between Italy, Austria and Hungary brought about by the Rome Agreements of 1934, and the series of agreements reached in the thirties between the 'Oslo Group' of nations, comprising Denmark, Sweden, Norway, Finland, the Netherlands, Belgium and Luxembourg, provide further examples of these attempts at regional economic co-operation. In the Americas the Pan American Conference attempted to deal with the problem of trade restrictions in the western hemisphere. The United States concluded a number of reciprocal trade agreements with Latin American countries in the years before 1939, and a number of trade liberalizing agreements were also concluded between pairs of Latin American countries. Owing to their relative importance in Latin American trade, even more such agreements were negotiated with European counties. Although, on balance, these regional agreements were probably trade diverting rather than trade creating in their effect on the international exchange of goods and services, they did help to revive business confidence and reverse the trend towards economic nationalism.

By far the most important regional economic pact of these years was the establishment of a general preferential system within the

British Commonwealth as a result of the Ottawa agreements of 1932. Under these arrangements Commonwealth countries agreed to extend to each other increased import preference. As for tariff reductions within the Empire, the results were meagre. What was achieved by way of increased trade within the Commonwealth was achieved not by the reduction of tariffs within the Empire but by raising them to those countries outside it. Moreover, although imperial preference increased Britain's share in the trade of Empire countries, it also deflected foreign competition into other markets where Britain's position was less favourable. The drawbacks to Britain of this changed pattern of trade only became apparent in the period after the end of World War II.

In colonial territories the open door policy formerly favoured by the chief colonial powers was gradually abandoned with the onset of the depression and the growing impact of Japanese competition in colonial areas in the Far East and elsewhere after 1931. Complete tariff assimilation between the mother country and its colonies constituted the policy pursued by France, the United States and Japan in relation to certain of their colonies. On the other hand, within the British, French (non-assimilated colonies), Portuguese, Spanish and Italian empires, tariff preferences were extensively employed. At the same time, import quotas and foreign exchange regulations provided convenient openings for discrimination in favour of intra-imperial trade.

INTERNATIONAL COMMODITY CONTROL SCHEMES

International commodity schemes constituted practically the only significant multilateral economic agreements concluded in the thirties. These intergovernmental agreements, between leading producing countries, or between the producing and leading importing countries as well, were concerned with matters relating to the production and marketing of certain primary products. Where only producers were involved, the object of these agreements was to control production and exportation so as to stabilize prices, or even to raise them. Some of these international agreements evolved from private cartels set up in the twenties to control the prices of certain products, such as rubber, tea, and tin, while others grew out of the attempts of individual governments to deal with the problem of surplus production and unstable prices. Cases in which international commodity agreements evolved through government sponsorship included coffee, sugar and wheat.

It was the collapse of these earlier control schemes and the depressed prices of primary products during the early thirties which led to the establishment of a number of international commodity agreements in the years from 1931 onwards. These included agreements covering tin and sugar (1931), tea and wheat (1933), rubber (1934) and copper (1936). All of these schemes covered 80–90 per cent, or even more, of exportable production, and, with the partial exception of the tin scheme, all relied on quantitative control of production. Pricing policy was largely one of opportunism or expediency. Overall, however, these schemes did not play an important part in the history of primary production during the thirties. Their influence was decisive only for tea, tin, and rubber, and they had some influence on the production and export of sugar and copper. Even if these achievements were confined to a limited field, however, the mere fact that control schemes were set up for so many products, and that their marketing was sufficiently well organized to enable the schemes to operate reasonably efficiently is important as a pointer to what might have been achieved had a more vigorous international economic policy been fostered by the major trading powers.

Because the interwar period with its falling prices and substantial excess capacity in many lines proved especially favourable for their development, private and government sponsored agreements between normally competitive firms located in two or more countries became more frequent in manufacturing industry. Thus at the outbreak of World War II, an American estimate placed the number of international cartels at 179, of which 133 involved manufactured and semi-manufactured goods, including steel, chemicals, electrical products, oil and aluminium. These cartels had as their central objective the reduction of competition so as to stabilize prices and, where possible, enjoy monopoly profits. They were also used occasionally as instruments of government policy. This happened in Germany in the 1930s, when various cartels dominated by German producers were used by the Nazi government to maintain German exports at the expense of other countries, and to assure the German economy of supplies of foreign currency.

Like all monopolies, cartels tended to restrict the volume of world trade and divert its channels. In particular, international cartellization tended to divide the world into spheres of commercial influence by allocating to the nationals of certain countries exclusive selling rights in certain territories. Thus in the cartel arrangements of the 1930s, American firms were normally assigned the American market, sometimes the whole of North America and, on occasion, part of Latin America. British firms laid special claim to Empire territory, while the growing strength of German firms in a number of cartels won them increasingly large areas of Europe as their exclusive market. It is perhaps in those situations where markets were allocated amongst the members of the cartel that the reduction of trade was most apparent, for example, where the United States market became the exclusive preserve of American firms, for under these arrangements potential trade is simply stopped at its source.

CONCLUSION

The world-wide depression of the 1930s, and the collapse of the gold standard which accompanied its onset in the early years of that decade, were responsible for the spread of financial and trade practices which severely restricted the exchange of goods between countries. Even when devices such as bilateral trading agreements promoted trade flows between countries which might not otherwise have taken place, the benefits derived from this increase in the volume of international trade were offset by the loss of welfare to its participants consequent upon the trade being conducted through bilateral rather than multilateral channels. Distortions of trading patterns and consequent loss of welfare were also characteristic of those regional economic blocs operating preferential trading arrangements. The net outcome of all these developments was a substantial slowing up in the growth of international trade during the interwar years which is examined in detail in the next chapter.

SELECTED REFERENCES

Ellsworth, P. T., *The International Economy*, 3rd edn. (New York, 1964).
Gordon M. S., *Barriers to World Trade* (New York, 1941).
League of Nations, *International Currency Experience* (Geneva, 1944).
Lewis, W. A., *Economic Survey 1919–1939* (London, 1949).
Rowe, J. W. F., *Primary Commodities in International Trade* (Cambridge, 1965).
United Nations, Dept. of Economic Affairs, *International Cartels* (New York, 1947).
Yeager, L. B., *International Monetary Relations* (New York, 1966).

Chapter 14

INTERNATIONAL TRADE DURING THE INTERWAR PERIOD

THE GROWTH OF WORLD TRADE IN THE INTERWAR YEARS

Between the two wars there was a sharp break in the expansion of world trade. Although the volume of foreign trade continued to grow, the rate of growth of total trade per decade declined from an average of almost 40 per cent in the period 1881–1913 to 14 per cent in the period 1913–37. The decline in *per capita* trade, from a decadal average of 34 per cent in the period 1881–1913 to 3 per cent in 1913–37, was even more striking. Given the economic difficulties of the interwar period, this decline in world trade is not surprising. What was disconcerting about foreign trade developments during these years, however, was that the retardation in the rate of growth of world trade was clearly more marked than that in the rate of growth of world product, whether measured on a total or *per capita* basis. Thus over the period 1913–37 the total product of thirteen developed countries grew 22 per cent and increased *per capita* 13 per cent compared with an increase of almost 11 per cent in total trade and a decrease of slightly more than 3 per cent in *per capita* trade.[1]

This tendency for output to grow faster than trade was not uniformly maintained throughout the interwar years, however. Largely on account of the expansion in the United States, industrial production emerged from the war less battered than trade. In the twenties, however, trade revived rapidly and was probably growing slightly faster than world output towards the end of the decade. This improvement in trade relative to output was maintained in the early years of the thirties when the loss in the volume of international trade because of the depression was less than the decline in world industrial output. But with recovery world production revived more rapidly than world trade and by 1937 industrial production had grown to

[1] See S. Kuznets, 'Quantitative Aspects of the Economic Growth of Nations: X—Levels and Structure of Foreign Trade: Long-term Trends', op. cit., Table 1, pp. 4–6. The thirteen countries covered by the statistics are the United Kingdom, America, France, Germany, Belgium, Denmark, Norway, Sweden, Canada, Japan, Italy, Switzerland, and the Netherlands.

104 per cent of the 1929 figure, whereas the quantum of world trade registered only 97 per cent.

These trends in world output and world trade suggest that the foreign trade proportion, that is, the ratio of world trade to world product, declined during the interwar period, despite an increase in the number of trading nations, largely brought about by the post-war political settlement in Europe. During the war years the world foreign trade proportion probably fell, but it had recovered to approximately the 1913 level by the later twenties, following the rapid post-war expansion of foreign trade, particularly that of Europe. It was the depression of the 1930s and World War II that sharply reduced the volume of foreign trade and the world trade proportion, so that by the late 1940s and early 1950s it was probably at its lowest since 1913.

THE DIRECTION OF WORLD TRADE BETWEEN THE WARS

World War I interrupted the customary flow of trade between continents and nations, bringing about a decrease in Europe's trade and an increase in that of the United States. The decline in Europe's share of total world trade continued during the interwar years, despite some recovery in the 1930s when the depression checked the expansion of American trade. Consequently, by 1937 Europe was responsible for just over half of world trade compared with almost two-thirds in 1913 (see Table 14). This decline in Europe's importance in world trade came about for various reasons. It was due

TABLE 14. *Distribution of World Trade by Geographic Regions, 1913–37*

	1913		Total	1928		Total	1937		Total
Region	Exports	Imports	trade	Exports	Imports	trade	Exports	Imports	trade
Europe[1]	58·9	65·1	62·0	48·0	56·2	52·1	47·0	55·8	51·4
North America[2]	14·8	11·5	13·2	19·8	15·2	17·5	17·1	13·9	15·5
Latin America[3]	8·3	7·0	7·6	9·8	7·6	8·7	10·2	7·2	8·7
Asia	11·8	10·4	11·1	15·5	13·8	14·6	16·9	14·1	15·5
Africa	3·7	3·6	3·7	4·0	4·6	4·3	5·3	6·2	5·7
Oceania	2·5	2·4	2·4	2·9	2·6	2·8	3·5	2·8	3·2
World	100·0	100·0	100·0	100·0	100·0	100·0	100·0	100·0	100·0

Notes: [1] Including Russia; [2] Canada and the United States; [3] Central and South America, including all colonial territories in the Western hemisphere.
Source: P. Lamartine Yates, *Forty Years of Foreign Trade* (London, 1955), Tables 6 and 7, pp. 32–3.

partly to the fall in the trade share of the Soviet Union, which accounted for close to 4 per cent of total world trade in 1913, but only some 1·5 per cent in the late 1920s and around 1 per cent in the late 1930s. It also reflected the continued growth in the importance of the North American continent in world trade, whose share in 1937 was larger than it had been in 1913 despite the set-back of the 1930s. An even more important cause of the shift in relative shares over the period was the continuous increase in the proportion of world trade of the largely underdeveloped regions of Asia, Africa, and Oceania. In 1913 they accounted for 17 per cent of world trade; by 1937 their combined share had grown to almost a quarter of the total trade.

The same trade picture is examined from a somewhat different angle in Table 15, which shows the changing shares of developed and underdeveloped countries in world trade during the period 1913–37, measured in constant prices and excluding the Soviet Union. Here it can be seen that the decline in Europe's share in world trade during the interwar years is accounted for solely by the decline in the share of Industrial Europe, since Other Europe's share was slightly larger in 1937 than it had been in 1913. The pattern for North America to be found in Table 14 is repeated here, with the region's share in total trade growing in the period up to 1928 and then declining in the 1930s. The trade of Japan and the newly industrializing areas of South Africa and Oceania expanded continuously as a proportion of world trade, as did the share of the Rest of the World, although the trade improvement experienced by the latter group of countries was largely concentrated in the period between 1913 and 1928.

Despite the various changes in the direction of world trade that occurred during the interwar years, the trade conducted between non-European nations only rose from just under a quarter

TABLE 15. *Shares of Developed and Underdeveloped Countries in World Trade, 1913–37*

Constant Prices (excluding the U.S.S.R.)

	Industrial Europe	U.S.A. and Canada	Oceania, South Africa, Japan	Others	Of which Other Europe	Rest of world
1913	54·4	14·5	5·4	25·7	5·7	20·0
1928	43·1	18·8	6·9	31·2	7·9	23·3
1937	43·8	16·5	9·5	30·2	6·3	23·9

Source: Kuznets, op. cit,. Table 2, p. 11.

to just over a quarter of the total world trade, and Europe still dominated the trade picture in 1938 as it had done before 1913 (see Table
16). Whereas intra-European trade fell substantially from 40
per cent of the total world trade in imports in 1913 to 29 per cent
in 1938, this fall was largely offset by an increase in trade between
European and non-European countries. In other words, the economic difficulties of the interwar years while restricting trade within
Europe tended at the same time to sustain and even encourage trade
between Europe and the rest of the world.

THE CHANGING COMPOSITION OF WORLD TRADE

The broad nature of the changes in the commodity structure of world
trade during the interwar period is illustrated in Table 17 and diagram 14, which describe the trends in the regional shares in world
trade in primary products and manufactures. As far as the world
trade in primary products is concerned, the most striking development during these years was the rapid growth of the export share of
the underdeveloped countries, from just over a third of the total in
1913 to around half in 1937. Taken together, these countries exported the whole range of tropical and temperate foodstuffs, as well as
all the non-ferrous metals and petroleum, the demand for which
was growing rapidly at this time. Even more striking, however,
was the heavy decline in Europe's share of the world export trade
in manufactures, from over four-fifths of the total trade in 1913
to approximately two-thirds in 1937. Within the total European
share, the United Kingdom's share continued the decline which had
begun well before 1913, but the decline in that of continental Europe
was a completely new trend which became apparent only after 1913.
Offsetting the falling European share were increases in the shares of
this trade originating in North America and Asia, chiefly Japan.

TABLE 16. *Percentage Distribution of World Trade in Imports, 1913–
38*

| | Per cent | |
	1913	1938
World trade	100	100
Intra-European trade	40	29
Imports to Europe from Non-European countries	22	27
Imports to Non-European from Europe	15	17
Trade among Non-European countries	23	27

Source: W. S. and E. S. Woytinsky, *World Commerce and Governments* (New
York, 1955), pp. 71, 80.

H

TABLE 17a. *Trade in Primary Products: Regional Shares, 1913–37*

	Per cent					
	1913		1928		1937	
Region	Imports	Exports	Imports	Exports	Imports	Exports
U.K. and Ireland	19·0	6·2	19·9	4·8	22·9	4·8
N.W. Europe[1]	43·1	25·2	34·2	14·5	33·7	15·6
Other Europe	12·3	14·7	10·5	16·0	8·5	13·7
U.S. and Canada	11·3	17·3	16·7	20·0	15·8	15·5
Underdeveloped and rest of world	14·3	36·6	18·7	44·7	19·1	50·4
World	100·0	100·0	100·0	100·0	100·0	100·0

As for the import trade in manufactures, the tendency for the share of the industrialized countries in this trade to decline was associated with an extension of the share going to the non-industrialized countries of the world.

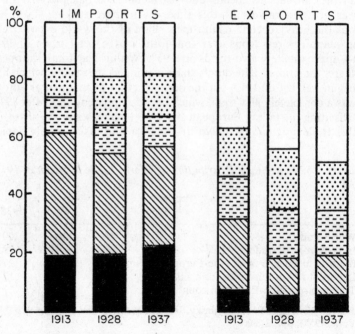

Diagram 14: Regional Shares in Total World Trade, 1913–37

(a) Primary Products

TABLE 17b. *Trade in Manufactures: Regional Shares, 1913–37*

Region	1913 Imports	1913 Exports	1928 Imports	1928 Exports	1937 Imports	1937 Exports
U.K. and Ireland	8·2	25·3	9·1	21·8	8·8	19·5
N.W. Europe[1]	24·4	47·9	17·5	40·9	17·5	41·8
Other Europe	15·4	8·3	15·7	4·6	13·3	5·8
U.S. and Canada	12·1	10·6	12·8	19·2	10·6	19·7
Underdeveloped and rest of world	39·9	7·9	44·9	13·5	49·8	13·2
World	100·0	100·0	100·0	100·0	100·0	100·0

(Per cent)

Note: [1] Includes Finland, Sweden, Norway, Denmark, Germany, Belgium, Netherlands, France, Switzerland, and Austria.
Source: Yates, op. cit., Tables 19, 21, 23 and 25,

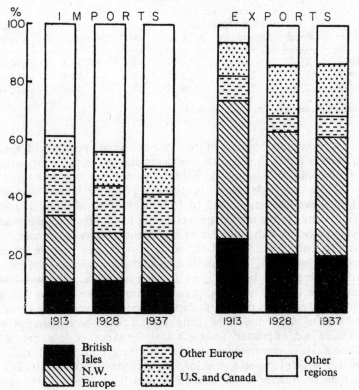

(b) Manufactures

Despite these changes in the commodity structure of world trade, the export trade of developed countries continued to be dominated by manufactures, while their import trade consisted largely of primary products. The reverse, of course, was still the case for the under-developed countries which, apart from Japan and India, continued to export mainly primary products. Moreover, within the developed countries, primary products continued to be a larger proportion of the exports and a smaller fraction of the imports of the United States and Canada than for the United Kingdom and Ireland and the other industrial countries of north-west Europe. Finally, the stability in the share of primary products in world trade noted earlier for the period before 1913 was maintained throughout the inter-war years (see Table 18).

TABLE 18. *Shares of Commodity Groups in World Exports, 1913–37* (*actual values*)

		Per cent				
		Primary products				
		Raw materials				Total
Year	Food	Agriculture	Minerals	Total	Manufactures	trade
1913	27·0	22·7	14·0	63·7	36·3	100·0
1927	24·3	21·5	15·8	61·6	38·4	100·0
1937	23·0	21·0	19·5	63·5	36·5	100·0

Source: Yates, op. cit., Table 16, p. 44.

This continued stability of the share of primary products in world trade was maintained despite significant changes in the composition of the commodity group. As Table 16 shows, the food and agricultural raw materials shares in primary products exports declined throughout the period 1913 to 1937, while that of minerals rose. This decline in the relative importance of foodstuffs in foreign trade was associated with a number of significant changes in the composition of world trade in food during these years. The trade in certain tropical foodstuffs, particularly cocoa, coffee, bananas and citrus fruits, increased substantially in the interwar years, both in volume and value terms. On the other hand, there was the relative stagnation of trade in certain non-tropical foodstuffs, especially cereals, which was partly due to the rising self-sufficiency of western Europe in these lines of primary production. In the export of dairy products New Zealand benefited immensely from the growing world trade in butter, which reached a peak of 615,000 tons in 1934–8. By 1937 it supplied a quarter of the world's exports. The volume of the meat trade also expanded during the 1920s, and suffered only a minor fall in the 1930s when, because of imperial preference and the fact that Britain took between three to four-fifths of the world's exports of meat, Australia and New Zealand grew at the expense of Argentina and Uruguay. Finally, Africa emerged as a major supplier of tropical foodstuffs, particularly cocoa, oilseeds and fats, a development which took place at the expense of traditional Latin American exports.

The depressed group of agricultural raw materials during these years included cotton, silk, and hides and skins. Their decline was due partly to competition between the various agricultural products themselves, for example, rubber replaced leather in a number of uses, and wood pulp in the form of rayon competed against cotton and silk. Competition also came from the mineral realm, where petroleum-based compounds made synthetic rubber and, later, nylon, and synthesized chemicals provided dyes and drugs previously obtained from the juices of plants. With the growing production of man-made fibres the European demand for raw cotton declined during the interwar years, being only partly offset by rising Japanses imports. The foreign trade in raw cotton was also reduced by the spread of cotton manufacture to countries, such as Brazil and India, which produced their own raw cotton. Among the raw cotton exporters, the salient changes were the rise of Brazil, the continued expansion of Egypt and India, and the decline of the United States. The growth of rayon production also brought about a heavy fall of raw silk exports from Japan and China. Unlike cotton and silk, the volume of the wool trade continued to grow in the twenties and held its own in the 1930s, and its greater stability compared to the other textiles may be put down largely to the lack of competition from synthetics. The world consumption of natural rubber also increased throughout the interwar period and was accompanied by a significant shift in the source of supply. Whereas, in 1909–13, 80 per cent of the rubber traded came from the Amazon basin, Central America and Central Africa, by the end of the 1930s it came almost wholly from south-eastern Asia.

The rise in mineral exports indicated in Table 18 is attributable to petroleum and, to a lesser extent, to nonferrous metals. Other significant changes in world trade in minerals during these years included the switch of the United States from being an exporter to an importer of copper, lead and zinc; Europe's growing deficiency of minerals; and the rising importance of Africa and Latin America as producers of minerals including copper, lead, zinc, iron ore and petroleum. For the newest of the non-ferrous metals—bauxite and aluminium—demand grew rapidly during the interwar years. Apart from America, mining was located mainly in Europe—Italy, Hungary, Yugoslavia and France. Some supplies were obtained from the Netherlands East Indies, and in the thirties a start was made in the Guianas. Among the fuels the growth of petroleum was spectacular. From virtually nothing in 1913 the trade grew to be worth $1,170m. in 1929. Europe was the main importer, with the United States, the Netherlands Antilles and Venezuela the main exporters. In international trade coal continued to be important, and as late as 1938 it was surpassed only by cotton. But whereas the combined exports of coal of continental Europe fell very little between the wars, Britain's exports of this product declined substantially.

The interwar years also witnessed significant changes in the commodity composition of world trade in manufactures, (see Table 19 and Diagram 15). The most striking change was the continued shift away from textiles and towards engineering products. Metals and chemicals showed a slight upward trend, while miscellaneous manufactures, composed largely of consumer goods, showed a downward movement after 1929. Indeed the trends in the various commodity groups included in Table 19 suggest that during the interwar years international trade in manufactures moved away from consumer goods and towards capital goods, with trade in manufactured materials remaining fairly stable. In support of this conclusion, it has been estimated that the combined shares of textiles and other consumer goods in the world export of manufactures fell from 52 per cent to 38 per cent between 1913 and 1937, while that

TABLE 19. *Commodity Pattern of Trade in Manufactures (Exports), 1913–37*

	Per cent		
	1913	1929	1937
Engineering Products	19·6	27·2	30·2
Non-electrical	9·7	11·4	12·9
Electrical	2·6	4·0	4·9
Transport	7·3	11·8	12·4
Textiles	28·2	23·2	18·2
Metals	13·8	12·7	16·0
Chemicals	8·5	8·1	9·5
All other manufactures	29·9	28·8	26·1
Total	100·0	100·0	100·0

Source: Cairncross, op. cit., p. 244.

of manufactured materials, including iron and steel, rose from 29
to 33, and of capital goods from 19 per cent to 29 per cent.

These changes in the composition of the export trade in manufactures were associated with a significant change in the direction of
this trade. Up to the early 1930s, the greater part of the expansion
in manufactured exports went to the non-industrial parts of the world,
trade in manufactures within the industrial group of countries
accounting for rather less than half the total increase. During the
remainder of the thirties, however, this intra-trade declined much
more heavily than did manufactures exported to non-industrial
countries, chiefly because the trade restrictions of these years affected
the intra-trade far more severely than exports to non-industrial
nations. As we have already noted, inter-European trade in manufactures fell precipitately during these years, a development which
was partly offset by a rapid expansion of trade in manufactures between the United States and Canada. The overall effect, however, of
a net decline in trade in manufactures between industrial countries
and an expansion of such trade between industrial and non-industrial
countries was that the share of manufactures in total world trade
changed very little during the interwar period.

Table 20 and Diagram 15 show the changing shares of the leading
exporters in world trade in manufactures between 1913 and 1937.
The picture they give is a familiar one. The shares of the United
Kingdom, France, and Germany in this trade declined through the
period, their combined share falling from just over 70 per cent of the
total world trade in manufactures in 1913 to about 52 per cent in

TABLE 20. *Shares of Leading Exporters in World Trade in
Manufactures, 1913–37*

| | Per cent | | |
	1913	1929	1937
U.K.	30·6	23·8	22·4
U.S.	13·0	21·4	20·3
France	12·7	11·1	6·1
Germany	27·5	21·9	23·4
Belgium, Italy, Sweden and Switzerland	13·1	14·3	15·4
Canada	0·7	3·4	5·0
Japan	2·5	4·1	7·5
Total	100·0	100·0	100·0
	£m. 1,292	2,342	1,723

Source: Cairncross, op. cit., Table IV, p. 235.

1937. On the other hand, the American share advanced from 13 per cent to 20 per cent over these years, despite a set-back in the 1930s because of the depression. Even more striking is the rise of Japan, and the equally rapid emergence of Canada as a large industrial exporter. In trying to explain these shifts in the relative positions of

Diagram 15: World Trade in Manufactures, 1913–37
(Commodity Composition and Country Share)

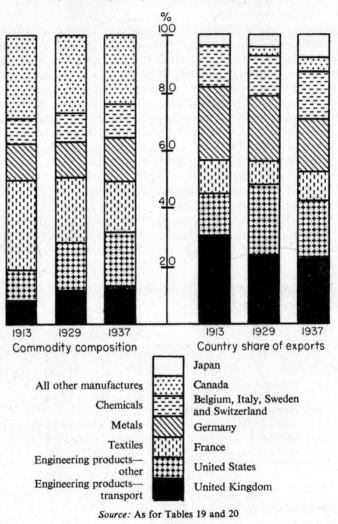

Source: As for Tables 19 and 20

the different countries engaged in exporting manufactured goods, the possibility suggests itself that those countries which gained most in relative importance in world trade in manufactures during these years—the United States, Japan and Canada—did so by concentrating on the export of those commodities, for example engineering products, which were growing in relative importance in world trade. This does not appear to have been so, however, since each of these countries advanced by improving its competitive position in different groups of commodities. The American advance was mainly in the expanding export lines, such as engineering products and transport equipment, Canada's in the stable group of miscellaneous manufactures, and that of Japan chiefly in the declining textile group. In short, the available evidence suggests that changes in the relative position of countries in world trade in manufactures during the interwar years was not so much due to structural shifts in the world demand for these exports as to each country's ability to compete in markets for individual groups of commodities. Thus it has been argued, for example, that the main reason for the fall in Britain's share in world trade in manufactures between 1899 and 1937 was her failure to compete in export markets for iron and steel and engineering products.[1]

DIMINISHING TRADE HYPOTHESIS

What impressed many economists during the interwar years, however, was not so much the poor export performance of individual countries as the declining importance of foreign trade generally. The slow growth of trade in manufactures between 1913 and 1929, the extreme declines in the volume of this trade in the depression years, and the tendency for the ratio of foreign trade to national income to decline in many countries lent support to the hypothesis of diminishing foreign trade. Stated briefly, this hypothesis implied that technological progress, the spread of industrialization, rising real incomes, and certain other forces at work in the international economy during these years would lead, other things being equal, to a decline in the volume of trade between nations. The technology of advanced industrialization, it was argued, is in part a technology of substitution, which replaces natural materials by synthetics largely produced from local resources. Technological progress also involves economizing in the use of raw materials, reductions in material wastage in production, as well as improvements in retrieving and re-using scrap. All these developments it was felt, would slow down

[1] H. Tyszynski, 'World Trade in Manufactured Commodities, 1899–1950', *The Manchester School* (September, 1951).

the growth in demand for raw materials, the trade in raw materials, and trade in general, relative to output.

The spread of industrialization was also thought by many economists to be a trade-reducing factor. Although it was agreed that, initially, industrialization would raise the level of trade in capital goods, the diffusion of technological knowledge throughout the world, it was argued, would eventually reduce the existing gaps in comparative cost advantages in such a way as to reduce trade. In particular the spread of industrialization was expected to lead to considerable import substitution with a consequent dampening of trade in manufactures. Of course, successful industrialization also meant rising living standards in newly industrializing areas, and for this reason other economists argued that on balance industrialization would be beneficial to foreign trade. Even so, it was conceded even by these economists that certain kinds of trade, including some of the traditional exports of the older industrialized countries, for example simple textile manufactures, would shrink.

Rising real incomes also entered the argument as a factor discouraging trade. Taking Engels' law, that foodstuffs is a declining fraction of rising *per capita* real incomes, and its corollary, that in advanced industrial countries the service component in the national output tends to rise, a case was made out for a contraction of world trade in foods and agricultural raw materials, and for a declining foreign trade ratio to total output because of a growth in the output of services—such as housing, mass education and government—which are mainly produced and consumed domestically, and which contribute very little to international trade. Another argument, which parallels that of the secular stagnationists of the United States concerning the closing of the American frontier and its impact on domestic economic growth in the 1930s, emphasized the gradual exhaustion of the trade expanding forces generated by the integration into the world economy of previously undeveloped areas. As more and more of these regions were absorbed into the international economy, through expanding world demand and improvements in transport technology, so the trade inducing forces of integration were played out, with a consequent slowing up in the rate of growth of foreign trade relative to total output.

Finally, it was argued that the increasing vulnerability of advanced industrial countries to economic instability would lead to growing political pressure for effective controls over economic activity which would have a harmful effect on international trade. To achieve economic stability, governments would find themselves compelled to extricate as much as possible of the national economy from a world market which they would not control and thus to expand the domestic economy which they could control at least to some extent. In the absence of effective international means of economic control and stabilization, these defensive actions, along with neo-nationalisms and autarchical postures, were bound to lower the foreign trade ratio and bring about certain of the trends in foreign trade to be observed in the interwar years.

These arguments pointing to a future contraction of world trade were never completely acceptable to all economists, however. For some critics of the diminishing foreign trade hypothesis, industrialization was felt to be beneficial to foreign trade by expanding world demand along new lines. Other economists, while conceding that it was becoming possible to produce almost anything anywhere, were nevertheless prepared to argue that there was little evidence that a significant narrowing of the gap in comparative cost advantages had taken place. The arguments based on Engels' law and the shifting structure of world demand were also thought to be exaggerated. In particular it was felt that the decline in world trade relative to world output was attributable much more to the build-up of barriers to trade and specialization than to any of the other factors advanced by the contractionists. There was also a sneaking suspicion that a rapidly expanding world trade demanded higher rates of economic growth generally than were achieved during the interwar years.

SELECTED REFERENCES

Baldwin, R. E., 'The Commodity Composition of Trade: Selected Industrial Countries, 1900–1954' *Review of Economics and Statistics* (February, 1958), pp. 50–71.

Cairncross, A. K., 'World Trade in Manufactures since 1900', *Economia Internazionale*, Dec., 1955. Reprinted in Cairncross, A. K., *Factors in Economic Development* (London, 1962), Chap. 14.

Cairncross, A. K., *and* Faaland, J., 'Long-term Trends in Europe's Trade', *The Economic Journal* (March, 1952), pp. 25-34.

Hilgerdt, F., *Industrialisation and Foreign Trade* (Geneva, 1945).

Kuznets, S., 'Quantitative Aspects of the Economic Growth of Nations: X—Levels and Structure of Foreign Trade: Long-term Trends', *Economic Development and Cultural Change*, Part II, January, 1967.

Lamartine Yates, P., *Forty Years of Foreign Trade* (London, 1959).

Svennilson, I., *Growth and Stagnation in the European Economy* (Geneva, 1954).

Tyszynski, H., 'World Trade in Manufactured Commodities, 1899–1950', *The Manchester School*, September 1951, pp. 272–304.

Woytinsky, W. S., *and* E. S., *World Commerce and Governments* (New York, 1955).

Part III

THE POST–1945
INTERNATIONAL ECONOMY

Chapter 15

WARTIME PREPARATIONS FOR THE FUTURE INTERNATIONAL ECONOMY AND POST-WAR RECONSTRUCTION

The 1930s witnessed the collapse of the multilateral trade and payments system which had emerged in the late nineteenth century. In the field of commercial policy, severe restrictions, often of a discriminatory nature, tended to prevail, while the international payments system degenerated into a multitude of exchange controls. In consequence, international flows of capital and labour were severely retarded, and the future of world trade appeared to be particularly gloomy. With the outbreak of war the financial and commercial restrictions on trade were intensified and trade between nations was further reduced. Even while the war was still in progress, however, it was realized that strenuous efforts to reduce trade and exchange barriers would be needed to ensure the proper functioning of the international economy in the post-war years. Preliminary discussions along these lines followed the signing of the Mutual Aid Agreement between the United States and Britain in 1941, which, although predominantly concerned with lend-lease arrangements, also committed the two countries to co-operate in international economic affairs after the war. Subsequently, numerous discussions were held in Washington and London with a view to producing a set of rules or a code of conduct in international monetary affairs to be implemented after the war. The outcome of these discussions was a plan for the establishment of a new and unique institution, the International Monetary Fund. At an international conference held at Bretton Woods, New Hampshire, in July, 1944, delegates from forty-four nations hammered out the Articles of Agreement of the proposed organization, together with another Agreement setting up the International Bank for Reconstruction and Development.

THE INTERNATIONAL MONETARY FUND

The ultimate goal of the Fund's operation was to create the conditions under which the transfer of goods and services from one country to another could take place unfettered by restrictions on trade or controls over international payments. To achieve this end, the Fund had three main objectives, each of which clearly reflected the lessons learnt during the interwar years. First, a multilateral system of payments based on a world wide convertibility of currencies was to be achieved through the elimination of exchange controls.[1] In addition, reasonable stability of exchange rates was to be maintained, competitive currency devaluations avoided, and where exchange adjustments were necessary, these were to be carried out in an orderly fashion. Finally, to enable member nations to pursue domestic policies of full employment, the Fund undertook the virtually impossible task of combining exchange rate stability with national independence in monetary and fiscal matters.

To eliminate foreign exchange restrictions and thus eventually to restore convertibility, members of the Fund were to refrain from imposing new exchange restrictions on current account transactions after the war, and to avoid practices that discriminated against any currency. But realizing that exchange controls might be necessary in the difficult early post-war years, the Fund allowed for a transitional period of re-adjustment and adaptation ending in 1952, after which members still retaining exchange restrictions were to consult with officers of the IMF about their continuance. Exchange restrictions on capital account transactions were not forbidden, but were retained as a guard against the de-stabilizing effects of flights of capital on a country's blance of payments. Indeed, the Fund expected members to introduce controls to prevent such capital movements. Currency discrimination was also to be sanctioned by the IMF under certain conditions, particularly where a currency was officially designated a scarce currency. As long as it was so designated, member countries were to be permitted to impose discriminatory exchange controls on the use of that currency.

To achieve stability of exchange rates and an acceptable mechanism of international adjustment, the Fund Agreement borrowed some elements from the gold standard and some from the rival system of flexible exchange rates. Thus, under the provisions of the IMF Agreement, each member country was obliged to establish a par value for its currency fixed either in terms of gold or of the dollar, and to peg the exchange rate of its currency against other currencies

---

[1] Convertibility of a currency is a term which has undergone a definitional change. Whereas under the nineteenth century gold standard it signified convertibility into gold on demand, since 1940, at least, it has referred to a situation in which there are no restrictions on the conversion of one currency into another for current account purposes.

within a range of 1 per cent above or below that par value. To deal with pressures on these exchange rates due to short-term disturbances in a country's balance of payments or to the difficulties associated with the early stages of more deep-seated payments problems, the Fund established a pool of currencies upon which members could draw. This was made up of the contributions of members, based on assigned quotas, the individual size of which was determined by the level of the contributing country's gross national product and its importance in world trade. The quotas themselves were to consist of two components: 25 per cent of the quota was to be contributed in the form of gold and dollars, and 75 per cent in the member's own currency. Apart from determining a country's drawing rights on the Fund, the size of its quota also determined a country's voting rights in the Fund's deliberations. The largest quotas were originally assigned to the United States ($2,750m.), Britain ($1,300m.), China ($550m.), France ($450m.) and India ($400m.).[1] Provision was made for a periodic review of quotas and changes in quotas could be made if the Fund deemed such a step desirable for the proper functioning of the international monetary system.

To deal with short-run balance of payments difficulties, members were to be allowed to draw on the foreign currencies held in the pool, so that these drawing rights, in effect, provided a form of reserves supplemental to the members' own international reserves. In making such a drawing, a member country would surrender domestic currency to the Fund equal in value to the foreign currencies withdrawn. A member drawing from the Fund was also expected to make a future repurchase of the domestic currency thus transferred to the Fund with gold and/or convertible currencies. A drawing within the gold tranche (up to the value of the gold subscribed by a member to the Fund) was to be automatic, but to obtain a larger drawing, a member would be required to gain the consent of the Fund. The repurchase provisions were included to preserve the efficacy of the Fund by ensuring that, in the short-run, its stocks of currencies in strong demand would not be rapidly depleted. However, where widespread drawings made a currency scarce in the Fund, additional supplies of it could be obtained from the scarce currency country in exchange for gold or by borrowing the currency from the member country. Alternatively, the Fund could declare the currency scarce, whereupon other member countries would be allowed to implement exchange controls on their dealings with the member in question, and the Fund would take steps to ration its meagre supply of the currency. These sanctions were to continue until the offending coun-

---

[1] Russia was given a quota of $1,200m., but declined membership of the Fund.

try introduced measures to end the continuous surplus in its balance of payments and thus to eliminate the cause of the scarcity.

In order to deal with a fundamental disequilibrium in a country's balance of payments the Fund turned to supervized flexibility of exchange rates. Members were to be allowed to change the initial par value of their currencies (i.e. devalue or revalue) only in order to correct fundamental types of disequilibrium. Such a change was to be approved by the Fund—unless the change altered the exchange rate by no more than 10 per cent of the currency's initial par value.

The new international monetary system was constructed on the supposition that each member country would experience fairly regular fluctuations in its balance of payments, with deficits in some years and surpluses in others. Over a period of several years, however, it was expected that surpluses would tend to offset deficits. When a particular deficit was very severe, and a country's international reserves fell to a dangerous level, it could approach the Fund for a drawing to carry it over its difficult period. But if the payments deficit persisted over a period of several years, and the country thus had to make frequent use of the Fund's resources, a devaluation of its currency would then become acceptable to the Fund, especially if the country's domestic economic policies were not the most immediate cause of the difficulties. A country with a persistent surplus in its balance of payments, on the other hand, would simply amass reserves, and would not be under any monetary pressures to rectify the situation comparable to those faced by the persistent debtor country whose reserves were being depleted. But the Fund's powers under the scarce currency clause were deemed sufficient either to deter the surplus country from continuing to amass reserves or to compel it to eliminate its payments surplus by an upward revaluation of its currency or by some other such measure. When the international monetary system was functioning smoothly, the Fund's operations were expected to be of minor importance. On the other hand, should imbalances and other difficulties arise, the Fund was considered to possess ample reserves and sufficient powers to return the world monetary system quickly to normalcy.

THE INTERNATIONAL BANK FOR RECONSTRUCTION AND DEVELOPMENT

The other institution set up at Bretton Woods in 1944 was the International Bank for Reconstruction and Development (IBRD), commonly called the World Bank. Originally designed to help finance post-war economic reconstruction, the Bank was later to help extend aid to the developing nations. At first it was intended that the Bank's loan capital, which was set at $10,000m., would be subscribed by member countries, each of which was asked to provide 20 per cent of its subscription (2 per cent in gold or dollars and 18 per cent in its own currency) when the Bank began operations. The other 80 per cent remained on call to meet the Bank's future obligations. By 1959, however, the Bank's capital had been increased to $21,000m., and the bulk of the Bank's lending resources was derived from borrowing in capital markets through the issue of bonds which were guaranteed by the governments of the countries in whose currencies the particular isues were denominated. Furthermore, the function of the Bank had been extended to cover development loans to member countries for specified projects. Such loans were normally tied to the direct foreign exchange costs of the imports needed for the completion of these projects, and the IBRD was given powers to stipulate the foreign country from which the required imports were to be purchased. These development loans were to be repaid in the currencies originally made available, and borrowers were to be charged rates of interest determined by the prevailing rates in capital markets where the Bank's bonds were sold. The Bank was also allowed to lend to private enterprise in member countries.[1] Finally, in addition to its lending function, the IBRD was given powers to offer technical assistance in the use of the funds it provided and to conduct general surveys to help member countries assess their economic potential and prepare development programmes.

POST-WAR RECONSTRUCTION

Many parts of the world experienced difficult times in the immediate post-war years. A long war had deprived consumers in many countries of basic commodities and semi-luxuries and personal savings had grown as a consequence of these shortages. When peace returned, therefore, consumers were anxious to use these savings to satisfy their unfulfilled desires for all types of goods and services. On the other hand, in other countries, especially in Europe, the war had reduced millions of people to desperate poverty. In addition, much of the productive equipment in the warring nations had been destroyed or replacement and new investment had been delayed, so that whole industrial complexes required rebuilding. As a result, the demand for goods and services for consumption and investment purposes outran the available world supplies, while the problem of increasing output was made all the more difficult by the problems

[1] It has always been the Bank's policy not to offer loans where funds are obtainable in private capital markets on reasonable terms. It aims at promoting private investment, not competing with it.

of the changeover from wartime to peacetime production. The consequent excess demand that persisted throughout the immediate post-war years produced tremendous inflationary pressures in many countries, which were only partly contained in some by the continuation of wartime rationing and other physical controls. Other countries were not so fortunately placed, and eventually currency reforms were needed to put a stop to runaway inflation. The shortage of fuel and the inability of the agricultural sector to provide the population with adequate supplies of food, added to the extreme economic difficulties which existed in Europe.

For several years after the end of the war, then, the international economy experienced abnormal conditions. The only major country to enter into world trade and commerce without undue stresses on its balance of payments was the United States, which emerged from the war in a highly favourable economic position. For a number of years many of its competitors in the industrial field were barely able to meet domestic requirements for manufactures and were thus unable to compete with American exports in foreign markets. Furthermore, European demand for foodstuffs, raw materials, and capital goods was such that the United States was able to benefit considerably from supplying part of the demand, and consequently recorded a highly favourable balance of trade with Europe.[1] Such a situation led directly to a dollar shortage which became almost universal in the late forties.

From 1945 to 1948 world production rose and economic recovery continued, but in Europe generally the rate of growth of industrial output was too slow to catch up with demand or to increase exports sufficiently to produce external equilibrium. In the late forties, however, two developments occurred which, perhaps more than any others, were responsible for transforming the economic situation in Europe. These were the European Recovery Programme, inaugurated in April, 1948, and the devaluations of September, 1949.

The European Recovery Programme was largely inspired by the fear that any further economic deterioration in western Europe would make the countries in the region easy prey for a Communist take-over. The Programme had its origins in a commencement address delivered by the American Secretary of State, George Marshall, at Harvard on June 5, 1947. Calling upon European nations to get together and agree on a common plan of action, he pledged America's help in formulating and financing a comprehensive programme for the economic reconstruction of Europe. In less than a year the European Recovery Programme—or the Marshall

[1] Other temperate zone countries also experienced large foreign demands for their primary products.

Plan, as it came to be called—began to take shape. To implement the programme, the Economic Co-operation Administration (ECA) was formed in the United States. In Europe, in 1947, a Committee of European Economic Co-operation (CEEC) was established to determine ways and means of guiding and co-ordinating recovery programmes in Europe. It led to the establishment in April, 1948, of the Organization for European Economic Co-operation (OEEC) consisting of the sixteen participating European nations of the Programme.

From April, 1948 to the end of 1951, over $11,000m. was provided through the ECA to Europe, where the major recipients were France ($2,570m.), Britain ($2,290m.), West Germany ($1,190m.), Netherlands ($1,140m), Italy ($1,060m.), Greece and Austria (each $800m.). Norway, Denmark, Turkey, Ireland, Belgium, Luxembourg, Portugal, Sweden, and Iceland (the other members of the OEEC) also received grants. After June, 1951, Europe received a further $2,600m. in Marshall Aid, mainly in the period up to mid-1953. The aid offered under the Programme took the form of grants of commodities produced predominantly in the United States. Initially the European countries demanded foodstuffs, fertilizers, fodder, and fuel, but by 1951 raw materials, semi-processed goods and machinery had risen sufficiently to account for over half the annual receipts of commodities under the Plan.

Although Marshall Aid represented only about 5 per cent of the recipient countries' gross national products, because of its strategic importance for industrial reconstruction, its economic impact on western Europe was quickly noticeable. Total manufacturing output in the OEEC countries rose by 13 per cent in 1949, and by 1952 was 39 per cent above the 1948 level. While many other factors undoubtedly contributed to European recovery over these years, the contribution of Marshall Aid remains a very significant one.

The other major event which helped the European recovery, and which led to an improvement in the balance of payments of several countries, was the widespread use of currency devaluation in September, 1949. In that month, nineteen countries, accounting for almost two-thirds of total world trade, devalued their currencies relative to the dollar by approximately 30 per cent. The basic reason for the devaluations was the distortions which had developed in the pattern of international payments. Even before the outbreak of World War II, exchange rates had not been sufficiently harmonious to produce high levels of production and employment in all trading countries, while the war and the abnormal conditions after 1945 had created new forces to change the trade and payments patterns in the world economy. For these reasons the initial par values established in 1946–7 of many currencies were out of line with each other and did not truly reflect the differences in domestic purchasing power of the currencies of the various trading countries. As a result the countries with overvalued currencies were not capable of earning the export receipts needed to buy urgently required foreign produced commodities.

The position in Britain, in particular, is worthy of special mention. During the war she had liquidated a large part of her overseas assets to obtain funds out of which to purchase war materials. War demands also forced her to incur vast debts to other countries in the form of accumulated sterling balances, as well as to borrow heavily from the United States. British dependence on American aid continued into the immediate post-war period. Late in 1945, when heavy military and financial commitments in Germany, Greece, and elsewhere, combined with the slow recovery of exports and a continuing need for dollar area imports threatened to exhaust Britain's international reserves, she was forced to seek further financial assistance from the U.S. Under the Anglo-American Financial Agreement of July, 1946, the United States undertook to advance $3,750m. to Britain in the next four years, while lend-lease and other debt obligations were consolidated into a lump of sum of $650m. Repayment of the total British debt of $4,400m. was to begin in 1952, and to be spread over fifty years with interest at 2 per cent. Canada also lent Britain $1,250m. on similar terms at this time. In return for this aid, Britain undertook to make sterling freely convertible on and after July 15, 1947. The size of the credit proved to be totally inadequate to Britain's needs, however. Within twelve months, over $2,000m. of the loans had been used up, and when the pound was made convertible in mid-1947, the rest disappeared almost overnight. By the end of August, with only $400m. left, the British government was forced to suspend convertibility. Sterling was not to attain full convertibility again until February, 1961.

Despite Britain's difficulties, economic recovery was rapid in Europe from 1947 onwards, and, confronted by sellers' markets, exporters had few problems with which to contend. By 1949, however, the picture was changing. The increased availability of goods in Europe and North America now favoured the buyer, and price considerations once again became decisive in export markets. Overvalued European currencies, not a serious hindrance to exports as long as shortages persisted, now became a major obstacle. A revision of exchange values was inevitable. Britain went first, devaluing the pound by 30·5 per cent on September 18, 1949. Within a few days, some 27 countries followed her example, including all the sterling area (except Pakistan) and 11 western European nations. Most of the countries devalued by the same amount; a few—notably Belgium, France, Italy, and West Germany—chose a substantially smaller figure.

The improvement in the balance of payments position of a number of countries that followed devaluation was helped by the outbreak of the Korean War in 1950, which raised the level of world demand considerably. In addition, European production continued to expand, thus reducing the region's dependence on foreign goods, especially those of the United States, at the same time as its export capacity was increased. Intra-European trade was also beginning to revive with the return to more normal trading conditions. By 1952 the international economic situation had improved considerably. Perhaps the most significant feature of the improvement was the disappearance of the American payments surplus in the second half of the year and the general increase in the gold and dollar holdings of other countries. Although the existing controls over trade and payments were to last in varying degrees of intensity from country to country for the remainder of the decade, by 1952 the extreme pressures of the immediate post-war years had almost disappeared.

SELECTED REFERENCES

Behrman, J. N., *and* Schmidt, W. E., *International Economics* (New York, 1957), especially Chaps. 16–18.

Ellsworth, P. T., *The International Economy*, 3rd edn. (New York, 1964).

Horie, S., *The International Monetary Fund* (London, 1964).

International Monetary Fund, *Annual Reports*, 1947–52.

Scammell, W. M., *International Monetary Policy* (London 1961).

Tew, B., *International Monetary Co-operation* (London, 1960).

Yeager, L., *International Monetary Relations* (New York, 1966).

Chapter 16

THE INTERNATIONAL ECONOMY IN THE 1950s

By the early 1950s the first stage in the post-war recovery of the international economy had been largely completed. A significant proportion of the displaced people of the world had been repatriated or resettled in other countries willing to accept them. The European economies had been reconstructed, chiefly by means of aid from the United States, and normal peacetime production had been resumed in most of them. Inflation had given way to price stability, and currency overvaluation had been corrected by widespread devaluation in 1949. With the revival of the economic fortunes of Europe came a rising world demand for primary products, much inflated by the requirements of the Korean War, which contributed to trigger off an upsurge of growth in the underdeveloped regions of the world. These signs of widespread economic improvement set the stage for a burst of economic prosperity which confronted the highly developed countries at least with a new kind of economic problem—that of affluence.

In contrast to the depressed conditions of the 1930s and the grim austerity of the war and post-war years, the 1950s was a decade of rapidly rising living standards for the greater part of the population in western Europe, North America and Oceania. This transformation in living standards is epitomized in the new and ever-widening range of consumer durables which quickly became an accepted part of the consumption patterns of the people in these countries. Where income levels did not allow immediate purchase of these goods, greater security of employment increased the attractiveness of living on credit, which permitted a more rapid accumulation of these material goods than would otherwise have occurred. In this age of affluence, advertising took on a new importance and television provided the advertiser with a new medium with which to practise his highly specialized selling techniques. But the increased importance of advertising not only reflected the existence of affluence, in the sense that people now had a larger part of their income left over to spend on other things once their basic needs had been met, but it was also a necessary adjunct to modern industrial technology.

The new techniques which brought about the rise in industrial productivity that largely supported the rise in living standards apparent during these years almost inevitably demanded large-scale operations. In secondary and tertiary industries, bigness became a necessity and oligopoly perhaps the predominant form of market structure. With production concentrated in a few large firms, each with heavy investment in plant and equipment, the need to maintain its hold on its share of the market, and increase it if possible, became the principal objective of the individual firm's market policy. Since the size of the competing firms and the large financial resources over which they had command, plus the need to guarantee some minimum level of profitability to satisfy share-holders, ruled out competitive price-cutting, firms resorted increasingly to competitive advertising, the promotion of after-sales service and other forms of non-price competition. The result was the setting aside of large funds for the sole purpose of advertising. Innovation was another form of inter-firm competition, since product improvement and the development of completely new products quickly gave a firm an advantage over its rivals. In a period when the pace of technological change was stepped up considerably, the threatened loss of markets and of profits was more than enough to keep most large business enterprises abreast of current technical developments and, in so far as these changes could be affected by what the firm itself did, particularly by its programme of research and development, the level of investment in the enterprise was raised correspondingly. Investment was not only the means of ensuring the short-run efficiency of the firm's plant and equipment, but it also became the means of promoting the long-run growth of the firm.

This shift of emphasis from short-run to long-run considerations evident in the investment behaviour of large-scale businesses is also to be found in contemporary theorizing, where discussion of the short-run problem of full employment has given way to considerations of the long-run problem of economic growth. Having achieved fairly high and stable levels of employment in most developed countries, attention has turned in recent years to ways and means of increasing a country's productive capacity, in the sense of raising the level of output that can be produced when all factors of production are fully employed, through varying both the quantity and quality of its available stock of capital as well as by improving the quality of its human resources. For reasons of political power or prestige or because of the consequent rise in living standards, securing high rates of economic growth has become an important object of economic policy. At the same time, the tendency to compare the performance of different countries by comparing their growth rates, with the fastest growing nations being regarded as the most successful, has given these growth policies an irrational element that has led some writers to dub the last decade or so as an age of 'growthmanship'.

Beneath the welter of affluence and growthmanship there has been present in the post-war years a desire to improve the economic welfare of the poorer countries of the world. This desire was the outcome of several motives. The threat posed to their affluence by the poverty and misery that abounded in these underdeveloped regions was keenly felt in most Western countries, especially as this fear was reinforced by the appeal of Communism as a political ideology and an economic model for the political, social and economic development of the underdeveloped world. It was also felt that, while a few advanced countries with special positions to protect might be hurt by the changes brought about by successful economic development, the economic benefits to be gained from an all-round rise in living standards and the greater opportunities for trade between nations that would arise as countries became richer would more than offset these losses. There is also no doubt that part of the interest of people in developed countries in the fate of people in the underdeveloped countries stems from genuine altruism, a fact which is perhaps most in evidence in the succession of voluntary appeals for food, medical supplies, and clothing for the inhabitants of the strickened areas of the world. Whatever the motives, however, the channelling of aid from the developed to the underdeveloped countries of the world represented a major change in the field of international capital flows as compared with the pre-1939 period, while the current efforts to overcome the problem of economic underdevelopment remain of immense significance for the future of the international economy. It is against this background of increasing affluence in the West and the first attempts to increase the rate of economic development in the rest of the world that changes in the international economy during the 1950s must be viewed.

POPULATION GROWTH AND MIGRATION

Between 1950 and 1960 the world population rose from 2,509m. to 3,010m., or at an average annual rate of growth of 1·8 per cent. During these years the European population grew by only 0·8 per cent per annum, chiefly because of a declining birth rate and because emigration was running at a high level throughout the decade. All the other continents recorded annual increases above the world average, the highest being experienced in South America, Oceania and Asia. Immigration contributed substantially to the growth of population in South America and Oceania, but in many of the countries in these two regions natural increase rose above its pre-war average and served to make the population growth even greater. In Asia, medical improvements and a public health revolution lowered the death rate drastically, and with hardly any fall in the birth rate, population grew rapidly.

Between 1945 and 1960 the major source of migrants was Europe, notably the British Isles (2·2m.), Germany (1·5m.), Italy (1·3m.) and Spain (0·7m.). Altogether just under five million people emigrated from Europe during the fifties. Although this figure is larger than that of the 1930s and forties, it is much smaller than the totals of each decade from 1880 to 1930. The chief countries of destination were the United States, Canada, Australia (each of which absorbed more than a million people), Argentina, and Brazil.[1] In some respects a pattern emerged in population flows similar to that of the 1870s and 1880s, to the extent that northern Europe contributed more people than other regions and the temperate zone countries absorbed most of the migrants. In other respects, however, there were great differences. The more recent period was characterized by restrictions on the inflow of people into the United States and other recipient countries. Moreover, whereas the European emigrants of the nineteenth century enabled the receiving countries to expand their supplies of foodstuffs and raw materials for the European market, the bulk of the emigrants of the 1950s entered manufacturing or tertiary industries in the immigrant country, some of which were competitive with European export industries.

In addition to wartime displacement, emigration from Europe stemmed from the desire to avoid future wars and to escape from the political oppression which afflicted a large part of the continent. The unfavourable economic conditions prevailing in many European countries during the late 1940s also stimulated the outflow of population during these years. But with the revival of industrial activity and the steady improvement in living standards in western Europe, a decline in the rate of emigration set in, although the outflow from the British Isles ran at a high level throughout the 1950s. Britain's economic difficulties were far more deep-seated than those of many of her European rivals, and the need to resort continually to imposing economic restrictions on domestic growth in order to preserve the country's international financial position limited the improvement in her living standards. On the other hand,

[1] See Woodruff, *The Impact of Western Man*, pp. 106–7. These figures do not include the estimated net movement of 9·2m. migrants from European to Asiatic Russia.

the relatively more affluent state of the main recipient countries, their high growth rates and well-defined immigration policies, at times selectively biased in Britain's favour, provided strong pull forces on the potential emigrant.

INTERNATIONAL CAPITAL FLOWS: PRIVATE INVESTMENT

In the late 1940s, the United States alone was in a position to export capital on a large scale. Compared with 1938, when it stood at $11,700m., American private foreign investment rose to $32,800m. by 1960. The bulk of this increase in foreign investments, about $15,000m., occurred after 1952, when the private capital outflow accelerated to over $2,000m. annually. Undistributed profits contributed a further $8,800m. to the value of American real assets abroad. The regional breakdown of the destinations of the outflow shows that over $12,000m. entered other industrial nations, of which Canada received $7,400m., Europe $4,000m., and Japan and Australia $700m. The less developed countries received about $6,500m. Of this total, Latin America absorbed $4,200m. (Venezuela alone attracting $2,300m.), and south-west Asia $1,000m. Much of this private investment in the developing regions of the world went into mining, especially oil. Another $2,300m. was invested in international shipping enterprises and in the dependencies of Western countries.

Mainly because of their greater attractiveness, large industrial countries tended to absorb the greater part of American private investment funds. American investors have always tended to look upon investment in industrially advanced countries as less risky than investment in the developing regions of the world, in which profits may, even if only initially, tend to be relatively low, where political instability, including the possiblity of nationalization of foreign-controlled business organizations, added to the risks of investment, and in which indigenous labour had to be trained for specialized production. The underdeveloped countries with mineral resources provide the main exception to this rule.

Approximately 70 per cent of total American investment in western Europe was direct, and within this category over half went into manufacturing industry and a quarter into oil-refining. Within this region, the present Common Market (EEC) countries became the most important recipients of American funds after 1957, when the prospect of supplying a market of 160m. people and the need to overcome the common external tariff of the region to be applied to American exports stimulated heavy investment in these countries. In 1950 they received only $637m. of American private funds, in

1957 $1,680m., but by 1964 the inflow had risen to $5,398m. The most attractive Common Market country in the eyes of American investors was West Germany, and the increasing attention paid to the EEC occurred at a time when Britain was declining relatively as a recipient of American private investment funds.

While the total value of British private investment abroad amounted to about $23,000m. in 1938, over a third of this value had to be realized during the war to obtain foreign currency for the purchase of urgently needed war materials. In the 1950s, however, Britain invested over $6,000m. abroad, a large proportion of which went to Commonwealth countries. During the same decade, private capital inflow into Britain, mostly from the United States, reached close to $3,000m. The other major capital exporters were France, Germany and the Netherlands. France invested large sums in the overseas member countries of the franc area, mainly those in Africa. Germany and the Netherlands concentrated their attention largely on the other members of the OEEC and on the United States. Much of this was portfolio investment. Switzerland was another country which invested abroad during these years, particularly in loans floated in America. Italy, on the other hand, remained a large net importer of capital throughout the decade.

An important feature of direct investment after 1945 has been the rapid increase in the importance of the multi-national corporation. This is a form of business organization which operates on a large scale in a number of foreign countries as well as in its own domestic market. Although statistical data on the activities of such companies are meagre, a considerable proportion of the direct investment undertaken since 1945 can undoubtedly be attributed to these international corporations, many of which have their origins in the United States. They cover numerous manufacturing industries, including chemicals, vehicles, oil, computers, and foodstuffs. Obviously the entry of such firms into a country confers many benefits on it in terms of increased production, investment and employment, the introduction of new managerial skills, and export expansion or import replacement. The diffusion of technology is also promoted. At the same time, the concentration of a number of these international firms in a particular country may pose serious problems for the government of that country, especially if a significant part of the country's exports can be attributed to these firms. These include the possible re-allocation of export orders from the branch in such a country to another branch somewhere else in the world, or the movement of liquid assets out of the counry if it happens to be experiencing foreign exchange difficulties, thus compounding them. Alternatively, the unwillingness of the home office to allow a foreign subsidiary to export may also pose difficulties for a country endeavouring to broaden its export base. The importance of such corporations may be evidenced by the fact that in 1960 nearly 7 per cent of British exports came from American international companies operating in Britain, and that probably almost as much again arose from other international corporations producing in the country.

INTERNATIONAL CAPITAL FLOWS: FOREIGN AID AND OFFICIAL LONG-TERM LOANS

Strictly speaking, foreign aid refers to grants or gifts of money or goods from one country to another for development purposes. However, it has become conventional to broaden the definition to include long-term developmental loans granted to one country by another and aid provided for military purposes. Thus defined, foreign aid may be provided by individual countries, by regional organizations consisting of a number of countries, or by international bodies such as the World Bank.

Between 1945 and the end of the fifties approximately $26,000m. was granted in the form of financial aid and loans to poor countries by the advanced nations. The United States gave $16,000m., France $4,500m., Britain $1,750m., and West Germany, Holland and Belgium together $300m. The international agencies provided a further $2,900m. This aid was divided among the continents in the following way: $5,000m. went to Latin America, $14,400m. to Asia, and $6,700m. to Africa (of which $4,250m. was supplied by France to her African colonies). In addition, aid from the Communist bloc amounted to almost $6,700m. during the 1950s, of which Communist China received over $2,000m., India $850m., French West Africa $800m., the United Arab Republic $620m., and Indonesia $460m.

The United States is the major donor of foreign aid in the Western world. It began its foreign aid programme in earnest by underwriting the massive European Recovery Programme under which $13,000m. of aid crossed the Atlantic between 1949 and 1954. Thereafter, in response to the growing demand of the poor nations of the world for development capital the bulk of the aid went to countries in Latin America, Asia and Africa. Thus nearly three-quarters of the total American aid from 1955 to 1960 went to Asian countries, chiefly India, South Vietnam and Nationalist China. Latin America absorbed most of the remainder, while Africa, on the whole, was left to receive aid from other nations, notably France.

France was the second most important donor between 1945 and 1960, and contributed $4,500m. to less developed economies. Of this total, $4,250m. was granted to French colonies in Africa ($1,600m. to Algeria, $800m. to French West Africa, and $700m. to Morocco and Tunisia), and the rest went predominantly to French territories in Latin America. The United Kingdom began its aid programme on a small scale in 1945, when a Colonial Development and Welfare Act provided for £120m. to be made available over a ten-year period to implement development plans in the colonies. Three years later, the Colonial Development Corporation was set up with powers to borrow from the Treasury to invest in industry, agriculture, or any other profit-making field in the colonies. Throughout the fifties, therefore, British colonies were the major recipients of British aid— $300m. going to Latin America, $700m. to Asia, and $750m. to Africa. Of the other European countries, West Germany contributed $150m. towards development in Argentina and India, and the Netherlands provided $100m. for her Latin American territories and Dutch New Guinea.

Regional arrangements for promoting aid to the underdeveloped countries came into operation only in the late 1950s, when the European Common Market countries began operating a European Development Fund (1958) to assist the Associated Territories, most of which were former French, Belgian and Italian colonies in Africa, and the Organization of American States created the Inter-American Development Bank which started functioning in 1960.[1]

International financial aid was initially channelled through the World Bank, which began its operations in 1946. In its early years it was involved in assisting post-war reconstruction in Europe, but because of the size of the problem and the smallness of the Bank's resources, the Marshall Plan completely overshadowed the Bank's lending, which amounted to a mere $500m. The Bank was more successful with its developmental loans. From 1946 to 1960 it approved 260 loans amounting to a net figure of $5,050m. Almost 75 per cent of these loans was made available for the provision of basic services, including electric power, transportation and communications. Another sixth of the total loans went into manufacturing, and a twelfth into agriculture. A major function of the loans was to relieve bottlenecks in production and marketing in recipient countries, while it was also believed that the provision of basic services would stimulate industrial growth and thus promote an expansion of private investment. The Bank's efforts at promoting economic development were not completely successful, however, partly because it was limited by a lack of flexibility in its powers, and partly because the floating of its development loans in capital

---

[1] The Inter-American Development Bank makes long-term loans to member countries, especially for social overhead projects, such as a town water system.

markets placed undue emphasis on the short-run profitability of aid projects. To overcome these deficiencies, therefore, two new institutions, both affiliated to the Bank, were created. These were the International Finance Corporation (IFC) and the International Development Association (IDA).

The IFC began operations in July, 1956, with a membership of some thirty countries and a total authorized capital of $100m. The main purpose of the IFC is to promote and encourage the growth of private enterprise in the member countries by making loans to private firms. While its limited financial resources have prevented the IFC from having any significant economic impact on developing countries, by encouraging outside private investors to participate in its investments, the Corporation has often stimulated a flow of private investment into projects in underdeveloped countries. The International Development Association, on the other hand, was established in September 1960, for the purpose of extending aid on a wider basis than the World Bank and on more liberal terms. It provides finance for projects which may not be revenue earning or directly productive, for example housing projects, health and sanitation, but which are nevertheless important for the recipient country's long-run development. It offers interest-free loans, the repayment of which is spread over fifty years. Because IDA's loans require no repayment for the first decade, its resources have to be replenished frequently by calling upon the rich donor countries to grant additional funds to the organization.

In addition to the World Bank and its affiliates, the United Nations has provided aid through a number of its organs in the form of technical assistance to developing countries, relief aid, and investment in education and research. In relation to the efforts of the other international organizations, the monetary value of the aid given by these bodies has been relatively small, but in most instances it has been used very effectively.

TECHNOLOGICAL CHANGE AND WORLD TRADE

The increased emphasis placed on trade as a mechanism for promoting economic development in recent years leads naturally to a consideration of the ways in which technological change has influenced the post-war pattern of world trade. Partly because of the backlog of promising but unused innovations built up during the adverse economic conditions of the 1930s, and partly because the exigencies of war stimulated further research in many industrial fields which was to have considerable peacetime significance, technical progress has been very rapid in the period since 1945. Moreover, innovative capacity has been sustained at a high level during the post-war years by an enormous increase in the funds, both public and private, devoted to research. In the United States the proportion of gross national product spent on research rose from 1 per cent in 1950 to 2·8 per cent in 1960, and in Russia over the same period, it grew from 1·2 per cent to 2·5 per cent. In Britain the percentages for 1955 and 1960 were 1·7 and 2·5 respectively. The picture is repeated in most other developed countries.

The end result of all this innovative activity was an ever-growing range of new raw materials, production processes, energy sources, and production and consumption goods. The period witnessed the introduction of the transistor, plastics, synthetic resins, man-made fibres, new metals and metal products of aluminium and alloy steels, and whole ranges of antibiotics and other life-saving drugs. New production processes were installed in most industries, including steel, cotton, glass, shipbuilding and construction. Prefabrication became a common method of production. Nuclear energy provided a new form of fuel for possible use in transportation and other industries in the future. Many types of electronic devices, including television and radar equipment became objects of everyday use, while computers and transfer systems, which are the basis of auto-mation and cybernetic methods, were more widely adopted. The list is far from complete, but it is long enough to indicate the nature of the far-reaching technological changes that have occurred since 1945.

While technological progress in the production of goods provided increased opportunities for trade, transport improvements continued to assist the international movement of commodities and people. Railway construction remained an important form of transport investment in most underdeveloped countries between 1945 and 1960, but in the highly industrialized nations the importance of the railway declined in the face of growing relative efficiency of road transport. The growing use of motor transport (and of the aero-plane) enormously increased the consumption of petroleum, and this was reflected at sea by the rapid enlargement of oil tanker capacity. Another feature of sea transport during these years was the accelera-tion in the changeover to motor ships. In 1938 they represented just under a quarter of the world's gross registered tonnage; but by 1960 the proportion had almost doubled. Towards the end of the 1950s, considerable attention was being paid to containerization as a means of speeding up the handling and transportation of goods. Increas-ingly after 1945, air transport of people and goods by domestic and international airlines made greater and greater inroads on land and sea transport. In particular, air travel made possible the rapid exten-sion of the international company, by providing the necessary face

I

to face communication needed to administer complex affairs with appropriate speed and at a reasonable cost.

What effects did these changes in production and consumption have on world trade? The answer lies, perhaps, in the extent to which trade increased during the 1950s. Trade amongst the rich nations was stimulated not only because it provided a channel for the diffusion of the fruits of technological progress between the industrial countries, but also because manufactured products became much more sophisticated and consumers' tastes varied with respect to the different brands of products being produced in different countries. Thus, for instance, American cars are sold in Britain and Europe, and British and European cars are sold in the United States. In other respects however, inventions and discoveries have been detrimental to the trade of several countries. Wartime shortages had stimulated the search for new synthetic products to replace natural raw materials, and these efforts were continued in the post-war period with new discoveries in the field of chemistry and other branches of the natural sciences. Substantial economies were also made in the industrial uses of natural materials, for instance, through electrolytic tin-plating and the systematic recovery and reprocessing of metals. These developments have had severe repercussions on many primary producing countries. The demand for such staple exports as crude rubber, silk, indigo, nitrates, jute, hemp, vegetable oils, hides and skins has certainly declined in recent years—in most cases as the result of recent advances in the chemicals industry. Despite the fact that the synthetic materials may have advantages over the natural products, it is unfortunate that some developing countries are losing valuable export markets while, at the same time, rich countries are gaining new export industries.

CONCLUSION

From 1945 to 1960 international economic relations became more complex and more extensive than in any previous period. International co-operation produced large flows of resources, commodities, ideas and technology. In a number of respects, however, the period differed from that of the second half of the nineteenth century. Whereas the degree of interdependence which existed between the industrializing European nations and a number of underdeveloped countries in other parts of the world was a major feature of the nineteenth century world economy, in the 1950s such interdependence was much less evident, and consequently industrial countries had fewer economic incentives to aid less developed countries. Except for oil and the other minerals in short supply in industrial countries, few primary products have attracted the attention of investors in the rich countries to the extent that they did in the nineteenth century. Another contrast is to be found in the lack of a major trading nation willing or capable of pouring capital (at a rate of 4 per cent of national income per annum) into the less developed economies as Britain did in the period after 1870. In addition, the absence in the 1950s of widespread convertibility of currencies and a multilateral settlements network to smooth the working of the international economy provides another major difference between the two periods. On the other hand, foreign aid filled part of the gap in capital flows to less developed countries, although in volume it could not compare with British investment in the nineteenth century. Despite these differences compared with past and the many frictions which emerged in trade and commercial relations during the 1950s, the decade was still one of the most successful in the history of the international economy.

SELECTED REFERENCES

Kindleberger, C. P., *Foreign Trade and the National Economy* (New Haven 1962).

Lilley, S., *Men, Machines and History* (London 1965).

Little, I. M. D. *and* Clifford, J. M., *International Aid* (London, 1965).

Meier, G. M., *The International Economics of Development* (New York, 1968).

Postan, H. M., *An Economic History of Western Europe 1945–1964* (London, 1967).

Wexler, I., *Fundamentals of International Economics* (New York, 1966).

Woodruff, W., *The Impact of Western Man* (New York, 1966).

THE INTERNATIONAL MONETARY SYSTEM, 1945-60

In turning to consider the workings of the international monetary mechanism after 1945 it is convenient to divide the period into two parts, because in many respects 1952 can be accepted as the year in which the abnormal trading and commercial relations of the immediate post-war years gave way to the more normal trading conditions of the later fifties.

PERFORMANCE OF THE SYSTEM 1945-52

The International Monetary Fund

The first annual meeting of the Board of Governors of the International Monetary Fund was held in late September, 1946, in Washington, when measures were taken to ensure that the Fund could commence exchange transactions early in 1947. Member countries were asked to submit the initial parity values of their currencies, being requested specifically to consider the exchange rates for their currencies prevailing on October 28, 1945. Members were also expected to pay their subscriptions to the Fund before it began its operations on March 1, 1947.

Due to widespread inflation and the other problems associated with post-war reconstruction, the IMF was confronted with abnormal conditions in trade and commerce during the early years of its existence. In particular, it had to deal with a large demand for dollars, which would have been even more intense had trade and exchange restrictions not been adopted by many countries under the transitional period provisions of the Fund Agreement. However, despite the considerable international payments difficulties that existed for some time after 1947, the Fund's currency transactions over the first five years of its operations amounted to only $851m., of which $606m. was drawn in the first year of the Fund's existence. The Fund's activities were limited partly because members were expected to rely largely on exchange controls during the transitional period. In addition, when Marshall Aid began, the Fund adopted the policy of disallowing recipient countries access to its resources. American aid and loans to other areas than Europe also acted to reduce the demand for dollars from the Fund, as did the devaluations of September, 1949. Finally, to further ease the pressure on its dollar holding, the Fund increasingly emphasized the need for member countries to implement suitable monetary and fiscal policies to combat inflation.

During these years the IMF also endeavoured, with moderate success, to recreate a multilateral system of trade and payments. Apart from encouraging the elimination of exchange controls on current account transactions after the transitional period had passed, the Fund was concerned with eradicating import restrictions and discrimination in the form of multiple exchange rate practices.[1] However, multilateralism could be fully realized only when current account convertibility was general, and this could come about only when member countries could amass adequate reserves of convertible currencies with which to conduct their international transactions. Consequently, with the dollar already fully convertible into gold or other currencies, it seemed desirable to ensure that sterling, the only other currency previously attractive enough for other countries to hold as international reserves, should also become convertible as soon as possible. Unfortunately the difficult economic position of Britain in the immediate post-war years, with its large external short-term debts (sterling balances) accumulated during the war and its severe shortage of dollars, proved enough to make the first attempt at sterling convertibility, in mid-1947, a catastrophe, and set Britain back many years in its move towards the permanent elimination of exchange controls on current transactions. Another major step towards convertibility of currencies could have been provided by the currency devaluations approved by the Fund in September 1949, but the outbreak of the Korean War in the following year and the resumption of inflationary pressures in many devaluing countries were severe impediments to a return to convertibility. In addition, Marshall Aid had only just begun the work of restoring industrial production in Europe, and the basis for an expanding trade had yet

[1] Multiple exchange rates were in use mainly in Latin America. They arise when a country offers different rates for foreign currency according to the way in which it is earned and charges different rates for foreign currency according to the way in which it is to be spent. A country could also use different rates of exchange in its international transactions with different countries. These practices were obviously discriminatory in their effects on foreign trade, and they were also contrary to the basic IMF rule of officially established par values for foreign currencies. The Fund accepted the view that several years of consultation and modification were required to eliminate the practices altogether, and by the early fifties had made some headway in this direction.

to be laid. By 1952 then, a multilateral payments system was almost as remote as it had been in 1947.

European Monetary Affairs—Regional Payments Arrangements

Until 1948 post-war monetary dealings in continental Europe tended to be very unsatisfactory. Both France and Italy adopted multiple exchange rate practices and Germany suffered severe inflationary pressure reminiscent of the 1920s. In 1948, however, the situation began to improve, following currency reforms in Germany and the abandonment of discriminatory financial practices by France and Italy. There now began a movement towards regional monetary co-operation within Europe which was to have important implications for the future of the international economy. This co-operation was partly the result of the implementation of Marshall Aid, which demanded greater flexibility in intra-European payments if it was to work effectively. After the setting up of a number of short-lived schemes aimed at easing payments settlements within Europe, the problem was finally solved with the creation of the European Payments Union (EPU), which began operations in mid-1950.

By incorporating automatic clearing of all deficits, regardless of size, and the automatic settlement of reciprocal deficits, the EPU was a decided advance on the earlier schemes. It also contained machinery for correcting intra-European balance of payments disequilibria. All OEEC countries, and the overseas territories of Belgium, France, Portugal and the United Kingdom were included in the Union, and the Bank for International Settlements (BIS) acted as the agent of the member countries. Briefly, the operation of the EPU involved establishing the monthly net overall financial position of each member country with the Union as a whole by offsetting its deficits with some members against its surpluses with others. Once this net position was determined by the BIS, a settlement between each member country and the Union was necessary. A country in debit to the Union was expected to surrender gold, dollars and credits to the EPU according to an agreed formula, whereas a country in surplus with the Union would receive these media of settlement from the EPU.[1] To ensure that the EPU would not be depleted of gold and dollars, the Marshall Aid administration provided an initial sum of $350m. for the undertaking.

The original agreement ran for two years, but subsequent renewals allowed it to remain in force until the end of 1958, when it

---

[1] 'Credits' were IOUs expressed in terms of the borrower's currency or the EPU's unit of account, which was purely an accounting device and bore the same gold value as the dollar. Credits were not transferable from member to member and could only be held for future settlements with the Union.

became redundant because of the widespread acceptance among members of non-resident convertibility. Apart from providing the means of accommodating intra-OEEC payments disequilibria, the EPU offered an incentive to members to correct their balance of payments positions because certain amounts of gold and dollars were required to settle monthly deficits. Moreover, because multi-lateral liquidity was provided by the EPU, reductions in trade restrictions were encouraged and discrimination against imports from within the region was less needed. The consequent improvement in the European trade and payments position was not achieved without some difficulties, however, and in its early years the European monetary system weathered some major crises, including the German crises of 1950-1, and the French and British deficits of 1951-2. But by the second half of 1952 a greater degree of economic stability was evident in Europe, and some relaxation of exchange controls became possible. Moreover, with the easing of the intra-European payments situation, the OEEC's efforts to liberalize trade began to bear fruit. In October, 1950, agreements were signed to remove import restrictions in a non-discriminatory way from 60 per cent of intra-bloc imports, and in 1952 the OEEC aided the setting-up of the European Coal and Steel Community.

A curious feature of the formation of the EPU was the attitude of opposition to it adopted from the start by the IMF. The explanation of this opposition is probably to be found in the fear amongst American Treasury officials that the EPU might come to rival the IMF in certain monetary spheres and that, in the event of this happening, the United States would be unable to exercise the influence over the EPU's activities that it had over those of the IMF. Whatever the reason for the IMF's attitude, however, its policy towards the EPU was a major factor contributing to the decline in the reputation of the Fund in the 1950s. It was also responsible for the continued tendency for European countries to develop their own methods of monetary co-operation outside, and largely independent of, the Fund. Moreover, the role which the IMF could have played in the EPU was assumed by the BIS, the organization whose death -knell had been supposedly sounded at the Bretton Woods Conference in 1944.

The Sterling Area

The outbreak of war inevitably produced a rapid contraction of the loosely formed boundaries of the Sterling Area, which came to include the British Commonwealth (except Canada), the Colonial territories, Eire, Egypt, the Sudan, Iceland, and Iraq. In addition, the need to conserve gold and dollars for war purposes led to the introduction of exchange controls in 1939 which remained in force until the late 1950s and which were the main formal link binding the wartime Sterling Area. The principle underlying the system was simple. All gold and foreign currency earned was directed into a single pool, the Exchange Equalization Account, and all external payments were made from that pool.[1]

Within the Sterling Area itself there was free movement of currencies, whereas payments into and out of the Area were subject to regulation. Outside the sterling bloc, the British exchange control distinguished between countries according to whether they would accept inconvertible sterling (inconvertible into gold or other non-Sterling Area currencies) or not. For those which would accept inconvertible sterling a Special Accounts system was formed. Countries included in this Accounts system could use their sterling receipts for payments to Sterling Area countries but not to other countries. As a result a number of countries with large export surpluses with the Sterling Area accumulated large amounts of inconvertible sterling, partly in the belief that sterling would become convertible immediately after the war. Although initially all neutral countries were treated in a similar fashion under the new system of exchange control, from July, 1940, the sterling accounts of the United States and of Switzerland were given special treatment. America would at that time only supply war material on a 'cash and carry' basis, and all sterling accounts of the American (and Swiss) banks were therefore treated as Registered Accounts, with all payments between the Sterling Area and the United States being made either in dollars or in convertible sterling through a Registered Account. This distinction between foreign countries which would accept inconvertible sterling and those which would not was the historical origin of the post-war distinction between soft and hard currency countries. Later, in 1944, Britain negotiated a series of bilateral payments agreements with European countries under which these countries signified their willingness to accept sterling which could be used freely throughout the Sterling Area. These agreements resembled the Special Accounts arrangements but differed from them in that they were more liberal and allowed for such limited transfer of sterling to non-sterling area countries as might be granted by the Bank of England. Some of them also provided for the settlement in gold of mutual indebtedness over an agreed amount.

With the return of peace, attention was directed to the problem

[1] On becoming the Sterling Area's common pool of gold and foreign currencies, the Exchange Equalization Account abandoned its earlier function of acting as an official agency for buying and selling sterling in the gold and foreign currency markets.

of dismantling exchange controls within the Sterling Area and resuming sterling convertibility. Working to this end, in July, 1945, a number of Central American countries (previously grouped together and treated on a bilateral basis) were included with the existing American Registered Accounts to form a composite group known as American Accounts. Current payments made into these Accounts both by residents of the Sterling Area and of other countries were to be freely convertible into dollars on demand. The next step occurred in the first half of 1947 when, following negotiations with a group of countries which included Argentina, Brazil, Uruguay, a number of European countries, Egypt and the Sudan, Ethiopia, Canada and Newfoundland, Transferable Account status was introduced. The most important feature of Transferable Accounts was that they provided for the fostering of sterling as an international currency, since the countries classified in this category agreed to accept sterling in payment for goods and services from all countries and to hold it as an international reserve until they needed it to buy imports or to make other current payments.

These substantial modifications of the Sterling Area's system of exchange control were largely the outcome of the Anglo-American Loan Agreement of 1946, under which Britain was committed to the abolition of exchange restrictions on current account transactions much sooner than was necessary under the IMF Agreement. The abolition of exchange controls on American transactions was to be effective as soon as the Loan Agreement came into force, and on transactions with other countries within a year of the commencement of the loan. But these provisions were not to apply to already existing sterling balances which could remain blocked by mutual accord and gradually converted over a number of years or written off altogether. When the new convertibility measures were introduced in mid-1947, the conversion of sterling into dollars occurred on such a scale that the Anglo-American loan proved vastly inadequate to the needs of sterling convertibility and the Sterling Area's supply of dollars was soon gravely threatened. Consequently, on August 20, the right of Transferable Account countries to use sterling for current payments to American Account countries had to be suspended. This retreat from sterling convertibility was so grave for Transferable Account countries that their monetary agreements required renegotiation. Some returned to bilateral agreements, while others retained their Transferable Accounts status without the right to transfer sterling to other than Sterling Area countries.

Thus for the British monetary authorities there were now four monetary areas in the world. Countries were classified into the Sterling Area, the American Account, the Transferable Account, or the Bilateral Agreements group. Sterling Area countries possessed freedom of payments within the bloc but controls on outside payments; American Account countries faced no restriction on convertibility of sterling into dollars once sterling reached the United States; for Transferable Account countries, sterling was inconvertible but could be used for current payments to other Transferable Account countries or to members of the Sterling Area; bilateral countries also could not convert sterling into gold or dollars. In the remaining years up to 1952 there were few changes in these arrangements.

Concluding Observations, 1945–52

At Bretton Woods it had been expected that post-war reconstruction and the restoration of normal trading and commercial relations between countries would be largely attained by 1952, and that consequently the transitional provisions of the Fund Agreement would then be unnecessary. In actual fact, by the end of that year, general convertibility of currencies was no nearer than it had been towards the end of the forties. There were many good reasons for this state of affairs, including the set-back suffered by Britain following the premature sterling convertibility of 1947, the failure of deficit countries to cope satisfactorily with inflation, the effects of the Korean War on many countries which had expected to achieve external equilibrium as a result of the 1949 devaluations, and the continuing predominance of the United States in world trade. Indeed, the situation would probably have been even more critical than it was had it not been for Marshall Aid, for the IMF was not intended to cope with the problems of industrial reconstruction, and the World Bank's resources were too meagre to deal with the economic problems of the post-war years. Even when it could provide assistance, however, the IMF proved very reluctant to give it. The unwillingness of the Fund to participate in the foundation of a European monetary system, or to allow Marshall Aid countries to use its facilities, and its limited activities during the first five years of its existence, all meant that by 1952 the prestige of the organization was at a low ebb.

PERFORMANCE OF THE SYSTEM, 1953–60

From the beginning of 1953 to 1956, world trade expanded rapidly and the international payments situation improved for many non-dollar countries, notably those in western Europe and amongst the developed primary producers. Inflation was being more effectively dealt with in these countries and consequently the improvement in the European payments situation with the United States resulted not so much from an increased demand in America for European imports as from the growth and increasing competitiveness of European export industries, as countries such as Germany, Italy, Belgium, Holland, and France began to regain their pre-war positions as manufacturing nations and as exporters. In bringing about this overall improvement in the economic condition of western Europe, American aid and foreign investment and the continued good work of the EPU, which facilitated further reductions of barriers to trade and payments within Europe, were other major contributing factors. Primary producing countries over this period tended on the whole to record lower rates of growth in their exports than did the industrial nations. The difference in the rates of export growth between these two groups of countries widened more in value terms between 1953 and 1955 than it had done between 1950 and 1953, mainly because of the declining importance of foodstuffs in total consumption, and the expansion of agricultural production in industrial countries. To a significant extent these trends in growth rates also reflected declining agricultural prices. In this respect, countries exporting petroleum, rubber and metals were more favourably treated by the vagaries of world prices than were those producing foodstuffs and animal and vegetable fibres.

Restrictions on foreign payments tended on the whole to be relaxed considerably during this period of relative prosperity in the international economy, and the possibility of the adoption of currency convertibility by a number of countries seemed very likely. Even so, dollars were still scarce in several parts of the world, particularly in the Sterling Area, and although some European countries experienced external surpluses for several years in a row, their total reserves were still considered too small on the basis of past experience to allow them to experiment with convertibility. Moreover, there was always the possibility that the existing exchange controls were contributing somewhat to the ability of these countries to maintain favourable payments balances.

In 1956 and 1957 inflationary pressures were once more apparent in a number of countries and new difficulties arose for several countries, including Britain, which experienced a series of exchange market crises, the most severe of which resulted from the Suez affair of mid-1956. By the end of 1957, however, the boom conditions of the past year or so began to disappear and the abnormal exchange market situations abated. The following year, 1958, marked a turning-point in the post-war history of international monetary relations, for the United States ended the year with its first major payments deficit of the post-war years, and a massive outflow of dollars and gold to the rest of the world resulted. This deficit was a culmination of a deterioration in the American trade account,[1] an expansion of its foreign investments and the continuing high level of government outlays abroad.

It was this large outflow of gold and dollars from the United States which facilitated the concerted move abroad towards greater currency convertibility. In December, 1958, thirteen European and fifteen other countries announced their adoption of non-resident convertibility,[2] which meant that, in future, the exchange regulations of these countries would apply only to their residents, whereas foreigners would be able to shift funds for current account purposes freely from one country to another. Thus, by the end of 1958 the first important step towards the complete liberalization of payments on current account had occurred. Few international monetary disturbances resulted from the adoption of non-resident convertibility and, although the British balance of payments deteriorated somewhat in 1960, by the end of that year the foreign reserves of most west European countries had risen considerably. Consequently, on February 15, 1961, the IMF's transitional period was finally brought to an end when ten countries, namely, Belgium, France, Germany, Eire, Italy, Luxembourg, Netherlands, Peru, Sweden and Britain, signified their acceptance of full current account convertibility of their currencies.

The International Monetary Fund

Between 1952 and 1956, the Fund's prestige in international monetary affairs was at a low ebb. Despite the fact that exchange problems were still widespread, annual drawings from the Fund remained small, totalling $440m. in the six years 1950–5. This inactivity on the part of the Fund occurred even though it had introduced a system of stand-by credits in February, 1952, designed to speed up the machinery for granting drawings to members when they were required. Under these arrangements, a member predicting the possibility of a drawing within the immediate future, could approach the Fund for a stand-by credit of a specified amount, which, if granted, could be drawn on immediately if needed, and up

---

[1] The Suez crisis in 1956 had diverted much trade in the direction of America, and the redirection of this demand back to its normal markets after the crisis had disappeared was the major cause of the fall in United States' exports in 1958.

[2] These countries were Austria, Belgium, Luxembourg, Denmark, Finland, France, Germany, Italy, the Netherlands, Norway, Portugal, Sweden, Switzerland, and Britain. Only Britain and Germany adopted full non-resident convertibility. All the other countries maintained bilateral payments arrangements with certain countries, while France and the Netherlands adopted limited non-resident convertibility by extending convertibility to certain countries only.

to its full value. Few countries availed themselves of these facilities until after 1956, when it became fashionable to negotiate such credits to ensure that impending drawings would be automatic.

In 1956, coinciding with the appointment of Per Jacobbson as Managing Director, the Fund adopted a more active monetary policy, and in this way increased its stature in the world economy. Because of the Suez crisis, the United Kingdom drew $561·5m. from the Fund, while total drawings in 1956 and 1957 amounted to $692m. and $977m. respectively. In the remaining years up to 1960 drawings were not large, and they were restricted mainly to primary producing countries. Towards the end of the fifties, however, an increase in the Fund's financial resources served to enhance its standing in the international economy. With world trade increasing rapidly, and with the Fund's resources being used more frequently, the first review of members' contributions to the Fund took place in 1958. It resulted in a general 50 per cent rise in the size of the original quotas, though Canada, Germany and Japan increased their quotas by larger percentages. As a result of the general increase in members' subscriptions, the Fund's financial resources rose by $5,100m. to approximately $14,500m. Thus when the post-war transitional period ended early in 1961, the Fund, with larger resources and greater prestige, was in a position to start operating as it was intended to at Bretton Woods.

The European Payments Union

No changes in the structure of the EPU occurred until 1954, when the formula for settling the monthly payments deficits and credits of members was changed so that settlements were henceforth to be transacted in equal amounts of gold (or dollars) and credits. In August, 1955, a further alteration occurred and the ratio became 75 per cent gold and 25 per cent credits. Finally, when, at the end of 1958, non-resident convertibility was accepted by all participants in the EPU, the Union was liquidated and replaced by the European Monetary Agreement (EMA), the function of which was to ensure that monetary co-operation among OEEC countries continued after convertibility of the major European currencies was achieved. One feature of the new Agreement was the setting up of a European Fund to provide short-term credit for up to two years to any member country whose balance of payments difficulties appeared to be a danger to intra-European trade.

The Sterling Area

In the years after 1952 sterling made slow, if not uninterrupted, progress towards convertibility. In May, 1953, certain controls over the London foreign exchange market were relaxed, and almost a year later, in March, 1954, the London Gold Market was reopened to gold buyers who resided outside the Sterling Area and who were able to pay for gold in dollars or other convertible currencies. The supply of gold for the market came from the Sterling Area and from other countries willing to accept payment in sterling. Part of the demand came from the Bank of England on behalf of the Exchange Equalization Account, while the other purchasers included mainly holders of American Account sterling. As for the convertibility of sterling, in March, 1954, it was also possible, because of the improved economic condition of the Sterling Area, to convert bilateral status countries to the Transferable Account, thus reducing countries with which Britain had financial dealings to membership either of the Sterling Area, American Account, or Transferable Account.

The return to convertibility of sterling was interrupted in 1956 by the Suez affair and the external difficulties created by this event, and again in 1957, when sterling suffered another major crisis. Nevertheless, these events were largely accidental, and once their effects wore off the way was open, at the end of 1958, to the adoption of non-resident convertibility status. This step involved the fusion of Transferable Account and American Account sterling into an External Account. The status of Resident Sterling remained unchanged throughout the post-war period until full current account convertibility was accepted by Britain in February 1961.

Concluding Remarks

The whole of the period up to 1960 was needed before the international monetary system could function in the manner envisaged by its Bretton Woods architects. During this period, such 'accidents' as the Korean War and the Suez crisis delayed improvements in the monetary sphere. Some blatant errors of judgment, such as the abortive attempt at sterling convertibility in 1947, also proved to be detrimental to international monetary relations. Furthermore, the IMF failed to demonstrate its full capabilities until Per Jacobbson arrived on the scene in 1956. By then, however, many European countries had resorted to regional devices for overcoming their payments problems. Yet, despite the numerous difficulties and weaknesses in the functioning of the international monetary system in the fifties, and the persistence of controls over foreign exchange dealings and of restrictions on imports during these years, the growth of world trade proceeded at a rate far greater than the most optimistic forecasts of economists in the 1940s. This success in the field of foreign trade was not without its problems, however, and towards the end of the fifties the structure and functioning of the international monetary system were being brought into question, especially by international monetary experts such as Robert Triffin.[1] With world trade and foreign capital flows reaching massive proportions and continuing to rise, it was felt that, in future, trading nations would become susceptible to wider swings in their balance of payments positions and would thus require larger reserves of gold and foreign currencies. Unfortunately, the annual additions to the supplies of gold entering official reserves were not increasing at a rate comparable to the rate of growth of trade. Moreover, as Triffin pointed out, if increases in gold supplies are inadequate, it becomes necessary for the supply of internationally acceptable currencies, such as dollars and sterling, to increase if the demands of central banks for international reserves are to be satisfied. But this entails key currency countries running deficits in their balance of payments thus bringing about a progressive softening of their currencies. Eventually speculation against these currencies could gravely affect the efficacy of the system. Triffin's answer to the problem lay in an expanded, more autonomous, IMF with the ability to create additional reserves. Since Triffin's proposals were put forward, numerous other plans have been forthcoming in an effort to find a long-term solution to the current international monetary problem.

SELECTED REFERENCES

The literature on this topic is large. However, the references to Chapter 15 provide a good coverage, if to this list is added:

Johnson, H. G., *The World Economy at the Crossroads* (Oxford, 1965).

[1] R. Triffin, *Gold and the Dollar Crisis* (New Haven, 1961).

Chapter 18

INTERNATIONAL COMMERCIAL POLICY, 1945–60

The IMF's efforts to re-establish multilateralism by removing all restrictions on international payments would have been defeated if trade controls, over which it had no authority, replaced arbitrary controls over international payments. But experience in the 1930s had underlined the close connection between exchange controls and trade restrictions, and consequently between 1943 and 1945, when the setting up of the IMF was under consideration, American, British and Canadian officials were also discussing the possibility of extending the principle of international organization into the field of commercial policy. Subsequent efforts in the post-war years to reach international agreement on the removal of trade barriers achieved a measure of success which went a long way to encouraging the expansion of foreign trade that occurred in the period before 1960.

THE INTERNATIONAL TRADE ORGANIZATION

The proposed International Trade Organization (ITO) was the outcome of a conference convened to consider proposals advanced by the United States for the expansion of world trade and employment. The conference met in London in the latter part of 1946, changed its location to Geneva in the next year, and concluded its deliberations in Havana in the winter of 1947–8. Out of these discussions came the Havana Charter for the setting up of the International Trade Organization subject to the Charter's ratification by twenty of the fifty-three countries represented at the conference. The Havana Charter was never ratified, however, chiefly because intense opposition to ratification arose in the United States, and because the American failure to ratify the agreement was enough to deter most other countries from approving it too. It has been argued that solutions to too many problems were attempted in the agreement. Had it concentrated on methods of restricting trade, and thus complemented the IMF provisions relating to exchange controls, it may have been acceptable, but it also included provisions relating to full employment policies, international cartels, and the stabilization of primary product prices, and by trying to legislate for too many specific circumstances, its free trade principles tended to be buried under escape clauses, exceptions, and special cases. At the same time, the success of the first GATT session in 1947 did much to reduce the urgency for the creation of an ITO.

THE INAUGURATION OF GATT

During the war years trade was tightly controlled and after the war, the threat of inflation and the excessive demand for foreign products led to the retention of wartime controls in many major trading countries. In addition, because the dollar was scarce in the non-dollar world, and because the United States experienced large trade advantages, such controls were generally highly discriminatory. In the United States, however, the Trade Agreements Act[1] was renewed in 1945 for a further three years to allow the administration to negotiate tariff reductions up to 25 per cent from the rates current at the beginning of that year. It was under these arrangements that the first GATT was organized, for the United States proceeded to invite a number of countries to participate in discussions aimed at effecting reductions in tariffs and other trade barriers. Eventually twenty-three countries were represented in the negotiations conducted in Geneva in 1947 concurrently with the discussions on the ITO. The procedure adopted at the negotiations involved bilateral bargaining between delegates on a product by product basis to obtain the maximum reductions possible in existing duties. Reduced rates agreed to in this manner were generalized by being granted to all other countries participating in the conference through the adoption of the most-favoured nation principle. Altogether, 123 sets of negotiations covering 50,000 items were completed and incorporated in the General Agreement on Tariffs and Trade (GATT), which was signed on October 30, 1947.

The code of conduct incorporated in GATT involved two major principles: first, a multilateral and non-discriminatory approach to international trade, and second, condemnation of quantitative trade restrictions. The first of these principles was implemented through the inclusion in the code of the most-favoured nation clause. Under this clause GATT prohibits any preferential trade arrangements

[1] The Americans had embarked on a programme of trade liberalization in the 1930s when, under the Reciprocal Trade Agreements Act of 1934, the President was authorized to sign commercial agreements with other countries reducing existing American duties by as much as 50 per cent, in exchange for parallel concessions.

designed to favour one nation over another. The main exceptions to this rule include those preferential systems existing in mid-1939, preferential arrangements that take the form of customs unions or free trade areas, and discriminatory treatment introduced by a member country for balance of payments purposes or by developing countries to aid growth. As for quantitative restrictions, the code forbids them in principle but allows for exceptions in certain circumstances—where countries are suffering from balance of payments difficulties, and where developing countries wish to protect infant industries. Finally, the code features an escape clause that allows member nations to raise tariffs or impose quotas if any of their domestic industries are materially injured by increased import competition.

Despite the diversity of interests among the contracting parties to GATT and the variety of commercial policies they pursued, the Agreement achieved considerable success in a number of fields during the 1950s. While the early success achieved in the 1947 tariff reducing negotiations was not again repeated in the later meetings at Annecy (1949), Torquay (1950–1), and Geneva (1955–6), some progress continued to be made, and by the mid-fifties it was estimated that a net reduction in United States duties of 50 per cent had been achieved since 1934 by tariff concessions alone, the greater part of which had been accomplished in the period after 1945. Even more striking has been the growth in the membership of GATT. Numbering twenty-three signatories in 1947, it now comprises over seventy nations that together account for over 80 per cent of total world trade. Equally significant is GATT's contribution to the peaceful settlement of commercial disputes. By providing a forum of consultation and discussion, disputes that might otherwise have caused continuing bad feeling, reprisals, and even diplomatic breakdown, have been resolved, often through the use of arbitration or adjudication.

Progress in dealing with quantitative trade restrictions was much slower than that with tariffs. This was partly because the economic difficulties of the late forties and the fifties made it imperative that many countries retain their controls over trade. Moreover, on the matter of quantitative trade restrictions, GATT's powers were relatively weak, for it could only consult members in an endeavour to persuade them to reduce their restrictive measures. Despite this limitation, however, GATT's constant review of the commercial policies of individual countries, and its persistent attempts to obtain a relaxation of trade restrictions must have contributed something to the general, if gradual, elimination of restrictions that took place in the late fifties. In addition, GATT's existence may have prevented the introduction of new preferential arrangements along the lines of those adopted in the 1920s. Late in the fifties, however, the growth of regional trading blocs did much to erode GATT's powers under the no new preferences rule.

The general improvement in trading conditions between the Western industrial nations evident in the latter part of the fifties led to increasing dissatisfaction among many of the primary producing countries in GATT which were inclined to look upon the organization as one designed largely to introduce commercial policies favourable to the advanced nations. Consequently, a panel of experts was appointed to investigate and report on the failure of the trade of less developed countries to grow as rapidly as that of the industrial nations, the excessive short-term fluctuations in the prices of primary products, and the widespread resort to agricultural protection in the developed countries. The Haberler Report was presented to GATT in 1958. Generally speaking, the report favoured the adoption of measures to stabilize markets in primary products, and further investigations into methods of reducing barriers to trade in such products were called for in order that the relative decline in the growth of exports of primary producing countries, which it had verified, could be arrested. As a result of the recommendations of the Haberler Report, the 1958 Session of GATT established three Committees to follow up certain aspects of the report. The Tariff Negotiations Committee was given the task of exploring the possibility of further tariff reductions and this body was instrumental in preparing two rounds of tariff reductions—the Dillon Round (1961) and the Kennedy Round (1967). Another committee was asked to investigate other avenues of trade for maintaining and expanding the export earnings of less developed countries. These investigations led, in 1964, to GATT waiving the no new preferences rule so as to allow any advanced country which so wished to discriminate in its tariff in favour of less developed countries. A third committee was set up to examine the question of agricultural protection. This committee has consulted with member countries on their agricultural policies and their effects on international trade. It also played a part in outlining the agricultural policy of the European Common Market.

The agricultural provisions of GATT remain one of its most controversial features. These provisions have aims similar to those of the other provisions in the General Agreement, namely, the elimination of quotas and other restrictive devices on imports. At the same time, a member country can impose quotas on specified agricultural commodity imports provided that it concurrently introduces equally restrictive measures on production and/or marketing of the corresponding domestically-produced commodities. Under such arrangements, foreign suppliers can expect to maintain roughly the same share of the domestic market, and unmanageable surpluses are unlikely to emerge to create marketing difficulties. During the fifties, however, several industrial countries introduced quotas on imports of certain agricultural commodities without at the same time regulating domestic production. Such actions were a great source of annoyance to many primary producing countries affected by these limitations on their exports. Other problems of great concern to primary producers included the methods of dumping or otherwise disposing of agricultural surpluses and the subsidizing of agricultural exporting industries in several industrial countries. Some of these problems were partially overcome under the new Agreement contracted in 1955, when greater emphasis came to be placed on prior consultation before agricultural surpluses were disposed of. It was also agreed that export subsidies on primary production should not be used to obtain for the exporting country more than an equitable share of the world market after taking into account previous trends in trade and any special factors which might arise. The committee on agricultural protectionism set up in 1958 was the latest attempt by GATT to deal with these problems.

DISCRIMINATION IN TRADE RELATIONS

One of the primary aims of GATT is the eradication of discriminatory treatment in world trade. When GATT was established, it was recognized that some tariff barriers would remain indefinitely, even if others could be substantially lowered by concerted and repeated negotiations under the Agreement, but it was agreed that such tariff barriers should be applied in a non-discriminatory manner. Consequently, while existing preferential trading arrangements were allowed to continue, member countries were expected in future to follow a no new preferences rule, which could, however, be waived in certain specifically defined circumstances. Despite the acceptance of this principle by the member countries of GATT, discrimination in international commerce has grown since World War II for a number of reasons.

One cause of trade discrimination was the dollar shortage, which developed in the early post-war years and persisted in varying degrees of intensity right up to almost the end of the fifties. The formation of regional trading blocs was another potent cause of trade discrimination during these years, even though, according to GATT, the creation of such permanent regional entities was an acceptable exception to the rule of non-discrimination. At the time the Agreement was signed, however, no one expected such unions to produce major trading blocs and, in any case, it was considered that when formed, they would prove beneficial to other countries by improving the welfare of the participants and creating new opportunities for trade. But with the establishment of large customs unions, it has been found necessary to consider not only their trade creating potentialities, but also their trade diverting effects, that is, the extent to which the formation of a customs union will lead to the diversion of the trade of one member country from third countries to another member of the union. Obviously the rest of the world would benefit from the setting-up of the customs union only if the creation of new trade opportunities exceeded the extent of trade diversion.

Discrimination as a method of protection against Japanese exports was adopted during the mid-fifties by a number of countries, including Britain, France, Belgium and the Netherlands. Fear of Japanese competition also made these countries unwilling to extend the same tariff concessions enjoyed by other contracting parties to Japan when it was granted full membership of GATT in 1955. Despite earlier opposition to the idea by most of the industrial nations, discrimination in the form of preferential treatment granted to underdeveloped countries by industrial nations, with the object of aiding their economic development, also began to manifest itself late in the 1950s. With the acceptance of discriminatory regional trading blocs, the industrial nations were less able to refuse assistance to the poorer members of GATT through the granting of preferential treatment.

REGIONAL TRADING BLOCS

A number of small customs unions, France–Monaco, Italy–San Marino, Switzerland–Leichtenstein, and Belgium–Luxembourg, emerged unbroken from World War II.[1] After the war, the trend towards economic and/or political integration gathered pace. The first step was taken with the formation of Benelux in 1944, when the governments of Belgium, the Netherlands and Luxembourg agreed to establish first a tariff community with a common external tariff and reduced internal duties, then a customs union, and finally complete economic integration. After encountering many difficulties, the common external tariff was achieved in 1948. The second stage

[1] A customs union involves the economic integration of a number of countries in such a way as to produce free trade among members of the union and a common external tariff levied against all non-members; a free trade area differs from a customs union in that member nations follow independent tariff policies with respect to other countries.

had not been attained by 1957, however, when the three member countries were preparing to enter a wider customs union—the European Economic Community.

Meanwhile, the European Coal and Steel Community (ECSC) had been formed in 1952 by Belgium, Luxembourg, the Netherlands, France, West Germany and Italy in an attempt to prevent the re-establishment of the unsatisfactory pre-war cartel operations in coal and steel in western Europe. The 1950 Schuman Plan, which was the basis of this organization, aimed at opening up the markets in coal, iron and steel in each country to all members of the Community, and at placing these industries under a supranational authority. The common market in these products was to be attained by the gradual removal of duties, subsidies and other restrictions and discriminatory practices. Workers were to be allowed freedom of movement from one country to another. The High Authority of the ECSC was given power to determine limits within which external duties levied by members were to be set, the right to borrow funds, co-ordinate investment programmes, impose fines, and to regulate the industries as it saw fit. The ECSC aimed to improve efficiency and at the same time to assure each member access on equal terms to raw materials and final products.

To establish the ECSC, a waiver of GATT's no new preferences rule was required. Although opposition came from Denmark, Norway and Sweden which relied upon prospective ECSC members for supplies of iron and steel, a conditional waiver was allowed, containing rules and conditions under which the ECSC was to function. Later annual reviews were adopted within GATT because of complaints from certain non-members of unfair treatment. The ECSC operated particularly well during the fifties. Perhaps the major benefit conferred on the members of the Community by its existence was the impetus provided for investment in steel, the production of which greatly needed modernizing.

The ECSC was only the prelude to much bigger things. In 1955 discussions commenced on the formation of a customs union in Europe embracing Belgium, France, Germany, Italy, Luxembourg, and the Netherlands, which was to have far-reaching implications for the international economy. European co-operation in trade and payments had previously asserted itself in the fifties in the OEEC, the EPU, and the ECSC. In addition, as we have just seen, three of these countries—the Benelux group—were already forming a customs union. Thus the proposed economic union was in a way simply a widening of horizons in the region. The structure of the European Economic Community (EEC) was finally agreed upon in March, 1957, and incorporated in the Treaty of Rome, the provisions of which came into operation at the beginning of 1958 after recognition of the regional trading bloc had been established in GATT.

It was the aim of the EEC, by establishing a common market and progressively approximating the economic policies of the member states, to promote a harmonious development of economic activities in the region, a continuous and balanced expansion of each member's economy, increased economic stability, and an accelerated improvement in the living standards of the population in the union. At the same time, political unity formed a long-term aim, even if it was no more than implied in the Treaty of Rome. Other features of the Treaty provided for the free movement of people, services and capital within the area, common agricultural and transport policies, and the co-ordination of the economic policies of the member states. A European Social Fund was to be set up to improve employment possibilities within the region and to help raise living standards, and a European Investment Bank was also planned. In addition, the Treaty provided for an association of the EEC with the dependent territories overseas of France, Belgium, the Netherlands and Italy. The trade and economic development of these territories were to be encouraged by the preferential treatment of their exports to the EEC, and by the setting up of the European Development Fund by the EEC countries for the purpose of extending financial help to their overseas associates.

The EEC aimed at the gradual establishment of a single unified market of over 160m. people. Within the Community, the Council of Ministers was the most important policy decision making body and consisted of one representative from each country, while the administrative arm of the EEC took the form of a Commission made up of fourteen representatives drawn in varying numbers from the individual member states. A unified market was to be achieved through the elimination of tariffs on intra-EEC trade, which was to proceed in three stages, each covering a period of four years. The Treaty also specified the actual amount of each tariff reduction to be made during each stage. Thus, by the end of the first stage (1958–61), tariffs were to be reduced by at least 25 per cent from their 1957 levels; and by the end of the second stage (1962–5) they were to be 50 per cent lower than in 1957. Any remaining tariffs were to be completely removed by 1970. By the end of 1960 two reductions, each of 10 per cent on all products had been completed, and the changeover was proceeding so smoothly that at the beginning of 1961 it was decided to accelerate the programme. At the same time, a timetable for the introduction of a common external tariff was drawn up with three stages which coincided with those of internal tariff dismantlement. Except for certain raw materials and foodstuffs, for which future negotiations were to be held, the common external tariff was taken as the arithmetic average of the customs duties in force on January 1, 1957, in member countries. By December, 1960, the end of the first stage had been reached. On items for which the national duties of January 1, 1957, did not differ from the proposed common external tariff by more than 15 per cent, the common external tariff was brought fully into operation. In all other cases the difference between national basic rates and the common external tariff was reduced by 30 per cent. From the inception of the EEC all member countries recorded high rates of growth in production and incomes and considerably improved their balance of payments positions. The major successes of integration in western Europe belong to the 1960s, however, and are beyond the limits prescribed for this book.

In the early stages of the EEC's formation, Britain was approached on the question of possible membership, but favouring a wider free trade area, she refrained from joining the discussions. With the formation of the EEC, however, steps were taken by the European countries outside the Common Market to set up their own trading bloc. The European Free Trade Association (EFTA) Convention was signed in Stockholm in November, 1959, and came into effect in May, 1960. Its membership consisted of Austria, Denmark, Norway, Portugal, Sweden, Switzerland, and the United Kingdom, often spoken of as the 'Seven'. Under the Convention, each member was committed to a reduction of its tariffs on other members' goods, but could follow an independent policy with regard to import duties on goods coming from other countries. In July, 1960, EFTA members undertook their first mutual tariff reductions (on manufactures only) of 20 per cent. By the end of 1962 duties on industrial products within EFTA had been reduced to 50 per cent below their early 1960 level. Thus western European countries, after the unified efforts of the OEEC, split into two trading areas in the late fifties, one of which was to become an integrated customs union, the other a more loosely constructed free trade area.

The example provided by the formation of the EEC and EFTA paved the way for the establishment of further regional trading blocs in other parts of the world, and the movement towards economic integration far exceeded anything envisaged at Geneva in 1947. Many countries quickly recognized the fact that membership of a regional bloc may have decided advantages over the pursuit of an independent commercial policy. It was argued in support of these developments that while regional economic unions may have detrimental effects on non-member countries, the more countries there were involved in regional systems, the greater would be the advantages for all. Some sceptics, however, considered that the implications for the multilateral trade system may not be so clear-cut.

Among the major regional blocs which came into existence towards the end of the fifties were the Latin American Free Trade Association (LAFTA), finalized in February, 1961, by Argentina, Brazil, Chile, Mexico, Paraguay, Peru, and Uruguay, and the Central American Common Market (ODECA), comprising Costa Rica, El Salvador, Guatemala, Honduras and Nicaragua, which expected to become an integrated customs union by the end of 1967. In Africa, two regional trading blocs were agreed upon in 1959: one comprised the former French West African Federation countries, namely Dahomey, Ivory Coast, Mali, Mauritania, Niger, Senegal, and Upper Volta; the other was the Equatorial Customs Union, consisting of Chad, Gabon, and the Central African Republic. With the spread of these regional trading arrangements in the late 1950s and early sixties, one of the fundamental principles of GATT, that of non-discrimination, was rapidly undermined.

INTERNATIONAL COMMODITY AGREEMENTS

One of the major problems confronting many primary producing countries is the tendency for the prices of their exports of foodstuffs and raw materials to fluctuate far more widely than those of manufactured products. Severe fluctuations in export prices greatly affect these countries by increasing inflationary pressures when prices are high, and by retarding economic growth when they are low. This problem is especially significant for a country with a narrow primary product export base or for one for which these exports constitute a relatively large proportion of its national income. While it is obviously in the interest of such countries to avoid these price fluctuations, industrial countries, despite being importers of foodstuffs and raw materials, also have an interest in ensuring that a high level of export receipts accrues to primary producing countries which form a major market for their manufactured products. Thus for the purposes of stability it is often desirable for both primary exporting and importing countries to prevent or to moderate such price fluctuations. Since World War II, therefore, attempts have been made to preserve orderly marketing and these have resulted in international commodity agreements covering four commodities: wheat, sugar, tin and coffee.

For those who believe in the merits of commodity control as an instrument of stability, the experience of the post-war years could hardly be much more depressing. Of the four international commodity control schemes introduced before 1960, the sugar scheme had been suspended and the tin scheme was out of control by the early

1960s, while the coffee agreement failed to prevent coffee prices from declining because of an expansion of production and the large proportion of total coffee production not covered by the agreement. Indeed, none of these agreements achieved price stability for more than relatively short periods. The record of the wheat agreement is very much better, but this success has come about largely because the two biggest exporters, the United States and Canada, have adopted national stockholding policies which amount to a behind the scenes control of prices. During the interwar years, and again during the 1950s, experience has shown how difficult it is to sustain international commodity agreements. If an agreement is limited solely to producers or consumers of the product, it is necessary to ensure almost all countries producing or consuming the commodity are members if it is to be effective. On the other hand, when both consumers and producers are represented, consumers become reluctant members when prices are low, and when prices are high, producers favour the elimination of controls over production and exports. Since most international commodity agreements are concerned with preventing large fluctuations in prices, the progress of any commodity agreement is always likely to be subjected to extreme pressures of these kinds.

CONCLUSION

Immediately after World War II a concerted effort was made to set up a multilateral trade system through the elimination of controls over trade and commerce and a reduction in the amount of protection afforded to domestic industries. The most-favoured nation principle and the no new preferences rule was intended to prevail in the tariff field. All discriminatory devices were to be scorned by all participants in Western trade. By the end of the 1950s the situation was, in practice, almost the complete reverse. As the result of escape clauses in the GATT, and the inclusion of what was considered at the time to be a relatively minor exception to the general rules governing trade liberalization, the international economy was heading towards regionalization to such an extent that, within each regional free trade area, the most-favoured nation principle and the no new preferences rule were being side-stepped, as individual member countries within these free trade regions discriminated in favour of other members and against outsiders. While it is still too early for us to assess the full significance for world trade and payments of this reversal of commercial policy, what is obvious is that since the formation of the EEC, the member countries have achieved their best-ever rates of economic growth. In addition, the setting up of the customs union was at least partially responsible for the subsequent large inflow of foreign private capital, especially from the United States, as outside manufacturers attempted to overcome the increasing discrimination against their exports within the EEC by setting up subsidiaries within the bloc.

A major source of grievance within GATT has been the comparatively poor export performance of many primary producing countries during the 1950s. While some of the reasons for this state of affairs are to be found in the domestic policies of the primary producing countries themselves, many of them, nevertheless, believe that the developed nations have used the exceptions in GATT to protect their own relatively inefficient agricultural industries to the detriment of the exports of foreign primary producers. Furthermore, until the Kennedy Round, agricultural products did not enter into discussions with respect to tariff reductions. Whether rightly or wrongly, the less developed countries have looked upon GATT as a 'rich man's club', and in the 1960s were to turn to the United Nations, the only forum in which they possessed considerable voting strength, for an answer to their trade problems. The result was the establishment of UNCTAD, the United Nations Conference on Trade and Development.

SELECTED REFERENCES

Behrman, J. N. *and* Schmidt, W. E., *International Economics* (New York, 1957).

Curzon, G., *Multilateral Commercial Diplomacy*, (London 1965).

Ellsworth, P. T., *The International Economy* 3rd edn. (New York, 1964).

GATT, *Trends in International Trade* (Geneva, 1958).

Johnson, Harry G., *The World Economy at the Crossroads* (Oxford, 1965), especially Chap. 4.

Patterson, G., *Discrimination in International Trade, The Policy Issues, 1945–1965* (Princeton, 1966).

Rowe, J. W. F., *Primary Commodities in International Trade* (Cambridge 1965).

Chapter 19

TRADE AND GROWTH IN THE INTERNATIONAL ECONOMY, 1945–60: THE DEVELOPED ECONOMIES

TRENDS IN TRADE

Total Trade

Despite the restrictions on foreign trade which existed in one form or another from the end of World War II to 1960, the total value of the exports of the non-Communist countries rose from $53,300m. in 1948 to $112,300m. in 1960, or at an average annual rate of growth of over 6 per cent. This was a remarkable achievement, especially when it is realized that the prices of traded commodities were about the same in 1960 as they were in 1948. The different regions of the world did not share equally in this rapidly expanding trade, however. The rate of growth of trade of the highly industrialized countries of Europe, North America and Japan was higher than the world average, and as a result these countries increased their relative share in total world exports from 61 to 70 per cent. Other developed countries in Europe, Australasia and South Africa experienced a reduction in their share from 9 to 7 per cent, and the share of the less developed countries fell from 30 to 23 per cent.

These various trends in total and regional trade largely reflect the different rates of growth in the output and exports of manufactured goods and primary products. If we ignore the boom in primary product exports up to 1950, and consider the trends in trade between 1953 and 1960, which enables us to include estimates of the trade of the Communist countries in our total figures, the value of world exports rose from $78,300m. to $126,000m., or by 61 per cent. Over the same period, trade in primary products increased from $41,800m. to $56,200m. (34 per cent), and in manufactures from $35,600m. to $68,600m. (93 per cent). Prices changed very little during these years, primary product prices declining by 7 per cent, while those of manufactured goods rose by an average of 5 per cent.

If we ignore price changes, the volume of manufactured exports rose by 83 per cent, and of primary products by 44 per cent. On the other hand, during the years 1953 to 1960 inclusive, the volume of world production increased by 44 per cent, with agricultural output growing by 22 per cent, and mining and manufacturing output by 54 per cent. It is thus apparent that world trade in both primary products and manufactures expanded at faster rates than world production in both categories of commodities—a phenomenon that had not been experienced since the late nineteenth century, and one which was to continue into the 1960s.

The fact that since 1953 world trade has grown faster than world output has meant that the foreign trade proportion has risen during these years. Indeed, according to one estimate, the world foreign trade proportion in 1963 was more than a fourth higher than it was in 1953. Yet, despite the impressive growth in international trade since 1950, it is still not possible to say whether this trend heralds a new stage in the growth and development of the international economy. Nor is it possible, on the basis of experience in the 1950s, to refute completely the diminishing foreign trade hypothesis advanced during the 1930s. The expansion of trade in the 1950s contains a large element of recovery from and catching up with the lags produced by the depression and the second World War. Moreover, in spite of the rise in the world foreign trade proportion between 1953 and 1963, it still falls short of its 1913 and 1928 levels.

The Direction of Trade

The differences to be observed in the rates of growth of trade recorded by different groups of countries during the 1950s is reflected in the shifts in the direction of trade during these years. Trade within the group of highly industrialized countries, and trade amongst the centrally-planned economies themselves and between them and the industrialized West tended to grow at the expense of the trade of the underdeveloped countries. By 1960 the pattern of trade between the different groups of countries was along the lines depicted in Table 21. The bulk of the world export trade was conducted between the highly industrialized countries, and, with the exception of the centrally-planned economies, whose trade consisted largely of intra-group exchanges, the highly industrialized nations also provided the main market for the exports of the other regions.

When we examine the export performances of the chief industrial nations since the late thirties, we find that, despite some significant shifts in the direction of this trade in the fifties, the relative importance of the different countries was much the same in 1960 as it had been in 1937 (Table 22). The one major change that had occurred

TABLE 21. *Matrix of World Exports, 1960*

Exports to of	Industrial countries	Other developed areas	Under- developed countries	Centrally- planned economies	Total
Industrial countries[a]	37	5	16	2	60
Other developed areas[b]	4	n	1	1	6
Underdeveloped countries[c]	14	1	5	1	21
Centrally-planned economies[d]	2	n	1	8	12
Total	57	6	23	12	100

Notes: n negligible (less than 0·5 per cent); discrepancies in totals due to round-
ing;
a Includes the EEC countries, Austria, Canada, Denmark, Japan,
Norway, Sweden, Switzerland, the United Kingdom, and United States;
b Includes 'Other Europe' (including Yugoslavia), Australia, New
Zealand, and South Africa;
c Less developed countries which are members of the IMF.
d Both in Europe and Asia.
Source: IMF, *Direction of Trade*, Vol. 2, 1960–4.

between these two dates was the increase in the American share
of the total trade. Up to 1950 this increase was achieved at the expense of Germany and Japan, but later, when these two countries
began to regain their pre-war trading status, the increased share of
the United States was maintained largely at the expense of the trade
of the United Kingdom. Moreover, despite the tremendous export

TABLE 22. *Distribution of Total Export Trade of the Industrial
Countries, 1937–60*

	Per cent of total exports		
	1937	1950	1960
U.K.	20	20	14
France	7	10	9
Germany	16	6	15
Other Western Europe[1]	20	20	21
Canada	8	9	7
U.S.	23	32	28
Japan	6	3	5
Total	100	100	100

Note: [1] Includes Belgium, Luxemburg, the Netherlands, Italy and Sweden.
Sources: Maizels, op. cit., pp. 426–7; IMF, *Direction of Trade*, 1960–64.

performances of Germany and Japan in the 1950s, they were still barely able to match their 1937 shares of the total trade.[1]

The Composition of World Trade

The trends in the direction of world trade ran parallel with the changes in the composition of total exports. As Table 23 and Diagram 16 show, the increased importance of manufactures in world exports was matched by a corresponding decline in the importance of trade in food and raw materials. In the raw materials category, both agricultural and mineral products experienced a relative decline after 1937. Nevertheless, within the minerals group, fuels especially oil became increasingly more important in world trade over most of the fifties, and in the total exports of the less developed countries they increased their share from 19 to 30 per cent between 1950 and 1960.

TABLE 23. *Shares of Commodity Groups in World Exports, 1937–60*

		Per cent of total exports			
		Primary products			Total
Year	Food	Raw materials	Total	Manufactures	trade
1937	23	40	63	37	100
1950	23	34	57	43	100
1960	18	29	47	53	100

Sources: Yates, op. cit., Table 16, p. 44; D. W. Slater, *World Trade and Economic Growth: Trends and Prospects with Applications to Canada* (Toronto, 1968), p. 29.

TABLE 24. *Commodity Pattern of Trade in Manufactures, 1937–59*

		Per cent of total			
Product category		1937		1950		1959
Engineering products		26·5		34·9		41·3
Machinery	16·0		20·7		24·8	
Transport	10·5		14·2		16·5	
Textiles		21·5		19·9		11·1
Metals		15·3		12·9		13·5
Chemicals		10·6		10·5		12·0
All other manufactures		26·0		21·9		22·1
Total		100·0		100·0		100·0

Sources: See Table 19; and Slater, op. cit., p. 14.

[1] It should be noted, however, that Germany suffered a reduction in geographical size between 1937 and 1950. Only West Germany is considered in Table 22 above in 1950 and 1960.

Diagram 16: World Trade in Manufactures, 1937–60
(Commodity Composition and Country Share)

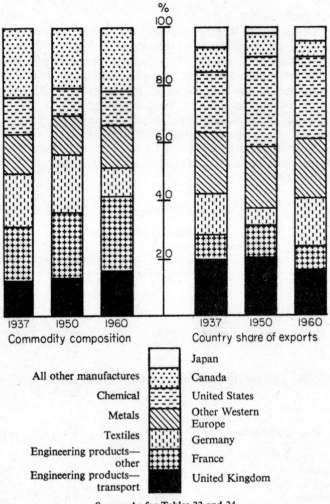

Commodity composition   Country share of exports

All other manufactures — Canada

Chemical — United States

Metals — Other Western Europe

Textiles — Germany

Engineering products— other — France

Engineering products— transport — United Kingdom

Japan

Source: As for Tables 22 and 24

The changing composition of trade in manufactures followed the pattern established in the late nineteenth century and continued during the interwar period. The shift away from textiles towards machinery and transport equipment was intensified, chemicals continued to improve their position, and 'all other manufactures' tended on the whole to hold their own (Tables 24 and Diagram 16). There was thus a continuation and intensification of the movement away from consumer goods and towards capital goods which had begun in the interwar years. Such a trend is consistent with the accentuation of trade among the highly industrialized nations that occurred during the 1950s.[1]

Conclusion

It is apparent from the above account of the growth of international trade in the 1950s that the rich industrial countries were able to obtain greater benefits from it than most other countries. The relative shift in the foreign demand away from food and raw materials and towards capital goods produced a change in the direction of total trade in favour of inter-industrial country trade and against the exports of the less developed counties to the developed nations. This fact tends to contradict the predictions advanced by some economists in the thirties that, as nations developed and their factor endowments became relatively more uniform, the need for trade, based on the uneven distribution of factor endowments, would decline. The historical record outlined above shows that trade in the postwar period grew at annual rates never before experienced and, what is more significant, it was the trade among the highly industrialized group of countries which possessed similar ranges of factor endowments that rose the fastest. A number of reasons have been advanced to explain this apparent divergence between economic theory and historical fact.

First, it has been argued that much of this increased trade between industrialized countries was merely a return to a more normal state of foreign economic relations following the lowering of restrictions on trade and payments. Second, some of the expansion of trade within the group of highly industrialized nations merely reflects the high rates of economic growth achieved by these countries. Increased *per capita* incomes, it is said, lead to a substantial diversification of consumer demand, while continuous advances in technological knowledge encourages widespread innovation. Because rapid and uneven technical innovations produce a continual process of adjustment in the comparative advantages enjoyed by any one industrial country in its many fields of industrial production, and because demand patterns become more diversified as incomes rise, a more complex and shifting pattern of commodity trade among industrial

---

[1] During the interwar years, when this trend first revealed itself, it was associated with a substantial decline of trade between roughly the same group of countries. On this occasion the trade in capital goods was chiefly with the newly industrializing nations.

K

countries, as well as a growing trade, became possible. In other words, it appears that once technology is introduced as a type of factor endowment, it no longer follows that trade among advanced countries must necessarily decline because their factor endowments in other directions have become much more uniform over time.

Moreover, since patterns of domestic demand are influenced to an important degree by income, countries having similar income levels are likely to trade with each other more intensively than they are with countries having different income levels. Thus a highly industrialized nation producing an output of manufactured goods in excess of its domestic requirements is more likely to find a market for its surplus production in other highly industrialized high-income countries than in countries with much lower income levels where the demand is for less sophisticated manufactures. There may be some overlapping, of course, since there will be some demand for sophisticated manufactures even in an underdeveloped economy. But given the fact that *per capita* real incomes are growing faster in the industrial economies than elsewhere, the trade in manufactures could be expected to grow faster than the trade in primary products as a result.

ECONOMIC GROWTH IN THE DEVELOPED ECONOMIES, 1945–60

The Record of Growth

World production was more severely affected by World War II than by World War I, but reconstruction in the years after 1945 was much more rapid, and in most countries the 1938 levels of gross national product had been exceeded by 1950. The major exceptions were West Germany and Japan, both of which did not better their pre-war economic performances until the mid-fifties. On average, industrial countries in western Europe recorded an annual compound rate of growth of gross national product of nearly 5 per cent between 1950 and 1960. The fastest growing economies in this region were West Germany (close to 8 per cent), Italy (6 per cent), and the Netherlands (5 per cent). Britain and Belgium, on the other hand, were relatively poor performers. Other rapidly growing economies included Japan, which averaged a phenomenal 9 per cent per annum, and the Soviet Union, which achieved an average annual rate of growth of gross national product of close to 7 per cent. The high rates of growth in some of these countries came about partly because they were slow to reconstruct after World War II. By 1950 their recovery had not been completed, and therefore this year represents an abnormally low base from which to judge the extent of growth over the ensuing decade. On the other hand, countries which experienced low growth rates in total production during the fifties had, by the end of the forties, expanded appreciably beyond their prewar productions levels. For instance, the United Kingdom increased total production by 14 per cent between 1938 and 1950, Belgium by 25 per cent, and, more significantly, the United States by 79 per cent and Canada by 92 per cent. All four countries experienced relatively low increases in industrial production in the fifties, with America averaging just over 3 per cent per annum and Canada close to 4 per cent. Amongst the semi-industrial nations, Australia increased its volume of production during the 1950s by approximately 4 per cent per annum, New Zealand by 3 per cent, and South Africa by close to 3½ per cent.

Factors Influencing Growth Rates

Economic growth in many parts of the world economy was undoubtedly significantly influenced by the rapid expansion of industrial Europe during the 1950s, if only because the region's foreign trade rose faster than that of other countries and regions. At the same time the foreign demand for industrial Europe's exports was a major factor influencing the high growth rates recorded in a number of European countries. Progressive tariff reductions and the continuous elimination of other restrictive trade barriers, especially within Europe itself, also contributed a great deal towards the growth of the region's trade.

Another feature of the European economy in the post-war period was the high ratio of investment to national income. Investment generated, directly and indirectly, substantial additions to gross national product by raising demand in many sectors, increasing the amount of capital per worker, and allowing a high degree of innovation. But this high rate of investment itself cannot be treated as the primary cause or the all-determining factor of growth and improvements in productivity even if it was an important element. Continuously high investment was made possible by the existence of other factors such as high levels of domestic and foreign demand, substantial supplies of relatively cheap domestic and foreign savings, a high degree of confidence in the continuation of prosperity, rapid changes in technological knowledge, which produced incentives to introduce new products or to modernize production methods, changes in the entrepreneurial capabilities of management, and a progressive approach towards the fostering of economic growth by the public sector.[1] It also appears likely that readily available supplies of

[1] M. M. Postan, *An Economic History of Western Europe 1945–1964* (London,

low-wage labour, in the form of the domestically unemployed or foreign migrant workers, partly explains why output and exports grew more rapidly in Germany, Italy and Switzerland than in Britain, Belgium and the Scandinavian countries, where labour was in relatively short supply.

Thus many factors, reflecting both favourable demand and supply conditions, were responsible for the unprecedented growth rates experienced by most industrial European countries during the fifties. While many of these growth forces were domestic in origin, others had their origin in the international economy. In particular, the growth of foreign demand for European manufactures was of considerable importance in stimulating an expansion of industrial capacity in the region, which, in its turn, was partly sustained by an inflow of foreign capital (plus its associated technology) and labour.

The United States and Canada tended to record lower growth rates in the 1950s than most European countries. This was partly because both countries experienced large increases in production between 1938 and 1950, and especially after 1945, when Europe was generally depressed. For this reason, European economic growth in the 1950s involved an element of catching up with America. In addition, the dollar shortage inevitably led to restrictions being placed on imports from North America, and although other countries shared the gains to be derived from lower tariff barriers, such discriminatory treatment led to a lesser degree of benefit from trade liberalization accruing to America. From 1950 to 1959, therefore, the American share of world manufactured exports declined from 27 per cent to 21 per cent. On the other hand, Germany increased its share from 7 to 19 per cent, Japan from 3·4 to 6·6 per cent, and the Netherlands and Italy also increased their relative proportions substantially. Moreover, American long-term investment, while fostering economic growth in the recipient countries, may have hindered somewhat the expansion of American exports, to the extent that these investment funds were used to support import substitution in the capital-receiving countries. Two other factors may have contributed to the apparently poor performance of the United States over the decade, First, American production around 1950 was influenced favourably by the outbreak of the Korean War, but in 1960 the economy experienced little expansion of total production. Canada was similarly affected. Second, with a very large gross national product and high *per capita* income, it became increasingly more difficult to sustain high rates of growth of output from year to

1967), especially Chaps. 4 and 5. Postan provides detailed arguments with respect to each of these influences on European economic growth in the fifties.

year, for the incentive to do so may be less urgent than in countries which were still reconstructing their industries and attempting to raise *per capita* incomes.

Japan did not regain its pre-war level of gross national product until well into the 1950s. Nevertheless, the country experienced explosive growth thereafter, at annual rates above 8 per cent. This momentous effort was achieved through unprecedentedly high levels of investment, a labour supply expanding faster than population growth, a shift of labour out of low and into high productivity industries, a growing demand for Japanese exports, the ability of export industries to remain highly competitive, an absence of economic waste through low military expenditure, and significant advances in education. In the remaining industrial countries, including Australia, New Zealand, and South Africa, annual rates of growth were below those of Europe and Japan. As with the United States, these countries grew rapidly in the years immediately following World War II and, in addition, 1950 was an exceptionally good year for them because of the high foreign demand for their exports. With 1950 such a high base year, it was difficult for these countries to maintain average growth rates comparable with those recorded by other countries in the fifties. Moreover, most of these countries were still heavy exporters of primary products, and consequently their growth was retarded to some extent in the years after 1950 by declining terms of trade. Towards the end of the 1950s they were also faced with further difficulties in the form of tariffs imposed on their exports by other industrial countries.

Economic Fluctuations

The high rates of economic growth attained by most advanced countries in the period after 1945 significantly altered the character of the economic fluctuations experienced by them. Between 1945 and 1960 the United States suffered three recessions, in 1954, in 1957–8, and during the second half of 1960. Each setback, however, was followed in the succeeding year by higher than average percentage increases in gross national product. Western Europe, on the other hand, recorded recessions in only two years, 1952 and 1958. Moreover, it was in those two years alone that world trade declined, if only slightly. Apart from their short duration and the fact that they were invariably followed by an immediate and substantial recovery, these post-war recessions were also marked by changes in rates of growth rather than by fluctuations in absolute levels of economic activity characteristic of previous recessions and depressions. They also featured a weak transmission of cyclical downturns between the United States and Europe. In all these ways the post-1945 recessions contrast markedly with those experienced during the interwar period.[1]

The 1952 European recession, which was accompanied by a smaller reduction in the American growth rate, resulted primarily from the restrictive measures introduced to overcome inflationary forces introduced in 1951 by the outbreak of the Korean War. Within Europe, only Britain, Belgium, and the Scandinavian countries experienced absolute reductions in gross national product. As for trade, although the values of European and American imports from each other and from non-industrial countries declined, the volume of imports remained virtually unchanged. Non-industrial countries, however, recorded declining terms of trade, and recessionary impulses were transmitted to them from the two large industrial areas. Nevertheless, the expected reflection back of these deflationary forces to the industrial nations failed to occur, mainly because the imports of the non-industrial nations were maintained in the face of their declining export receipts by an inflow of foreign capital, especially from the United States. In addition, the decline in the non-industrial countries' import trade when it did come, came with a year's lag in 1953 by which time Europe had resumed its high rate of growth. The rapid revival of the European economy was also assisted by an American balance of payments deficit, which helped to ease the current world-wide dollar shortage. Further aids to recovery included the relaxation of restrictions on trade which quickly followed the passing of the crisis, the failure of intra-European trade to decline at all in 1952 while increasing significantly in 1953, and possibly the existence of the European Payments Union agreement, which prevented restrictions being placed on imports from other member countries by major European deficit countries.

The 1954 American recession was transmitted abroad via reductions in imports from most areas of the world, but industrial activity in these regions was sustained at a high level despite the deflationary pressures emanating from the United States. Western Europe was able to divert its exports elsewhere and increase its intra-regional trade by relaxing quantitative import restrictions within the EPU. Europe also acted as a buffer against the transmission of the recession to third party countries, since non-industrial countries more than offset their declining exports to the United States by taking advantage of the increased European demand for their exportable products. The American recession of 1957–8 also had little impact on Europe, and the recession experienced by Europe in 1958 was

---

[1] See A. Lamfalussy, 'International Trade and Trade Cycles, 1950–60', *International Trade Theory in a Developing World*, eds. R. Harrod and D. C. Hague (London, 1963), Chap. 11, for a comprehensive treatment of the period.

more the result of inventory reductions and government anti-inflationary policies than an outcome of the slowdown in American economic activity in the previous year. On the other hand, the deflationary forces generated by the American and European recessions of 1957–8 were transmitted to other countries. Primary product prices fell by 6 per cent during these years and the value of exports of third countries to the industrial nations declined in 1958 and 1959. But the implementation of an expansionary programme in the United States and the relaxation of government policies in Europe quickly restored world trade to normal levels.

Finally, it should be noted that throughout the 1950s the United States possessed considerable gold reserves and thus did not need to restrict imports or to reduce capital outflow because of balance of payments difficulties. Thus the international economy was stronger in the 1950s than it was in the thirties, when restrictions on American imports and a drastic fall in the capital outflow from America helped to spread economic depression throughout the world.

SELECTED REFERENCES

Kindleberger, C. P., *Europe's Postwar Growth: The Role of Labour Supply* (Cambridge, Mass., 1967).

Lamfalussy, A., 'International Trade and Trade Cycles, 1950–60', *International Trade Theory in a Developing World*, eds, R. Harrod and D. C. Hague (London, 1963).

Linder, S. B., *An Essay on Trade and Transformation* (New York, 1961).

Maddison, A., 'Economic Growth in Western Europe, 1870–1957', *Banca Nazionale del Lavoro Quarterly Review*, Vol. XII, (1959).

Maddison, A., 'Growth and Fluctuations in the World Economy, 1870–1960', *Banca Nazionale del Lavoro Quarterly Review*, Vol. XV (June, 1962).

Maddison, A., *Economic Growth in Japan and the U.S.S.R.* (London, 1969).

Maizels, A., *Industrial Growth and World Trade* (Cambridge, 1963).

Postan, M. M., *An Economic History of Western Europe 1945–1964* (London, 1967).

Slater, D. W., *World Trade and Economic Growth: Trends and Prospects with Applications to Canada* (Toronto, 1968).

Chapter 20

TRADE AND GROWTH IN THE INTERNATIONAL ECONOMY, 1945–60: THE DEVELOPING AND CENTRALLY-PLANNED ECONOMIES

THE DEVELOPING ECONOMIES

Economic Growth

It has been estimated that the developing countries as a whole increased their real gross domestic product at an annual average rate of 4·6 per cent between 1955 and 1960. On a regional basis, the rates of growth were 4·6 per cent for Latin America, 4·3 per cent for Africa, 6·5 per cent for west Asia, and 4·2 per cent for southern and south-eastern Asia. Of the 63 nations represented as developing countries, 21 recorded annual growth rates in excess of 5 per cent during the latter half of the fifties. Many of these were oil producing countries, whose growth was stimulated largely by the rapid expansion in the post-war world demand for petroleum. On the other hand, there were 25 countries with growth rates below 4 per cent, including 12 with rates under 3 per cent per annum.

Despite the apparently favourable growth rates of many of the developing countries, a different picture emerges when population growth is taken into account. The average rate of growth of population in developed countries of about 1·2 per cent over the 1950s contrasts sharply with the 2·2 per cent recorded in developing countries. Consequently, when *per capita* real incomes are calculated, the performances of the developing countries become less favourable than they appear on first glance, and the gap between the *per capita* gross national products of the developed and the developing groups of countries tends to widen during the decade. Thus in developed countries real gross domestic product *per capita* rose from $1,300 in 1955 to $1,430 in 1960, an increase of 10 per cent, whereas in the developing countries the increase was 4 per cent on average, with real product *per capita* rising from $137 to $142.

The growth of *per capita* real incomes in many developing countries was also slowed up by a deterioration in their terms of trade. In the late forties, the prices of foodstuffs and many raw materials rose sharply, reaching peaks in 1950 and 1951. Consequently, the primary product exporting countries experienced their best trade performances for many decades. Unfortunately, this favourable movement in the terms of trade of primary producers merely reflected an abnormal post-war boom in the demand for certain of their products, and by 1952 this excess demand had disappeared. Thereafter, except for short recoveries in the prices of primary products in 1954 and 1956, the terms of trade of most less developed countries tended to decline relatively to those of the industrial nations, the prices of whose manufactures remained comparatively stable throughout the fifties.

Foreign Aid and Economic Development

In the period before 1960, economic growth in the developing countries was assisted by a massive inflow of foreign capital. In addition to the influx of private capital, which went mainly to mining and oil producing countries, a further $26,000m. was provided by the governments of the Western industrial nations, either directly or indirectly through various international agencies. Another $9–9,500m. in aid originated within the Communist bloc, the bulk of which went to other Communist countries, many of them underdeveloped.

Foreign aid enabled a recipient country to overcome two obstacles which might have frustrated its efforts at economic development. If the country's development programme entails greater investment than can be sustained by the level of domestic savings, then it can undertake the additional expenditure without inflation only if the excess of domestic expenditure over current output is covered by external financing. On the other hand, a trade or foreign exchange gap will appear when a country's shortage of foreign exchange becomes an effective barrier to its economic development by denying it access to imported commodities, especially capital goods, essential for its economic growth. Foreign assistance is then needed to allow the projected investment of the development plan to take the desired form—that is, investment may require necessary imports that cannot be alternatively supplied from substitute domestic sources. If domestic saving does not result in an adequate increase in exports (through reducing the demand for domestically produced goods, thus freeing them for export) or reduction in imports of consumer goods so as to provide sufficient foreign exchange for the imports needed to support the higher rate of capital formation, foreign assistance will then be required for balance of payments reasons quite distinct from the need for aid as an adjunct to savings. Thus a country in which savings are relatively abundant may still experience a foreign exchange gap. It should also be pointed out that whereas a savings gap requires a transfer of external resources in the form of aid, a trade gap may be filled by foreign exchange obtained in a number of ways, for instance, through aid receipts, improvements in the terms of trade and/or higher export earnings.

Fears have been expressed that developing countries will come to depend upon foreign capital assistance, and that this state of dependence will never end. But assuming that the foreign capital is used successfully to promote economic development, the consequent increase in productivity and income will create a source of potential saving that can at some point take over the burden of supplying the capital needed for continuing development. In order to achieve successful growth, the foreign capital should make a net contribution to a country's development. It must not lead to a diversion of domestic investment funds into inventory accumulation, luxury building, speculation or military expenditure. At the same time, a country's capacity to make effective use of foreign aid will depend on a wide range of conditions, including the stability and efficiency of government, the availability of complementary inputs, the size of the domestic market, the extent of social overhead capital —especially in transport and communications—so important for the mobility of goods and people, and finally, the prevailing social attitudes toward change and institutions and habits that influence growth. However, even if successful economic development is achieved, a country's increased savings potential may be absorbed by population growth or by wasteful government expenditure.

The foreign aid policies adopted by donor countries can also influence for good or ill the way in which their financial assistance to the developing countries is used. Thus tied aid, that is loans and grants which can only be used to purchase goods in the donor country, may deny the recipient country the opportunity of buying its imports in the cheapest market or of obtaining the collection of goods most suitable for its development requirements. Untied aid, which has no restrictions on the uses to which it is put, is obviously to be preferred. The fact that the Cold War has made aid-giving an instrument of foreign policy for most donor countries has also tended to reduce its economic effectiveness. Thus a substantial part of the foreign aid advanced since 1945 has taken the form of military assistance and has conferred little economic benefit on the countries receiving it. Moreover, political considerations have tended to produce gross distortions in the pattern of foreign aid. Thus India, which has a high capacity to import capital, has, relatively speaking, been starved of foreign funds because of its policy of political noncommitment. On the other hand, certain other countries, by adopting a particular political stance, have gained access to funds out of all proportion to their capacity to use them effectively. One way in which it is hoped that this sort of problem can be overcome is by channelling a greater part of the existing flow of aid to developing countries through international agencies rather than national governments.

Some aid to developing countries has been in the form of gifts with no repayment, but in other cases, it has involved loans with or without interest, with a short or long maturing period. Where interest (or dividends) have to be paid, and where loans have to be amortized, these payments constitute the direct cost to a country of borrowed capital. To meet the services charges on foreign capital, the developing countries must somehow generate a surplus of foreign exchange receipts that exceeds imports of goods and services by the amount of the service payments to be made. If a developing country achieves a rapid rate of economic development, the growth of new savings will ensure the release of a corresponding value of real resources, which can be exported or can be substituted for imports. Consequently there will appear a similar surplus of foreign exchange receipts over payments for imports, which can be used to cover debt service charges. If, however, development lags, or if population grows too rapidly, a borrowing country can only ensure that debt charges will be covered by directing foreign capital into the production of exports or of import substitutes, or by the imposition of restrictions upon both imports and consumption. As far as foreign aid to developing countries is concerned, the debt charges problem will obviously be minimized to the extent that assistance takes the form of gifts with no repayment, or of grants and very long maturing loans with graduated repayments and little or no interest.

The direction of foreign capital into one specific area of an underdeveloped country, for example mining or oil production, may lead to the emergence of a dual economy with one sector capital intensive, modern, and highly profitable, and the other labour intensive, traditional, and yielding relatively low returns to factor inputs. Here economic development is thwarted because, for reasons discussed earlier in Chapter 9, the technical and economic benefits of the modernizing sector are not diffused throughout the rest of the economy of the developing country.

Foreign Trade and Economic Development

Towards the end of the fifties the underdeveloped countries found that their efforts at development were being undermined by deteriorating terms of trade. It also became clear around about this time that because of the growing number of countries seeking aid and the ambitious targets set by development planners, even a substantially increased volume of foreign assistance would still be grossly insufficient to meet all demands. The future prospect of a short-fall in aid and the mounting debt servicing problem in some countries, made the developing countries turn to trade as the possible solution to their external problems.

Several reasons have been advanced to account for the relatively poor performance of primary producers in world trade during the 1950s, including the change in the composition of industrial production in the developed countries from light to heavy manufacturing (from industries normally demanding a high raw materials content in the finished product to those whose products have a low raw materials content); the tendency for the income elasticity of consumer demand for many agricultural products to be low; agricultural protectionism in the industrial countries; the achievement of substantial economies in the industrial uses of natural materials through improved methods of production; and the ability to displace natural raw materials by synthetic and other man-made substitutes. Declining prices, due largely to similar causes, also affected the export earnings of many of the primary producing countries. The consequently poor export performance of many underdeveloped economies placed severe constraints on their growth, and while foreign aid tended to alleviate these difficulties to a certain extent by allowing the less developed nations to import larger quantities of manufactures from industrial countries than their trading positions warranted, this offset to the relatively low growth of exports was far from complete for the group as a whole. As for the solution to the trading problems of the underdeveloped countries, although trends in demand and technical progress cannot easily be reversed, the developing economies felt that the protectionist and fiscal policies of industrial countries could be moderated to allow greater rates of growth in at least some of their trade. At the same time, they believed that a greater degree of stability in primary product prices could be achieved through commodity agreements and other such arrangements.

The protection given by the advanced countries to their relatively inefficient domestic primary producers has been a major cause of discontent amongst the underdeveloped countries. In addition, the European practice of governments raising part of their revenue by levying fiscal taxes on such agricultural products as tea, coffee, and tobacco has also caused concern. Since these taxes are often more severe than the customs duties already imposed on the products, they have a particularly damaging effect on the exports of certain developing countries. However, the criticisms levelled against the developed countries are not limited to the trade in primary products. The underdeveloped countries also feel that they are at a disadvantage in trying to increase their share of the world trade in manufactures. Particularly significant in this respect is the argument that the manufactured exports of the developing countries should receive preferential treatment by the major trading nations, since the most-favoured nation clause included in GATT is just only if all the trading nations have reached the same level of economic development. More specifically, it is felt that the manner in which tariff reductions are agreed upon in GATT, namely reciprocal reductions on the part of the negotiating countries, is inappropriate for the developing countries, since tariff reductions brought about in this way may adversely affect their development programmes. Moreover, the tariff structure in advanced countries is detrimental to the growth of manufactured exports of developing countries, because duties tend to be lowest on raw materials and highest on finished products. Such a tariff arrangement encourages even the basic refinements of raw materials to be conducted in the advanced country in preference to the less developed economies where the raw materials are produced. Additionally, the advanced countries' imports of labour intensive manufactures often carry higher duties than do more complex manufactures. Finally, the developed countries have made use of quantitative import restrictions to protect high-cost domestic producers against competition from the underdeveloped countries. While these quota arrangements cover a number of commodities, including leather and leather goods, manufactures of jute and coir, electric motors, and sporting goods, textiles form the major area of complaint, for it is here that the developing countries have had a moderate degree of success with exports.

The difficulties encountered by the underdeveloped countries in their trading relations with the advanced countries led to their growing disenchantment with GATT. The belief that the developed nations had used the escape clauses in the Agreement to protect their own relatively inefficient agricultural industries to the detriment of the exports of foreign primary producers, and that GATT tended generally to favour the major trading powers caused the underdeveloped countries to turn to the United Nations for a solution to their problems. At the same time, mounting pressure within GATT resulted in the setting up of a special committee in 1958 to investigate ways and means of increasing the trade of the less developed world. One outcome of all this activity was the establishment of the United Nations Conference on Trade and Development (UNCTAD), which held its first meeting in Geneva in 1964. Out of this conference came several proposals for changes in the commercial policies of the advanced nations—changes geared to the special needs of the developing countries.

Despite the growing emphasis placed on trade by the underdeveloped countries in recent years, it has been argued effectively that trade and aid are not alternative but rather complementary means to economic development. In particular it has been increasingly recognized that a greater part of foreign aid should be allocated in the future to improving export production in contrast to the earlier emphasis on industrialization and import substitution. All too often the 1950s witnessed the attempts of countries to industrialize behind protective tariffs with the consequent neglect of the possibilities of diversification of traditional exports. Moreover, the high cost of manufacturing production in the countries inevitably precluded the entry of industrial surpluses into international markets. Towards the end of the fifties, therefore, increasing attention was being paid by many developing countries to ways and means of improving and diversifying their traditional export lines.

THE CENTRALLY-PLANNED ECONOMIES

Economic Growth

The Communist bloc grew rapidly in size and economic importance in the years following World War II. Apart from the absorption by Russia of the Baltic countries (Estonia, Latvia and Lithuania), Communist governments came to power in Albania, Bulgaria, Czechoslovakia, Hungary, Poland, Romania, and Yugoslavia. The importance of the bloc in world production and trade was further enhanced by the success of Communism in China in 1949, while other Asian members of the bloc include Mongolia, North Korea, and North Vietnam. Cuba has also been included in the bloc since the late 1950s.

In Europe, the centrally-planned economies emulated Western progress during the fifties. Almost all of the countries recorded higher than 7 per cent annual increases in net physical product, and, because population in these countries rose very slowly, *per capita* net physical product growth rates in excess of 5 per cent per annum. The Soviet Union was the fastest growing planned economy, experiencing an annual increase of 6·7 per cent in net physical product *per capita* between 1953 and 1958. In Communist China, gross domestic product averaged 6 per cent per annum during the years 1952–7, or around 4 per cent *per capita*.

Foreign Trade and the Centrally-planned Economies

Ideological considerations apart, the rapid expansion of trade between the communist countries of eastern Europe after 1948 was due mainly to the strategic embargo placed by the West on its trade with the Sino-Soviet bloc. As a result, the share of western Europe and America in east Europe's export trade (including the Soviet Union) fell from 40 per cent in 1948 to 15 per cent in 1953, whereas the intra-bloc trade, which took the form largely of an exchange of food, fuel, and raw materials for steel products, machinery, and equipment, expanded from 44 per cent to 64 per cent over the same period. After 1953, however, the gradual relaxation of the trade embargo, which followed the death of Stalin, opened up trade opportunities with the West, and this was followed by some expansion of the bloc's trade with western Europe in particular. Trade with the developing countries also expanded rapidly from the mid-fifties onwards, even if in total it was still running at a low level in 1960, when exports to the centrally-planned economies accounted for only 4 per cent of the total exports of Latin America, 5 per cent of exports from Asia and 8 per cent of exports from Africa. The developing countries also do not figure prominently in the total imports of the eastern European countries, although their shares rise as high as 11 per cent in the case of the Soviet Union and 12 per cent in the case of Yugoslavia. Consequently, by the end of the 1950s intra-bloc commerce still accounted for the bulk of the foreign trade of communist countries.

Turning to the two major Communist countries, Russia and China, we find that Soviet trade grew in value by about 9 per cent a year after 1953. During these years Soviet trade was directed mainly towards the Communist bloc, which still accounted for around 70 per cent of the total in the early sixties. Nevertheless, there was a moderate trend towards increased trade with non-Communist countries, especially after 1955, when the Soviet Union followed an active policy of trade promotion among the newly independent nations of Asia, the Middle East, and Africa. Thus the share of Russian exports going to all non-Communist countries rose from about 17 per cent in 1950 to slightly more than 30 per cent by 1964, and that of imports rose from 20 to 31 per cent. Despite the shift of trade towards the less developed countries after 1955, two-thirds of the Soviet trade with non-Communist countries was still with the advanced industrial nations in 1964.

As for the composition of Soviet trade during these years, exports consisted mainly of fuel, raw materials, and machinery and equipment, and imports were comprised of almost equal shares of fuel and raw materials, machinery and equipment, and consumer goods. The dominant Soviet exports to the West were petroleum, coal, iron ore and cotton—with the bulk of the machinery, equipment and other manufactured goods going to the underdeveloped countries. In turn, the greatest part of Soviet imports from the industrial West has been in the form of machinery and manufactured commodities, whereas imports from the underdeveloped countries have consisted largely of crude rubber, raw cotton, cocoa beans, wool, and hides and skins. Within the Communist bloc, Soviet trade with East Germany and Czechoslovakia is particularly important, and largely involves an exchange of Russian food, fuel and raw materials for the other countries' machinery, equipment and manufactured goods.

All trade between Communist countries is carried out under the provisions of bilateral trade and payments agreements, which have the main purpose of insuring the availability of basic supplies needed to meet planned yearly output targets in the various countries. Until 1951 each member of the bloc negotiated annual trade agreements with other members, but from that year long-term agreements became fashionable. At attempt at broader economic co-operation within Eastern Europe was also begun with the setting up of the Council for Mutual Economic Assistance (Comecon or CMEA) in January, 1949.[1] It was not until 1955, however, that an elaborate scheme for the co-ordination of production and the development of a pattern of national export specialization was completed which was designed to eliminate duplication of output and achieve the benefits—of large-scale production. But political instability in Hungary and Poland in 1956, and opposition to the suggested specialization format by the less developed countries in Comecon during 1956–8 prevented a multilateral economic cooperation pact from materializing. Romania, in particular, objected to its proposed specialist role as a supplier of primary products, and began to pursue a remarkably independent foreign trade policy, expanding its imports of plant, equipment and machinery from the West and some Comecon members in support of a continuing national policy of industrialization. Consequently, from 1957 to 1962, trade and commercial exchanges within the bloc grew substantially, but little progress was made toward the multilateralizing of planning and trade. Thereafter, however, the Soviet leadership began a more vigorous push for the planned economic co-ordination of the entire Comecon region.

China's ability to obtain both credit and required imports from the Soviet bloc and her inability to obtain them from the non-communist countries were the most important factors in determining the

[1] The original member nations were the Soviet Union, Czechoslovakia, Hungary, Poland, East Germany, Bulgaria, Romania, and Albania. Later, following its open attacks on the Soviet Union, Albania withdrew. As a partial compensation for Albania, in 1962 Mongolia was brought into what had hitherto been a European organization.

direction of the country's trade during the 1950s. Thus during the first half of the fifties more than three-quarters of China's imports came from Communist countries, and by 1960 the Communist share was still around two-thirds of the total. The bulk of Chinese exports (over two-thirds of the total) also went to the other countries of the Communist bloc. These exports consisted largely of raw and processed agricultural products (about three-quarters of the total) whose composition changed significantly during the fifties as a decline in the relative importance of food exports was offset by a large increase in the exports of textile products. Communist China's imports prior to 1960 were confined largely to capital goods, raw materials for industry, and arms. Machinery and equipment for both industry and transport constituted about one-third of China's total imports in the late fifties. Foreign trade therefore played a strategic role in Communist China's economic growth between 1949 and 1959, and it has been estimated that the import component of investment undertaken during these years may have been 20–40 per cent, depending on what rates of exchange are used for converting imports of complete plant, equipment and machinery from the Soviet bloc to China. Not only was the import component of Chinese capital formation quite large, but the industrialization that took place in the 1950s almost certainly would not have been possible without the ability to import machinery and other kinds of capital goods for expansion of heavy industry on the mainland.

Foreign Aid and the Centrally-planned Economies

Economic assistance from the centrally-planned economies to less developed countries dates from 1954, when the Soviet Union established its first programme. Since then other east European countries and Communist China have set up their own assistance programmes. By the end of 1960 total aid commitments by these countries amounted to around $3,600m., mostly in the form of loans. Disbursements, however, lagged considerably behind commitments, and the total amount of aid actually disbursed during the period was only about $750m. In its early stages Sino-Soviet assistance came almost exclusively from the Soviet Union, and as late as 1960 its share of the total was about 85 per cent. The only other aid-giving countries of any importance in the bloc were Czechoslovakia and Red China. During these years over one-half of Communist aid went to southeast Asian countries, and about a third to the Middle East. The largest recipients were India and the United Arab Republic, who together received about 40 per cent of the total aid.

Communist bloc aid is generally directed towards specific projects. More than half of these were concentrated in industry, particularly in the fields of ferrous and non-ferrous metals, engineering and metal-working industries. At the same time, the level of technology attained by the aid-giving country determines to an overwhelming extent the form its industrial aid takes. Thus while Russia has been able to undertake projects such as the Bhilai metallurgical works at An-keleshwar in India and the Aswân High Dam in Egypt, the Chinese have placed emphasis on small, uncomplicated, light industrial pro-jects that can be put into operation quickly and which yield some tangible benefits promptly to recipient states. Taken overall, about four-fifths of the total aid commitments extended by the Sino-Soviet countries between 1954 and 1962 were for projects in industry, power, transport and communications. Non-project assistance accounted for about another 5 per cent of the total, and the remainder was for technical assistance programmes.[1] The Communist bloc, with the exception of East Germany and Communist China, also contributed to the United Nations technical assistance and relief agencies. Con-tributions have remained relatively small, however, and amounted to only $6.3m. (net) by 1963.

Although only some 6 per cent of total communist aid commit-ments to the underdeveloped countries have so far been in the form of grants, about one-fifth of Chinese aid has taken this form. More-over, Chinese loans have been largely interest free, and provide for repayment over ten years with a ten-year period of grace. The major-ity of loans by the Soviet Union carry an interest rate of 2½ per cent and are repayable over 12 years from the time of first disbursement or from the time of completion. However, there are also repayment schedules of up to fifty years. East European credits usually carry slightly higher interest rates (3–4 per cent) and have a shorter repay-ment period (5–8 years). Repayment is usually made in the form of local products, but most assistance programmes also provide for settlement in convertible currencies if no satisfactory form of repay-ment in kind can be found.

Except for armaments, for which no data have been released, the Soviet Union played only a modest role as intra-bloc creditor up to the end of 1955. During this period, Soviet credits to its east Euro-pean satellites totalled not more than $1,000m., including $154m. extended to Yugoslavia in 1947, which was barely touched before that country's break with Moscow led to its cancellation. The early

[1] A high proportion of Sino-Soviet technical assistance consists of services connected with the construction and installation of industrial plant and the value of this assistance is usually included in the general credit arrangements. In addition, technical assistance is provided through the training of specialists, qualified managers and technicians under a number of programmes which are not related to specific projects. There is also an extensive programme for the training in Communist countries of personnel from less developed nations.

loans took the form of credits in gold or foreign exchange and credits for the purchase of raw materials and foodstuffs in the Soviet Union, which were extended in a period when the east European economies were partly disorganized and when some of them were sending reparations to the Soviet Union at the rate of 40–50m. gold dollars a year. More significant, however, were the investment loans, which assumed real importance only from 1948, when the defection of Yugoslavia and the interest evidenced by Poland and Czechoslovakia in Marshall Aid forced the Soviet Union to adopt a more positive aid programme within the bloc. In the next few years a number of Soviet loans were advanced to other communist countries, including one to Poland of $450m. to cover machinery imports and the construction of a steel works.

Russia undertook few new loan commitments in the early 1950s, although the death of Stalin and the Berlin uprising that followed it led to the granting of a loan of $128m. to East Germany in August, 1953, and the annulment of $3,200m. of war reparations owing to the Soviet Union. 1956, however, saw the introduction of a massive Soviet aid programme following the Polish and Hungarian uprisings of that year. In the next few years the Soviet Union advanced loans to its European satellites totalling over $1,500m., and while the bulk of this aid went to Hungary, Bulgaria, Poland and Albania, almost every bloc country received some Soviet help in the years 1956–8.[1] Even Yugoslavia received a loan of $194m. early in 1956, which marked the beginnings of a thaw in political relations between that country and Russia. Furthermore, because of the violent nature of the crisis in Hungary, most of the other European bloc members, as well as China, sought to help the country with additional aid, which totalled at least $100m.

Soviet aid to the smaller Asian Communist countries, which began in earnest in the 1950s, totalled around $1,300m. in 1960, of which just over 40 per cent went to Mongolia, the remainder being divided equally between North Korea and North Vietnam. Soviet aid to China between 1950 and 1957 amounted to 5,294m. yuan, which has been variously estimated at something like $1,370m. to $2,240m. Beginning in 1956, however, China became a net exporter of capital, in part because of her repayment obligations and in part because she started to extend foreign aid to other countries. By the end of 1960, Chinese aid commitments amounted to over $1,000m., 87 per cent of which had gone to other Communist countries, mostly those in Asia. Of the small amount of aid extended to non-Communist countries, virtually all of it went to Asian countries

[1] In addition, roughly $2,500m. was provided in 1956–7 in the form of debt cancellations or other benefits.

along China's southern periphery (Cambodia, Nepal, Indonesia and Ceylon) out of a desire to limit American and Nationalist Chinese influence in these areas.

SELECTED REFERENCES

Brown, A. A., *and* Neuberger, E., *International Trade and Central Planning* (Berkeley, 1968).

Eckstein, A., *Communist China's Economic Growth and Foreign Trade* (New York, 1966).

Goldman, M. I., *Soviet Foreign Aid* (London, 1967).

OECD, *The Flow of Financial Resources to Less Developed Countries 1956–1963* (Paris, 1964).

Sherman, H. J., *The Soviet Economy* (Boston, 1969).

Wexler, I., *Fundamentals of International Economics* (New York, 1968), especially Chap. 19.

Chapter 21

EPILOGUE

The evolution of the international economy during the past century and a half has been largely by way of a response to the changes that have occurred in the political, economic, and technological environment within which economic relations between countries are conducted. The unique feature of the pre-1913 international economy is that it was dominated by one country, Britain. The first country to industrialize, to adopt the gold standard, and to accept free trade as its commercial policy, Britain set the pace for the growth of the international economy by providing the markets, capital and labour needed for the economic development of a large part of the world. After 1870, it is true, France, Germany, and to a lesser extent, the United States began to play a more important part in promoting the expansion of the international economy and shaping its character. Even so, Britain's continued pre-eminence in world financial affairs and her adherence to free trade, in a period when there was a general return to protectionism, gave her undisputed leadership in international economic affairs. It is perhaps mainly for this reason that international agreements on financial and other matters were largely unnecessary before 1913. In so far as any guiding influences were exerted on the growth and functioning of the international economy in the nineteenth century, these originated chiefly in Britain, whose influence on world trade and finance was paramount.

However, the first World War changed all this. The subsequent decline in Britain's international economic position, the emergence of the United States as the world's leading industrial and financial power, and the economic difficulties experienced by Europe in general, and Germany in particular, made a simple return to the pre-war international economic system impossible. The attempt to restore the gold standard made in the 1920s was a complete failure, and in the face of mounting economic difficulties, aggravated later by a world-wide depression and growing political insecurity, countries, or groups of countries, turned in on themselves in order to deal with their economic problems. Moreover, as governments were called upon to deal with these crises by playing a more active role in national economic affairs, international considerations were increasingly subordinated to domestic policies aimed at maintaining employment and output levels. With the collapse of the traditional framework of international economic institutions and the emergence of a more nationalistic approach to economic affairs, there was little hope of intergovernmental co-operation in the search for a multilateral solution to world economic problems, and while the demands of trade finally brought some international agreement to stabilize exchange rates, attempts to deal with trade and financial problems in the 1930s were predominantly on a bilateral basis or made within the framework of discriminatory regional blocs.

The success in obtaining international agreement on a wide variety of economic matters from the early 1940s onwards contrasts sharply with the more nationalistic outlook prevalent during the interwar years, and the much more limited forms of international agreement characteristic of the period before 1913. But this has not come about because countries are today any less actively concerned with domestic levels of employment and rates of economic growth than they have been in the past, rather the reverse. It is because governments will not allow domestic economies to be threatened by outside events that it has become necessary to create, as an act of deliberate policy, an international economic system within which it is possible for individual countries to exercise economic sovereignty without endangering the welfare of other countries. Moreover, the fact that the attainment of national economic goals of full employment and high growth rates may be helped by the existence of a smoothly functioning world economy has also contributed to making countries more willing to co-operate in the setting up of international economic institutions designed to eliminate the financial weakness and widespread impediments to world trade and commerce that brought about the collapse of the international economy in the 1930s. In a sense then, the emergence of a managed international economy since 1945 has been largely the result of the spread of the managed economy at the national level characteristic of the period since 1920.

This new stage in the evolution of the international economy has barely begun, however, and many difficult problems remain to be solved before national and international interests are fully reconciled within the new system. One of these problems concerns the series of crises that occurred in the international economy in the 1960s. These led some economists to claim that the establishment and subsequent development of the IMF have not removed the basic instability inherent in an international monetary system based on a gold exchange standard. As these critics point out, the inability of the world's gold production to meet the growing needs for international liquidity induced by a rapidly expanding world trade has meant that trading nations wishing to increase their foreign reserves can do so only by largely accumulating certain key currencies, such as the dollar or the pound sterling. But accumulation by foreign countries of a particular currency can be accomplished only if the issuing country is willing to run a deficit in its own balance of payments. Furthermore, such deficits if they persist over time can breed lack of confidence in, and de-stabilizing speculative attacks against, the key currencies themselves. By allowing other countries to accumulate dollar and sterling claims, the United States and Britain, in effect, expose their gold reserves to possible depletion in the event that foreign central banks and other foreign holders of these claims want to convert them into gold. On the other hand, should the key currency countries refuse to tolerate balance of payments deficits, and attempt to reduce or eliminate them, the chief source of international liquidity might well dry up, thereby jeopardizing the continued growth of world trade. Whether the current IMF scheme for the creation of Special Drawing Rights (SDR's or 'paper gold') will solve the problem of international liquidity has yet to be seen. What is obvious, however, is that some provision for the orderly generation of new liquidity is necessary to the healthy growth of the international economy.

Another problem centres on the underdeveloped countries, which have remained deeply dissatisfied with the functioning of the international economy in the 1950s. The failure of substantial foreign aid to generate high growth rates in these countries in the face of declining primary product prices and the consequent adverse movements in the terms of trade, and the difficulties experienced in expanding exports to advanced countries, with their protected agriculture and manufacturers, have been a continuing source of tension between the rich and poor nations. Yet the case for international specialization remains as strong today as it was in the nineteenth century, while the indirect benefits that international trade can bestow upon today's developing nations exceed, both in size and variety, those which could have been expected a century ago. The number of more industrialized countries is greater, the existing technology is far more advanced and diversified, and the opportunities for the international exchange of ideas and methods far more abundant than they were a hundred or even fifty years ago. Whether it will be possible through intergovernmental co-operation and the creation of effective international agencies to ensure that the benefits of modern technology are more fully shared by the underdeveloped countries remains one of the most challenging problems of our age.

Index